THE
YOUNG
GUNNER

*The Royal
Field Artillery in
the Great War*

DAVID HUTCHISON

Matador
9 Priory Business Park,
Wistow Road, Kibworth Beauchamp,
Leicestershire. LE8 0RX
Tel: 0116 279 2299
Email: books@troubador.co.uk
Web: www.troubador.co.uk/matador
Twitter: @matadorbooks

ISBN 978 1785893 230

British Library Cataloguing in Publication Data.
A catalogue record for this book is available from the British Library.

Front cover image: Passchendaele Battle 1917.
Trench Map marked with artillery barrage and infantry
objective lines for the first day.

Printed and bound by CPI Group (UK) Ltd, Croydon, CR0 4YY
Typeset in 12pt Aldine by Troubador Publishing Ltd, Leicester, UK

Matador is an imprint of Troubador Publishing Ltd

MIX
Paper from
responsible sources
FSC® C013604

This book could not have been written without the help of my family. Chief among those is Colin Hutchison's son Donald who owns the original manuscripts and photographs. The Keable-Elliott and Prescot families also provided much background information on their grandfather and were highly supportive.

I also need to pay tribute to Paul Evans, librarian of the James Clavell Library, at Firepower, the Royal Artillery Museum; to Laura Morris and Benjamin Buchan who gave me invaluable early guidance: to Michael Webster, formerly of the Kings Troop, Royal Horse Artillery; and to Denzil Sharp, retired brigadier, who patiently read early drafts and corrected the most glaring errors, pointing me in new directions. The staff of the National Archives at Kew were extraordinarily helpful. The War Diaries that I found in their collections are integral to the book.

And this book could not have been written without all the legions of contributors to internet web-sites, pertaining to regimental histories and background information on the war from 1914 to 1918. I have acknowledged the most significant of these in the text and I apologise if there are any unacknowledged. A big thank you to them all.

theyounggunnerrfa@hotmail.com

CONTENTS

MAPS

Public domain

★ Map researched and designed by Dr Damien Fenton and produced by Geographx, Wellington, New Zealand, 2013. Originally appeared in Damien Fenton, *New Zealand and the First World War* (Auckland: Penguin, 2013).

ILLUSTRATIONS

*Every effort has been made to trace and contact copyright holders of
maps and photographs prior to publication. If notified, the publisher
will be pleased to rectify any omissions at the earliest opportunity.*

Lieutenant Colin Hutchison, aged 21, in December 1914

PREFACE

'I think as a gunner subaltern, one sees more of what goes on than anybody else in the whole army.'

This is a history of the Royal Field Artillery in the Great War, based on the letters and journals of two men, writing home to England from France and Flanders. Their letters were lovingly tied up in bundles with red ribbon, and chronicle their inspiring personal stories of everyday life in the front line.

But more importantly, they tell of how Colin and Duke learnt the hard lessons of trench warfare; when they learnt them; and later, often much later, when the generals did. They describe the slow development of effective artillery tactics through battle after battle, this evolution summed up in the last chapter.

They explain why the vastly outnumbered British army was not overwhelmed by the German artillery in 1914; why the infantry had no effective artillery support in 1915; why a shortage of ammunition was not the main problem; and why the timed up-lifting barrages, supporting the infantry attacks of 1916 and 1917, were a disaster. They tell a story that can only be told by men who were there, and not by the generals who thought they were. As Colin said again and again, *'our whole method of warfare is wrong.'*

Colin describes his command of a single gun in 1914, a section of guns in 1915, a battery of guns in 1916 and a brigade of guns by the end of the war. He was in action in 13 battles, including Mons 1914, Ypres 1915, The Somme 1916, Passchendaele 1917 and Ypres 1918. He was wounded three times, and repeatedly gassed. He ended the war both alive and heavily decorated.

His uncle, Duke Marshall, joined up in 1915, arriving in France in time to serve at the Somme. He was severely wounded in April 1917, dying as a consequence less than two years later. Between them, they tell a story that has never been told.

INTRODUCTION

It was a very different world before the First World War. The British Empire was the greatest there had ever been, policed by the most powerful navy that had ever sailed the seas. The British monarch was secure on the throne and related to most of the royal families of Europe. Riches flowed to the British Isles from every corner of the globe. Society was stable, and with the benefits of the industrial revolution filtering through to everyday life, standards of living had never been higher.

The Hutchison family were well placed. David Hutchison had business interests in England, and his wife Emma had income from properties in Japan. So they could afford to educate their three sons privately. And Emma had the leisure time, as many at that time did, to spend an hour or two every day writing long letters to her family and friends, taking advantage of the superbly efficient postal system.

Her second son Colin had followed his older brother Alec into the Army. Both had been educated at Merchiston Castle, a public school in Edinburgh and both were bright enough to progress to the Royal Military Academy ('the shop')[1] at Woolwich, for which there was a tough entry examination. Alec had chosen to join the Royal Engineers and was already a serving officer. Colin chose the artillery, and after his year of technical training, was accepted into the Royal Field Artillery[2] as a 2nd lieutenant in early 1913.

---

1   Woolwich Royal Military Academy educated aspiring young gunners and engineers in a one year course. Sandhurst Royal Military Academy was the college for potential young infantry and cavalry officers.

2   There were three artillery regiments in the British army. The Infantry were supported by the Royal Field Artillery, and the Cavalry by the lighter guns of the Royal Horse Artillery. The Royal Garrison Artillery had the heaviest guns, which were 60 pounders, four guns to a division on mobilisation the next year.

But by 1914, Colin was causing his mother some anxiety. He was at Bulford Camp, an Artillery Depot, near Salisbury in Wiltshire and had just turned 20. He was generally quiet, but this quietness disguised a fierce intolerance of poor leadership, which from the earliest days he shared with his mother. By the summer of 1914, he had already upset his first battery commander[3] with his views and been transferred to another.

But he had an exceptional talent. He was a very fine rugby player and was selected, when at Woolwich, to play both for the Army and for the London Scottish, even then a prestigious club.

Colin with King George V after an army rugby match

---

3   A major commanded the whole battery of 6 guns, and the approximately 200 men and the 200 horses required to service them. Colin was one of three very junior subalterns, each commanding a two gun section in the gun line. A captain commanded the Wagon Line where the horses, two ammunition wagons and about 18 other storage wagons were kept behind the battery in action. Army life in barracks revolved around care of the horses. Every officer was allocated his own charger, and Colin prided himself on his growing proficiency in the saddle.

Only five foot ten, he was a fearless and accomplished fly half. A possible candidate to play for Scotland, his name was nationally known to those who followed the sport and many did. He was in a small way a celebrity.

In addition, he had a generous allowance from his father, which allowed him to run a motor bicycle and visit home (Hatch End in Middlesex) regularly. He was not from the very upper echelons of society or he would have joined an infantry or cavalry regiment, but he was socially adroit, went shooting and fishing every year in Scotland with his father, and even went skiing with younger brother Donald, still at school, in the winter of 1912. His more senior officers thought him a good chap.

Donald, Alec and Colin in 1913. Colin with Father David

Emma, understood the nuances of social responsibility that her second son needed to master to make a success of his army career. Suffice it to say now that her Colin in 1914 was in a dangerous phase, a bit too famous, a little arrogant, and only temporarily protected by his precocious talents from the hard realities of army life.

In the summer of 1914, Colin was blissfully unaware of this anxiety. Nor was he particularly aware of the momentous political events leading inexorably to War as Germany flexed her muscles. He was only a boy and life was a game.

But his mother's brother, Duke Marshall, aged forty, living and working in Japan, was deeply aware of events. He was reading both the papers and his sister's frequent letters. He knew at first hand the commercial and military might of Germany. He had no confidence in the British press reports forecasting a quick German humiliation. He longed to be back in England at such a momentous time.

And then war. Colin's letters to his Mother and Father start.

The letters on which this book is based are mainly Colin's to his mother, and later Duke's to his sister. Throughout, both play down the dangers using typical British understatement[4]. For instance, if Colin says he is having a *'warm time'* that means he is under fire and has to be careful. If he says he is having a *'hot time'* that means he is in serious danger and could be killed at any minute. Sometimes he is having a *'very hot time'*. If he says he is causing the enemy a *'certain amount of consternation'* that means he is killing them. And so on.

The journals are more explicit and ignore the censor[5] which clearly constrain them both at times. In the course of this correspondence (and in Colin's official writing as adjutant in 1915) they frequently describe staff or tactical issues which are worrying them. Put together, these offer a contemporaneous insight into the development of artillery tactics through the four years of war in Flanders. These developments will become clear through the book, and are summarised in the last chapter.

---

4   This habit of understatement was universal at the time and caused problems in the War itself. It was not unknown for a colonel to say in a message that he 'was in a certain amount of trouble', which was a scream for help in the Regular Army, but was interpreted as 'coping OK' by colonial or inexperienced staff officers!

5   Censorship of letters from abroad was introduced immediately on the outbreak of war.

Emma Hutchison, Colin's mother and Duke's sister – with letters.

CHAPTER ONE

1914 Mons, Le Cateau and the Retreat

130th (Howitzer) Battery, 30th Brigade, 3rd Division

'We consider ourselves as good as the Germans.
However, that remains to be seen.'

The Great War started in Europe on the 28th July 1914[1] and Colin's first letters date from the middle of that month. These give just a glimpse into his busy social life. Rugby was his winter sport, but this was now high summer.

On the 29th July, he was playing in a county tennis tournament at Trowbridge in Wiltshire. When he got back from his tennis, *'this order has just come in. They are keeping all officers and men in barracks just now.'* The political situation was serious, but Colin, with youthful optimism, did not worry about it too much.

'If this war business goes any further, then it really only means that we will all go over to preserve the neutrality of Belgium. I believe we would go

---

1   Books have been written about the origins of the war, but very briefly, the Balkan States were destabilised by the assassination of Arch-Duke Ferdinand of Austria in 1914. The Austro-Hungarian Empire, with German encouragement, used the opportunity to annex a part of Serbia, in the Russian sphere of influence, knowing that this would trigger a Russian declaration of War. Germany had an alliance with the Austro-Hungarian Empire to fight Russia, if she attacked (as she did). France had a similar Treaty with Russia to fight Germany if they came to war. England tried to keep out, despite having a similar Treaty with Russia.

After the Franco-Prussian War of 1870, the French had fortified their Eastern defences. So the German grand plan in the West was to move her army through Belgium to attack France from the North. England, as a naval power, could not allow a continental power to get control of their Channel ports. When the Germans violated Belgian neutrality, England declared War on the side of Belgium, France and Russia.

to some place not far from Ostend, which is rather the fashionable place to go at this time of year, isn't it? And what there is of the English army would sit there, preserve the neutrality of Belgium and await events. It would really be jolly good fun and I rather wish we could get over before things are settled.'

But a few days later, on the 4th August, the political situation was more than serious and Britain mobilised for war. He started to understand the reality of what was occurring. *'I don't think now we will go to Belgium, and I don't suppose we can move out of England within 10 days. The German fleet will have to be beaten first.'*

The next two weeks were filled with frantic activity at Bulford. Reservists were *'for the most part fairly old men, most of them with South African war medals, but they proved very useful in the way they influenced the younger and less experienced members of the battery.'* Officers[2] and men were shuffled. *'Both my No 1s'* (gun captains) *'left me, promoted to Sergeant Majors. This was rather a handicap as we had to work with two new men who did not know much about gun drill.'*

The first outing of their reorganised brigade[3] was not particularly auspicious. *'Our first full parade with our fresh horses and men, all with brand new equipment and harness was an impressive sight, rather spoilt by*

---

2   *'2nd Lt Johnstone went as orderly officer to the Colonel.'* (Lt. Col. Staveley) *Boylan who had only left the shop about 6 months, took over his Section of two guns. Lieutenant S.R. Wason, our Senior Subaltern, commanded the Left Section. He was the only one of us who had had any real experience. Major G.C. Stapylton commanded the Battery and Captain Newlands the wagon line.'*

3   A Royal Field Artillery Brigade was commanded by a colonel, and consisted usually of three horse-drawn Batteries, each of six guns, and one horse-drawn Ammunition Column. Each Infantry Division of about 18000 men was supported by four brigades of Field Artillery, only one of which was howitzers. A howitzer brigade was armed with QF (quick firing) 4.5 inch Howitzers, a modern home-produced gun, introduced in 1910, having a five foot barrel and a 35 pound high explosive shell. The howitzers fired like mortars, up and over.

The other three brigades in the division, were equipped with conventional 18 pounder field guns, which fired with a flat trajectory.

several of the horses refusing to move with the rest of their teams, and by one horse rearing and falling over backward. However, after about an hour, they were all induced to move, and we went for a short march along the Tidworth Road, returning shortly afterwards intact.'

But Colin was incapacitated for much of this time, first by a riding injury to his leg and then by the violent reaction to his inoculation against typhoid. And he was not alone suffering from the latter. *'Another 60 or 70 of our men were taken down and inoculated this afternoon, so that if we start within two days it will be a sorry battery during the journey, as these Tommies will imagine they are going to die. It's rather rotten work with half the battery laid up through the inoculation. I shall be pleased when we 'get a move on'.'*

He was just 21 and the family rallied round. Colin had lost his wristwatch and a reliable timepiece was an essential for a subaltern on active service. Younger brother Donald sent him his new one to take to war. Colin refused the offer and took his father's alarm watch instead.

His motorbike, his fishing gear, his guns, his golf clubs and his skiing kit were all at Bulford. His mother came over in the car to pick some of it up. Father had financial papers for him to sign. War was coming. He and the family had a lot to lose. Colin was keen to go to war. *'It is an experience that one will not get more than once in a lifetime.'*[4]

But his mother was not enthusiastic. He remonstrated with her, *'you don't seem to realise what a disgraceful thing it would be having three healthy sons and none going out. I am the lucky one of course,'* but a few days later he wrote a sober and reflective letter to his father.

'Dear Father, I'm very thankful you let me join the Artillery. I hope Mother and you don't feel too badly over my going. I have made no will of any kind, but Donald is welcome to anything of mine if this happens to go wrong. I have made out a blank cheque to you in the cheque book I am forwarding to you in case you need to get my money out. I hope that won't be necessary, but I suppose it's the proper thing to do, and of course chances have to be faced.

---

4   He lived to serve in the Second World War.

You need not be afraid of my doing anything foolhardy. I won't take any unnecessary risks. The necessary ones I hope I shall take.'

He thought he was almost organised. *'If you could send me a pair of clippers, I shall be completely and wonderfully equipped.'* But his mother was worried and tried to anticipate his needs. *'I can't think what I can have said about those slippers, but I could not possibly have taken them with me.' 'Many thanks for the chlorodine and stuff. I can't possibly get ill with all the medicines I am taking with me.'*

His father bought him a revolver.

By the 20th August, he was in France as part of the British Expeditionary Force (BEF) of 70,000 men and 300 guns.[5] This was a tiny army by European standards. The German army that faced them at Mons, the first British battle of the war, had 160,000 men and 600 guns, and this was only one of six.

'With any luck we might be back from this jaunt in time for Xmas. I rather hope so as it will get rather cold about that time if one is still in it.'

Colin's letters home during this first campaign are not very informative, and his mother asked him to write up his adventure as a journal, which he did during the course of 1915. This gives a detailed account of the BEF campaign from the view point of a very junior artillery subaltern. They left for France on the 19th August.

'The train journey to Southampton was accomplished without incident. Every village on the way had its crowd of children and civilians who waved to us and cheered. At Southampton we were split into half batteries, and after some little delay we embarked in one of the Irish Mail boats that had every convenience for loading a limited number of animals. We sailed about 8 pm

---

5   The BEF were marching to the aid of the small Belgian Army who were fighting valiantly to delay the German advance. But the Belgian Army was already almost cut off and the BEF met the Germans sweeping south at Mons in Belgium. Further East, France and Germany were squaring up with five Armies each, every one of these Armies twice the size of the British Army. The British Army to France, the BEF, consisted of only two Corps plus an independent Cavalry Division. There were two Divisions to a Corps.

and were very interested in all the searchlight and harbour defences which were a very pretty sight, going past the Isle of Wight. We were convoyed across by a destroyer and arrived off the mouth of the Seine in the early hours of the morning. We lay at anchor there until we were able to get up the Seine, as we were to disembark at Rouen. Our transport was of light draught and twin screw and consequently able to negotiate all the twists and turns of the Seine with the greatest of ease.

Notwithstanding the early hour of the morning, every village turned out and waved and cheered us all the way to Rouen. The soldiers were in fine fettle, but towards the end of the journey were getting a little tired of the continual hand waving and cheering.

We arrived at Rouen soon after noon, but had to lie in the middle of the Seine for two or three hours until there was room at the wharf. Disembarkation was effected without much trouble, though considerable difficulty was encountered before a man could be obtained to work a crane for us. We were apparently well before our time.

The march through Rouen was a triumphal succession; ours was one of the first to arrive with artillery and we excited a lot of interest. The soldiers were presented with fruit and flowers to their hearts' content, and every pretty girl in the town must have turned out to see us pass. We marched to our camp situated in some meadows about a mile and a half south of Rouen.

The other half of our battery did not turn up at Rouen that day.[6] They had had delays in starting and had had to wait for the tide at Havre, being on board a transport which drew much more water than ours. We rested at Rouen under canvas until Saturday 22nd.

---

6   The brigade diary reports that the 130th embarked on the 'Colleen Bawn' in the afternoon of the 18th, and sailed at 10 am on the 19th. They reached Le Havre at midnight. At 6 am on the 20th, the Brigade moved up river to Rouen. Only half the Brigade disembarked at Rouen that day. The other half had to wait. The French workmen would not work after 8 pm Most of the BEF went out to Belgium via Boulogne.

That day we made an early start[7] and arrived at the station fully 1½ hours before our train was due in. We took it in turn to have an omelette and coffee at a café close to the station. We also laid in a store of drinks for the journey. The whole battery was accommodated on the train. The train journey was a long one, and the timetable was not rigidly kept. We had great difficulty in getting our horses watered satisfactorily.

At Amiens we were supposed to have a full 15 minutes' halt and a great effort was made to get the horses watered. No notice was taken of the frantic whistles of railway officials as it was important that the horses should get water and the men's rations be distributed. The train began to move, but the whole battery was still off the train. As it began to gather momentum, we succeeded in getting most of the men aboard, but 10 or 11 were left behind. Some of these men we never saw again, but some seven or eight rejoined us after various experiences as infantrymen etc.

On arriving at Valenciennes at midnight, we were informed by the railway transport officer (RTO) that we were to go to Marly[8], a small station about three miles distant and de-train there in order to ease pressure at Valenciennes. He also told us that some Uhlans[9] had been encountered and that some half dozen had been brought in the previous day. This was the first piece of news that really brought home to me that the whole thing was not a delightfully organised field picnic.

This last three miles was very tedious, but we eventually arrived about 2.30 am and started to de-train. The facilities provided for us were not up-to-date, and no efficient lighting was provided. We were ordered to march straight to Mons with as little delay as possible, barely having time to water and feed the horses.

We were not allowed to take the direct road from Valenciennes, presumably to avoid congestion of traffic on the main road. We had had no sleep that night but did not mind this as we thought we were going to a rest camp.

---

7   The Brigade was not fully entrained till 8.30 pm on the 22nd and travelled the 280 miles to Valenciennes disembarking on the 23rd. Colin's 130th brigade was in the first train.

8   Now an eastern suburb of Valenciennes which is about 25 miles from Mons.

9   Uhlans were German cavalry troops. There had been a cavalry skirmish early on the 22nd.

Breakfast we had in the dark before leaving Marly. It consisted of a cake of chocolate and a mouthful of tea and we were hurried off. Lunch we had about 10.30 in a quaint little Belgian town just inside the frontier. Here we got a long bearded French infantryman as a guide. He had first to go and fetch his bicycle, say goodbye to his friends and then we were ready to start. We went by country lanes, and everywhere the inhabitants came out and presented our Tommies with all kinds of fruit.

About 12 noon, we heard the sound of guns in the distance, but it sounded very muffled and far away. The natives were very much alarmed, but we assured them everywhere that it was quite all right, little thinking what was in store for them.

It was a very hot summer day and we eventually emerged onto a pavé road, lined on each side with trees as is typical. Here we came on a scene of bustle. Columns of infantry were moving forward and we had to wait a couple of hours before we moved on. The dusty, tired infantrymen passing us every time we had to halt.

About 3.30 pm we arrived at the top of a hill and from there had our first sight of German high explosive shells and had a distant view over a very dirty looking piece of country, dirty because of the many unsightly slag stacks, which marred what otherwise might have been a passable view. The noise of the shells bursting and the sight of those black pillars of smoke, distant as they were made me realise the appalling terrors of real war. This realisation did not come all at once, it took probably five minutes – and left the previous five minutes ten years behind. I had looked on war as something to be desired, something that every soldier wants to see and experience. Such things as we heard and saw had never been associated with war. They shook the earth, and they were miles away from us, and we were going into that. One did not want much imagination to make one know fear. Of course a soldier ought never to be afraid, and the natural conclusion was that I ought never to have been a soldier – and consequently I wanted to get out of it and run.'[10]

---

10 This account of the campaign was of course written in 1915, nearly a year later. He wrote only field postcards from Belgium, which give no information at all. His first full letter was written on the 4th September.

They had arrived just south of the Belgian town of Mons, as part of the 3rd Division. It was the 23rd August 1914.

Mons today, from a slag heap south of the town and just north-west of Ciply.

'*Soon afterwards we got moving again, went through the little village at the foot of the hill and found ourselves off the pavé and on a shocking road. Soon we halted and prepared for action as per drill book, putting on the sight carriers as laid down, and fusing[11] our ammunition. The guns were laid out on a line in the middle of a field avoiding a hedge. [12] A telephone wire ran up to the major who was observing from the top of a stack. The teams and wagons were taken into a neighbouring field.'*

---

11 The shells they fired had detachable fuses which had to be activated and fitted to the shell case.

12 Colin added a post-script in 1915. '*Hedges now considered the only safe place.*' His howitzer battery in 1914 did not look for cover. The major was observing and directing the battery fire, so there was no good reason for being right out in the open. But in the next paragraph, they '*build gun emplacements*'. The artillery were the only wing of the army in 1914, who were trained to dig themselves in at every opportunity. This is a significant fact that colours Colin's tactical thinking throughout 1914.

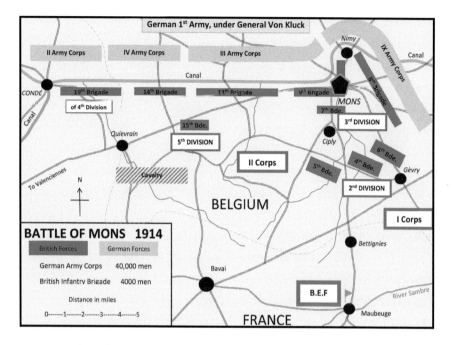

They advanced through Bavai to finish between Ciply and Mons

'General Wing[13] came up to the battery and went up to the observing post with the major and Wason. We were ordered to build gun emplacements, and during the intervals of not firing, busily started throwing up emplacements round the guns.' 'I believe we rather worried some Germans we caught in a column formation,[14]' he wrote later to his mother. I fear this was wishful thinking. His journal is more honest. 'We did not fire very many rounds that afternoon, and unfortunately started off with a very unfortunate incident, dropping a few shells amongst our own infantry.'

---

13 Brigadier General Frederick Wing commanded 3rd division artillery. To keep in touch with his brigades, he and his staff toured the positions during the battle. Major General Hamilton commanded the division.

14 Only the first German attacks, against Nimy on the right of the British line that morning, were in column formation. Later attacks in early evening, were in open order against the length of the canal. Column formation was Napoleonic as an infantry tactic. Even the British would not have attempted that!

'We were withdrawn that night after dark and soon saw signs of things not being well. We met an officer of the Fusiliers[15] *looking for his brigade headquarters, who said that his handful of miserably shaken men were all that remained of his battalion of 1000 men. They had had a terrible time lying in their shallow scrapes which gave no protection at all and faced by hordes which apparently were shot by the hundred, but came on in never-ending numbers.'* The German infantry had charged the British regiments who responded with rapid and very accurate rifle fire, together with artillery support.

The next morning, the battery returned to its position to cover the retreat of the British army, which had been forced by the retreat of the French army to their right. *'It was not long before columns of infantry, ambulances and transport began streaming past us. We eventually got the order to retire to a position on the left of the 3rd Division 60 pounders (the only type of heavy artillery*[16] *we had out with us).' 'We passed through the village of Ciply* (two miles south of Mons) *and prepared for action in the middle of a turnip field. Here we waited for about 2 ½ hours. Infantry went past us, the heavy battery retired, but 129*[th] *Battery*[17] *and ourselves stuck on.*

Presently a cavalry patrol came past and asked what the deuce we were doing. All our infantry had gone past, and as far as they knew the Germans were not very far behind. However, the colonel[18] *was perfectly happy, so we remained another half hour.*

We then got a report from the wagon line that a German battery could be seen coming into action about 3000 yards from us. We got the order to 'prepare to advance'.[19] *The horses came up and we had just hooked in when over came four ranging rounds from the German battery. We got the order 'Column of*

---

15   The 4th Royal Fusiliers lost very heavily in the battle.

16   Five inch guns. And very few of those. One battery of four guns for each of the four divisions.

17   The 129th battery of the brigade was on the second train from Rouen to Valenciennes and did not reach the battle at Mons on the 23rd. They arrived at Ciply at 4.30 am on the 24th. The 128th were in the last train and were probably still on the march at this stage, though the brigade diary suggests they got to Cipley.

18   Lieutenant Colonel Staveley, commanding 30th Brigade, Royal Field Artillery.

19   A later note explains that the word 'retire' was not used that day!

sections, from the centre, dismount the gunners! Walk, march'! We had about ½ a mile of absolutely open ground to cover to reach the road, and proceeded to do it at the walk. The next four rounds from the German battery (7.7 cm)[20] got our line and was also pretty fair for range. We continued to walk out of action and did so under their fire, getting about 20 rounds in all into us. Two men were hit, one poor devil had to be left behind.*

We were not out of trouble, until we got some houses between us and the German fire. And soon after that, there was a check in front. The major and I rode past the 129 Battery in front of us and we found the colonel examining his map. We were going in the wrong direction. The colonel decided to try his luck across country to strike the main Bavai road. We followed a wood, which marked the course of a small stream, but were soon held up by a wire fence on firmly driven iron stakes which defied our wire cutters. The Germans were now shelling pretty well all around us. It took precious minutes to cut a way through, the only successful implement being an axe used on the wire just where it went through the iron supporting stakes. Three such fences were encountered before we found a track and a narrow bridge leading across the stream and onto a narrow lane which went in the direction we wanted. We passed a line of infantry acting as rear guard. They were very surprised to see us, as they thought they were a long way the last. We arrived at last at the main road, only to see a never-ending column, all sorts of units mixed up, marching two columns deep.'

They moved to just south of Bavai, but the next day separated from the general retreat as a rear guard. *'Goodness knows where the rest of the brigade was.'* The brigade diary does not know where they are either!

'We halted and set up for action in a small field by some houses. The horses were watered and fed, and as things were fairly quiet, we settled down to a meal of bully and beans. The sergeants spotted some cows in the distance and milk was voted excellent. So they went over to them and after a great deal of exertion, and with tremendous applause from the battery, a beast was secured by means of a rope and hauled over to the battery. On arrival, some

---

20 7.7 cm Feldkanone 96 neuer Art, (7.7 cm FK 96 n.A.), was a German light artillery gun, mobile but firing a smaller 15 pound shell than the British Ordnance QF 18 pounder. It dated from 1904.

wag discovered the poor brute was a young bull, and the NCOs in question never heard the last of their famous effort.' Their rest did not last long. They were soon on their way again.

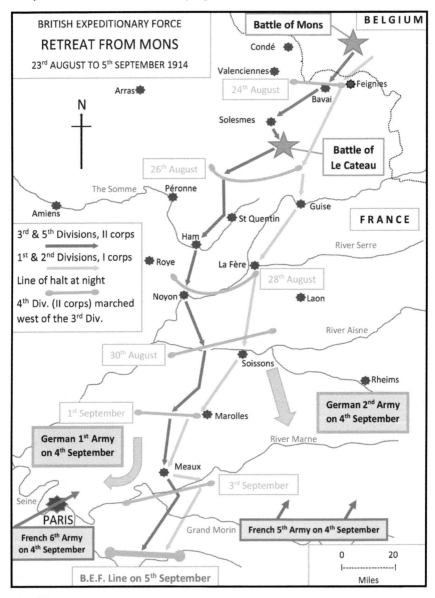

The 1st and 2nd divisions of I corps, and the 3rd and 5th divisions of II corps retreated the 200 miles from Mons to east of Paris in 12 days. The 4th division joined the retreating army at Le Cateau.

'*We eventually reached the outskirts of Solesmes,*' 25 miles south of Mons, where they fought a brisk little rear guard action. '*We came in to action at the top of a hill. There were a few infantry entrenched down the far side of the hill and a German horse battery shelling the plateau.*

The major[21], poor chap, this was the last I saw of him, went ahead down the hillside towards the Germans to observe. He gained a shallow trench, but he was shot by a shrapnel bullet between the eyes and was killed outright.

Things were by no means comfortable with the battery and were not improved by the infantry on our right all coming back at the double. We tried to stop them and make them form up again, but of course had our own work to do. Captain Newlands took command, and gave us the line and a range of 800 yards, as the Germans were apparently coming up the slope.

Owing to a wagon having stuck in a ditch at the side of a road and ammunition having to be fetched up to the gun from it, my detachment was very short-handed. So I served the gun during the action and was damned glad to have something to do which took my mind off the bursting German shrapnel which was making a most horribly uncomfortable whistling and singing noise.' The brigade diary records that two men were wounded in this action.[22] '*We finished every round we had, searching and sweeping and then got the order to retire. The horses and teams were brought up extraordinarily well under the quarter master sergeant who was acting captain[23]*' (ie much senior to him, a mere second lieutenant). '*He had been giving the drivers some driving drill, just as though*

---

21 Major G Stapylton. '*He never showed the least fear and was a gallant officer of the old type, refusing to hurry at any time, no matter what the Germans did.*'

22 The poor quality of the ordinance of the 7.7 cm Feldkanone 96, the standard German field gun, is not generally recognized in accounts of the battles of Mons and Le Cateau as a significant factor. Colin later compared them with the allied ordinance, '*Our own shells are better than the German. There is no comparison between the French and German field guns. The German field guns are useless.*'

23 By 1915 Q.M.S. Clarke had been commissioned as an officer and then wounded. One has to admire the panache of the brigade in the days after Mons, retiring under fire; on the 24th, they dismounted and walked half a mile to safety; that day, they calmly did parade drill prior to moving off. A panicky stampede would have been a disaster, of course, and they got away with all their guns, so it was not wrong, but it was not modern war.

they were on parade at Bulford, to keep them steady and they brought the teams up quite calmly.

My horse came up with one of the gun teams. I had a bit of a chase to catch him, but I mounted him and was standing watching my last gun get over the ditch when a German shell pitched clean under his legs. The horse covered some distance before I was able to pull him up. Probably not much effort was made to stop him at first!' If he said that, he meant it! He was a brilliant horseman.

The ammunition wagon stuck in the ditch had to be abandoned and a limber[24] which had been taken forward for the battery captain's protection, was also left behind. This was my fault. A good battery never leaves anything behind for the enemy. This I learned by overhearing the captain's remarks later. It did not strike me as being of such paramount importance while we were still on the Solesmes plateau. The last wagon and gun caught me up half way down the hill. The houses there gave me a certain sense of security.

I started on after the rest of the Battery when one of the horses came down with a crash and refused to get up. I thought he was killed and was all for cutting the traces, but the Quartermaster Sergeant was there and knew better. The horse soon got up when released of its harness and was harnessed in again. We followed on and caught the Battery up in the middle of the village.

It was getting towards dusk and the Germans had started shelling Solesmes with heavy stuff. I remember looking up a side street to see the whole front wall of a house bulge outwards and come down with a crash. While coming through Solesmes, French reservists attempted to climb onto our vehicles and would not get off until threatened with a revolver. It had to be done, we could not have carried them and had to make our own gunners walk to save the horses.'

The retreat continued to Le Cateau, now in France, where the corps turned and fought a rear guard action[25] on the 26th August, just two days into the retreat. *'We were ordered into action east of Caudry.*

---

24 A limber is a two wheeled carriage, comprising a box in which ammunition is stored. The horses are harnessed to it, and the gun towed behind. If required, two of the gun detachment can sit on it.

25 General Smith-Dorrien, commanding II Corps, decided to conduct a major rear guard action at Le Cateau.

We got out into the fields and advanced to a semi-covered position within shouting distance of a haystack, 200 yards north of the embankment. The guns were just behind the brow of a slight ridge, but still visible to the enemy.[26] We prepared for action, and soon afterwards opened fire. We got several good targets, infantry in close formation etc. It was not however my day as forward observing officer and I did not see much from the guns.'

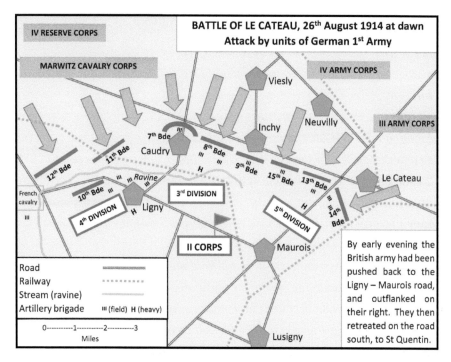

Colin's battery is behind 8th Infantry Brigade with the 18 pounder batteries forward of them on the brow of the hill. Each division had four field artillery brigades, and one heavy battery.

26 Where the infantry went, the artillery followed. There was a railway cutting and a 'ravine' behind them, both of which would hamper their withdrawal. A retreat under pressure was going to happen. But the British, sited their guns forward, very exposed to hostile fire from a huge army. They risked losing all their guns if their lines were broken. The British gambled, rightly as it happened, that the German artillery would not knock out the guns and that the infantry would hold, which they did – just.

We kept up a pretty useful fire for about 4 hours and a German field battery kept up a pretty useful fire on us. They had our range to within 25 yards, constantly bracketing us, but fired some rotten little high explosive shell which did no harm at all. They pitched one or two practically under the muzzles of a gun without doing any damage, but it made ammunition supply very uncomfortable. And they shelled the railway embankment behind us with what must have been 5.9s[27]. They came over four at a time and burst with a terrible demoralising crash. They frightened me terribly every time I heard them coming, with a fear which takes all the stuffing out of one. That four hours was just about as bad a shelling as I wish to remember.'

'At last General Wing[28] himself appeared and ordered us to get out of our position at once and to take up a position further back to cover the right (ie east) flank of the division where we were being seriously threatened.' 'We followed the battery slowly (the horses were pretty done pulling the heavy ammunition wagons over very heavy ground) picking up some rounds of ammunition on the way.' 'About 6.30pm, brigade headquarters discovered us and apparently we were to retire[29] still further.'

'I went forward with the adjutant to be shown the way. Coming back, I met the battery making for Ligny[30]. I failed to convince the captain to about turn, not through lack of volubility. I imagine I was very rude. Luckily we met a party of cavalry who put us right. We eventually got onto the road we wanted, but pretty well the last of our column again. The water cart was

---

27 *'Their common shell ammunition is not up to much,'* he said at the time. The German 15cm sFH 13 field howitzer, however, had rather more effective ammunition and fired a shell weighing 93 pounds, heavier than any of the British or French mobile guns. See note 47 and text.

28 General Wing, commanding 3rd division artillery, was up front, as he had been at Mons. He had to be – no telephones back to headquarters in 1914, so he knew exactly what his forward troops were enduring.

29 The British conducted a fighting retreat. They had lost about 5000 casualties, 38 guns (most on the right of the line) and 2,600 men taken prisoner.

30 Ligny was west, a few miles south of Le Cateau, back towards the Germans. They needed to go south.

lost here, something happened which made it necessary to tack the water cart behind a wagon. It came off somehow. Perhaps it is just as well it did, as the horses could not have managed the extra weight.'

The small British army had held the line in two battles, both rear guard actions against vastly superior numbers, as the French Armies on their right retreated.

'About 1 am that night we had been halted for about half an hour and it really seemed as though our promised billets had arrived. Exploring a large farm on the right of the road, it seemed there would be room for the whole battery[31] there.

So we started, under the colonel's orders, to pack the battery into this one farm; a real tight pack it was too. We eventually got all the horses watered and fed, and the men settled down for the night. We went into the farm, were given an omelette and some coffee, and then we settled down to sleep. We hadn't been asleep for more than an hour when we were awakened by a banging on the door and commotion outside. The rest of the division had left us behind, about one hour. We were on our own.

We had the deuce of a time waking our men up. However, the horses had been left harnessed, and we got out of that farm somehow. As I had packed them in, I was made to get them out. And to everybody's surprise they got out fairly easily, which was just as well for me. Of course, all this was done in the dark.'

'Up till now we had been more or less the absolute rear guard and had not had much marching in the column.' 'The whole of the next day was terrible. Every yard showed signs of equipment that had to be left behind because the men could carry it no longer. We got supplies from dumps left by the ASC.[32]

---

31 The battery had about 200 horses, 200 men, 6 limbers and guns, and about 20 supply wagons.

32 ASC The Army Service Corps was the service arm of the army and it grew through the war to a huge organisation. It performed a myriad of essential tasks such as organising rations and supplies, transport and timetables, administering the post, and staffing rest and transit areas. Colin refers to them with approving and good-natured disdain. They were generally very efficient, absolutely essential and not proper soldiers!

who were really wonderful. We marched from 3 am to 2 pm at about 1½ miles an hour, halting and going on all the time.' 'About 2 pm we arrived at Villeret[33] situated at a junction of three typical valleys.

Here we halted, and after watering the horses I was called and told to take some signallers and patrol out on our right flank. The divisional commander was rather anxious to know the whereabouts of the 4th Division which was somewhere around. I made for a farmhouse on a rise and on the far side of the hill was another column, but one could not tell if they were English or German. An infantry sergeant told me the column we could see was the 4th Division. [34] This was a great relief. I made up my report and started back.

Everyone was terribly jumpy and the Germans were reported close on top of us. I passed the 23rd Brigade and their colonel was not at all happy with the positions his batteries had been made to occupy and he gave me a message to this effect for the general. Going on, I ran across a couple of cavalry stragglers in a panic, who had been billeted somewhere and surprised by the Germans. They reported that their whole squadron had been 'cut up', and that the Germans were hot on their heels. They were beyond control and I could not stop them. At headquarters, I found General Hamilton[35] as calm and unmoved as a rock but all around were signs of absolute nerve strain and almost panic. Things seemed very serious and uncomfortable.

---

33 Villeret, a tiny hamlet ten miles on the Le Cateau – Péronne road. Map page 12.
34 At Villeret, the 3rd division found their route west to Péronne blocked by the 4th division who were moving south. So the 3rd division turned back east to the outskirts of St Quentin to find the 5th division had that route. They therefore went south by back roads to Ham, and on to Noyon, sandwiched between the other two divisions. Their routes were planned by the hour, rather than by the day.
35 Major General H.I.W. Hamilton CB, CVO, DSO, commanded the 3rd division. He was killed in action in October 1914. Colin refers to him with relative familiarity, seems to know all the officers in the division and talked to them, part of the reason why the small British army was so cohesive and effective.

The whole Third Division Infantry was bundled up in this little village. The Battery had been ordered to come into action[36] in a field just beyond the village. I found our Battery with every section pointing in a different direction, i.e. covering three fronts.'

The retreat continued for another twelve days. The brigade diary soon gives up attempting to say where the individual batteries are.

'The next three days we (the division) were retreating just about as fast as we could move, and we were marching mixed up with ambulance transport and infantry. This meant walking for perhaps 10 minutes, halt for three, start off again, concertina up again, and start off again, watering and feeding when it seemed that enough time could be snatched for the purpose.'

The night march from St Quentin to Ham on the 28th was the worst of the retreat. *'That night was a nightmare. After waiting an hour or two on the road we got going. It was now pitch dark, and a drizzly Scotch mist did not make things any pleasanter. Then disaster overtook us. I happened to be riding behind the battery, the other officers were all in front. After rather a longer halt than usual, I rode up towards the front of the battery and discovered that two sub-sections,'* two of the six guns, *'had been cut off by a battalion of infantry and a brigade of artillery. I was left behind with most of the battery, and thank goodness, the Quartermaster Sergeant (QMS).*

At a check the drivers would fall forward asleep on their horses' necks. Sometimes the horses moved on their own, sometimes they too fell asleep. I had to be continually riding up and down the column shouting and hitting the men to keep them awake.[37] Traces and bits of harness were constantly going wrong and causing halts. Men were falling off their horses and gunners were falling off their vehicles; quite a number of men were killed in this way.

---

36 *'Coming into action'* means deploying guns in readiness. It does not meant they were firing.

37 Only a week into the campaign and Colin is effectively in command of the battery. 1000 men and about 100 wagons were between him and the other officers up the road. Probably fortuitously, he had had no time to brood on his terror on facing shell fire for the first time, and his panic when his horse had bolted.

Just before dawn, an NCO rode up and told me that an officer had been run over. We got a water cart, the best conveyance we could find, and sent it back for him. Huish had fallen asleep on a limber, had rolled off and been run over. The wheels of the limber went right over his chest: how it failed to kill him I can't think.[38] We had to drag one poor devil who had been killed off the road – no time to bury him. He had been run over by several vehicles in the dark.'

'We had an extra long halt just when it began to get light and at once everyone fell asleep. I walked up and down to keep awake. Eventually mount was signalled. Using very bad language, I had to shout and curse and shake the men awake to get them on.' Colin is now assured. He knows what needs to be done and he does it. The uncertainties of the first few days are behind him. *'There was a horse standing at the side of the road and a man sitting on the doorstep of a house by it. Using very bad language, I started to rouse this individual before I discovered it was Colonel Maurice, General Hamilton's chief staff officer.'[39]*

At Ham, *'we halted for about an hour and a half on the main pavé road. This halt was of very little use to us as we were continually getting orders to mount and get ready and then having them cancelled. We were all*

---

38 Lieutenant Huish survived the experience and in 1915 was back in action in the Horse Artillery.

39 In this campaign Colin is still learning his trade and hardly alludes to the staff (see page 36 for a definition). But this episode, their tortuous route, and the near panic at Villeret cannot have been reassuring. Having said that, he wrote this journal in 1915, when he was scathing at the incompetence of the staff. This implies that he thought they did their job on the retreat, and the fact that the army stayed intact and disciplined speaks for itself. There are clues in the narrative as to why this was so. In 1914 all the officers knew each other. Colin, on reconnaissance reported to the general, not to his colonel. The Colonel of the 23rd brigade gave him a verbal message to pass on to the staff and Colin knew both him, and who to give the message to. He knew Colonel Maurice. At Le Cateau, Colin was not afraid to tell his captain he was heading in the wrong direction. There was little bureaucracy, almost an 'old boy network', the senior officers very close and talking to their men. Colin, a 2nd lieutenant, saw his divisional general, General Hamilton, occasionally, and his brigadier, General Wing, more regularly. It is no surprise that both were killed in action within the year.

absolutely exhausted after that awful night. We were eventually ordered to trot and started down the pavé. It was not long before two horses were down and I remained behind with the QMS to get them up. The horses were exhausted too and it was no easy job. To make matters worse, one of the horses was lying in the most extraordinary way with its body right under the limber, and with its two forelegs sticking through the wheel. Its disconsolate driver was sitting on its head and using most unparliamentary language. Eventually it was got out of its predicament with nothing more to show for it than a few scratches.'

'After a halt of about two hours during which we watered and fed our horses and also had a meal ourselves, we were ordered to march to Noyon, where we were to report to the brigade again.'

'A poor shepherd refugee passing with a flock of sheep told us to take and kill any we wanted, as he did not want the Germans to have them. We refused his offer.' 'It had now turned in to a glorious day and we were almost happy as we started off on our journey by the most roundabout route.[40]*'*

Unable to find their brigade, they *'decided to bivouac for the night in Noyon. The horses were watered and tied up on one of the boulevard avenues, and after a hasty meal (many did not wait for it) the men curled up on the pavements and slept.*

There was a little estaminet there, packed with our infantry, clamouring for refreshment. I got in the back, pulled the proprietress into a back room and explained to her that four officers were very hungry and very tired and wanted an omelette and anything else she could give us. I imagine I may have rather exaggerated the ranks of the officers concerned, as it was important to impress on her the great importance of our captain!

The good woman at once offered us beds and had omelettes prepared. Four very dirty, unshaven officers sat down to the meal. At first hunger overcame the desire to sleep. The effort to keep awake was painful, our forks dropped out of our hands as we ate, the clatter of it waking us to a fresh effort. But we were determined to sleep in the beds upstairs. We did not get up till 7.30, the only

---

40   It certainly was a roundabout route. From Ham they went on a 21 mile loop west almost to Roye, north-west of Noyon, and then headed almost east back to Noyon by back roads. Noyon is 13 miles south of Ham. Map page 12.

time on the retreat that we were not up at dawn. We got up to find that madame of the night before had fled at 5 am.' The Germans were close behind.

'We re-joined the brigade at about 10 am and spent most of the day in readiness, expecting to be sent into action at any minute. Towards 4 pm, we started to get a backward move on again. This was disheartening, as there had really seemed some hope that we were to occupy a line and hold the Germans here. It was a very tedious march indeed, right through the night. During the march, violent explosions were heard and this was the Royal Engineers blowing up the numerous bridges as we passed over them. Several we had crossed had been prepared for demolition.

We reached Vic Sur Aisne at about 3 o'clock in the afternoon' (about 15 miles almost due south of Noyon) *'and I was left behind to try to do some foraging for the mess. We needed several things including a complete new set of cooking utensils. The brigade cooks cart, which carried a large store of tinned provisions had unfortunately been lost.*

I would never have stayed behind if I had known I was going to have such a difficult task to find the Battery again. After what seemed a hopeless search, I eventually found them bivouacked just outside a pretty little village in a cornfield. The corn had been cut and bound, and was piled in bundles of sheaves in rows, prior to being brought in. As it was a glorious night we slept quite comfortably, hoping for a fairly late start for a change, as we had had no sleep the previous night at all. However, dawn found us once again on our weary way.'

The nadir of the army's retreat was the line of the River Seine, south-east of Paris. The 30th Brigade bivouacked at Liverdy-en-Brie, 40 kilometres from Paris, on the 5th and 6th September. They were allowed little time to rest and sort themselves out.

The small British army had to this point fought a very effective campaign. They had punched above their weight in this huge continental war and they had held together during the retreat with remarkable resilience. The fact that the whole army was able to go back onto the offensive from the River Brie with only one day's pause for thought is impressive.

But the British Expeditionary Force was an army equipped for open warfare. It had very few heavy guns, a cavalry division and an offensive mentality, led by infantry generals, who were looking for the quick victory the public and press in England expected.

The very speed with which events had moved meant that no time was allowed to analyse the battles and to learn from them. Everybody from General French downwards was tired and there were many political and practical distractions. They had lost neither of their two major battles despite being heavily outnumbered. At the time that seemed enough. But was it really practical to expect the war to be over by Christmas with a crushing victory? Probably not. But who had time to think?

Colin had only arrived in France seventeen days before. As he said, '*the retreat from Belgium was really rather trying.*'

CHAPTER TWO

1914 The Marne, Aisne and First Ypres

130th Battery, 30th Brigade, 3rd Division

'We have at last started to advance.'

It was now the Germans retreating in disarray. The weak French Sixth Army, based in Paris, advanced to threaten the flank of the German First Army on the west of the German line. In wheeling to face this threat, this First Army lost contact with the Second Army, leaving a wide gap in the German line. (See map page 12.)

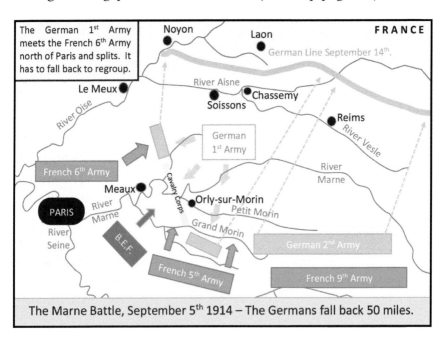

The German 1st Army meets the French 6th Army north of Paris and splits. It has to fall back to regroup.

Noyon

Laon

FRANCE

German Line September 14th.

River Aisne

Le Meux

Chassemy

Soissons

River Oise

Reims

River Vesle

German 1st Army

French 6th Army

River Marne

Meaux

Cavalry Corps

Orly-sur-Morin

Petit Morin

River Marne

PARIS

Grand Morin

German 2nd Army

River Seine

B.E.F.

French 5th Army

French 9th Army

The Marne Battle, September 5th 1914 – The Germans fall back 50 miles.

The German 1st Army was faced with annihilation on the right of their line of armies. It and all the other German armies fell back 50 miles, as fast as they had advanced. Only on the banks of the Aisne did they link up to form a defensive line.

The French Fifth Army and the British advanced against the German First Army which had to retreat fast to avoid encirclement. The other German armies retreated to maintain the line. This was the Battle of the Marne, where most of the heavy fighting was done by the French.

'Just a few lines while we are halted.[41] We have had really quite a peaceful time lately as far as actual fighting goes, but we have been making up for it in night marches.'

Colin was more worried with his own problems than those of the army. *'I am dreadfully pessimistic due to too many unripe pears which I ate three days ago, followed by a pill from the medical officer which performed its work only too well. I tried to cook some maize last night, but it was not ripe and was not the success it might have been.'* And worse, *'some vile fellow stole my sponge bag yesterday with my tooth brush, soap box and all. So far my efforts to replace them have met with no success. They don't seem to use tooth brushes in this country.'*

But it was not all bad. *'I shall be a very accomplished French scholar by the time I get back. I do all the foraging for the officers of the battery and have to coax chickens, butter, and eggs out of the country people. They are very good to us and would much rather we had them than the Germans.'*

'We have been advancing pretty fast. Two or three days ago I had my first experience of machine gun fire. I was sent with one gun into our infantry firing line to try and wipe out four or five machine guns which they left with about 800 men at a place called Orly.[42] No-one could locate the position of their machine guns so it was not much good us firing at all. However, we let off at where they might be and succeeded in drawing all their fire to ourselves. I can tell you I was jolly glad we have a shielded gun. We turned them out in time and apart from that little bit of excitement we have had quite a quiet time.'

The brigade diary of the 12th September dryly records *'one gun in action but could not do much because of machine gun fire.'* But their own 8th Infantry Brigade lost 100 men that day and it required 'J' battery of

---

41 From this point, the journal finishes and the narrative is taken from letters.
42 Orly-sur-Morin, on the Petit Morin which is a small tributary of the Marne.

the Royal Horse Artillery to clear the way for the crossing.[43] Only a few weeks into the war, and Colin had seen at first-hand the result of unsupported infantry attacking positions defended by machine guns.

The army moved on north to the River Aisne, in the battle of that name[44]. They were positioned on a high ridge just south of the river, looking north and west over it.

'I told Mother in my last letter that my section had been detached and that I was on my own. This has continued for 8 days now. I have built myself a draughty little observing station, which is very good for seeing all the surrounding country.' 'Must just stop for a minute and have a shot at some Germans building a trench on the opposite ridge … they have bolted to their shelters, so I will continue.' 'I come out at dawn, watch and shoot till dusk, and then retire, leaving my guns under guard, to a cave in an old sandstone mine which holds the officers and men of 3 batteries – 600 men and 520 horses.' 'During the day I drop shells into the trenches the Germans are making, break a bridge down over the Aisne whenever they mend it and generally make as much trouble for them as possible.'

'The Germans are gradually moving across our front. But they have selected a very strong position amongst some old forts built by the French after 1870.'[45]

Both sides had very strong positions. And as he was to say many times during the next four years, *'the blighters have started off again with their heavy guns and high explosives. It is the most damnable stuff and from the sound of it they must be near our batteries and not too far off my section. They are horribly accurate too.[46] I wish we had more heavy artillery.'*

---

43 The Royal Horse Artillery, who supported the Cavalry Division, used light and mobile 13 pounder field guns to harry the retreating Germans.

44 The Brigade Diary reports that the 130th Battery was in action, firing from Chassemy, contesting the bridge over the River Aisne at Condé on the 14th September, the Brigade losing 3 killed and 27 wounded. See map page 24

45 Colin was observing from Chassemy Ridge, which dominates the land south of Condé on the River Aisne. The Fort de Condé is on a similar ridge north of the river. There are many sandstone quarries and mine workings in the area.

46 The Brigade Diary recorded 3 casualties in the Quarry that day.

The British army in 1914 allowed for, and indeed demanded, that junior officers accept independent command and use personal initiative. This was making a virtue of necessity. Orders were passed by messenger, and telephones were only a recent invention. At Solesmes, the 130th Battery was acting independently of the brigade and fought its rear guard action on its own. Colin had to command the bulk of the battery on the retreat when it became separated from its senior officers. He was given a one-gun detachment at Orly. And now again on the heights just south of the Aisne he has command of his own independent section. This early responsibility forced him to observe, and assess his military options.

He had personally experienced the power of machine guns against infantry at Orly. Now he was destroying German positions, and watching British positions being destroyed by accurate artillery bombardment at the Aisne. So he made the assessment and drew conclusions. Well positioned artillery and machine guns could stop any infantry advance. And heavy artillery could make defensive positions very uncomfortable.

'The Germans have some very powerful heavy guns[47] *with them, and awful things they are. There is a crater of one of these monsters just 10 yards from where I am sitting now. If they hit anything direct, not very much remains.'* But they weren't quite as bad as they sounded. *'On the other hand, the action is very local and the pieces of shell rise very quickly. So that if you lie down, a shell might burst within 5 yards of you and do no damage. They give a lot of warning and we all drop into our pits the second we hear them coming.'* However, in a later letter he did remark dryly of these bigger guns that *'at 300 yards one is apt to get hit by splinters coming down again.'*

And as for the in-between distance; *'there is a huge shell crater just two yards off this trench. The gun that did it has been quiet for several days*

---

47 The German 15cm sFH 02 field howitzer, and the heavier 21 cm Mörser 10 heavy howitzer firing an 89 pound and 252 pound shell respectively. The largest British gun in the B.E.F. was the 60 pounder, one battery of four guns per division.

but started again this morning and burst a shell about 50 yards in front. I lay flat in my trench and when I heard it land, I jumped up to see where it had gone. There was a whizz and I ducked jolly quick again just in time to avoid a nasty jagged bit of shell which landed with a plop on the back of the trench. It has taught me to wait a little longer before I satisfy my curiosity. It would have got me square.'

Colin was a young man and all this danger gave him a sweet tooth. Not only that, *'munching chocolate isn't bad as a temporary measure to keep awake. It hurts less than pins.'* So almost every letter included a plea. *'I wonder if you could get some substantial chocolate and send it out. There is none to be got anywhere.'* But parcels were delayed or perhaps looted. *'Wrap a pair of drawers round them to pretend they are something else. There are a terrible lot of thieves about and no unmistakeable packets of chocolate get through.'* He had to do without.

'I am on a high knoll above the Aisne. I can see 12 miles of the front of the battle and numerous German trenches. We are up against a stiff proposition in the way of position here.' This is 'General' Hutchison reporting. *'This is a battle, but rather different from the first two we had. It has been going on for 18 days now.'* He was recognising the sea-change in tactics, from open to fortified trench warfare.

But what did the real generals think? *'I get all the generals up here to be shown round.' 'Just five minutes ago, Sir H Smith Dorrien was here for about 20 minutes and seemed quite pleased with the view. The infantry, he said, amuse themselves by making dummy figures on the end of a pole, and sticking them up – signalling back bull's-eyes or outers depending on where the Germans manage to hit their figures.'*

On the 26th September, *'Sir John French and his staff were here. They surprised me with my eye glued to a telescope. I just had time to seize my hat and coat as they arrived. I don't allow anybody in untended and I object to a crowd as the Germans have very sharp eyes. General French was very good about it and made most of his staff stay behind, while he was conducted round.'*

General Sir John French,
Commander in Chief BEF

General Sir Horace Smith Dorrien,
Commanding II Corps.

Junior officers did not usually tell General Sir John French, commander in chief of the British army, what to do! But anyway General French did not like what he saw of the German positions either, and one week later, the whole British army handed their positions over to the French and moved west towards the sea. Unsurprisingly the German generals reached the same conclusion and moved likewise. Both sides thought they had stolen a march on the other and the two armies met in the confused western offensives known as the 'Race to the Sea'.

'We left our cave on the Aisne, on the 5th October and marched for three nights to our place of entrainment[48]. The rolling stock was very ancient and both the doors of our carriage were broken before we started. The horse trucks were very slippery through not having been cleaned and one of my drivers fell and is in hospital. We then marched from Abbeville to here and pretty hard

48   Le Meux, west of Soissons, 60 kilometres north of Paris. See map page 24.

going it was too, marching all night and hiding from aeroplanes[49] *all day.'*

Colin finally got his chocolate. *'Many thanks for the parcels, which are all turning up now. I am inundated with chocolate, as I laid in a stock in town.'* The British army was now quite close to the Channel ports and the reliability of the post, even at this early stage of the war, was impressive. He had a new requirement. *'I have absolutely run out of silk handkerchiefs. I wonder if Father has any more to spare. I would be awfully glad of a few.'* Father's reaction is not recorded.

He mused on the tactical situation. *'We don't know what we are going to run into up here, but as usual I expect we will find the Germans reinforced and it will be a question of taking up a position, digging hard and staying in the same place all day.'*

Colin, like many, had been on the receiving end of both artillery and machine gun fire. He had also bombarded vulnerable infantry targets. As a consequence, he had learned the dire consequences to the infantry of open order advance against artillery and machine guns. He knew that the British army was outnumbered and outgunned, but he was confident that they could hold a line. But 'staying in one place' was the last thing on the mind of General French. They were an offensive army.[50]

They rode forward about ninety kilometres across country to the vicinity of Neuve Chappelle[51], first coming into action on the 12th October. *'We came up with the Germans about 8 days ago. They had no big guns against us, and we had three days close fighting, then a couple of days following up.'*

---

49 Even at this stage in the War, air power was significant. The BEF had six flying corps squadrons attached for reconnaissance purposes. The gap which had opened between the German armies at the Marne was exploited following air reconnaissance, the first time in history a battle had been influenced by air power.
50 The British High Command did not expect a long war and despite the small size of their army went for outright victory. The BEF did not even at this stage issue digging tools as standard to the infantry. Only the artillery had a tradition of digging themselves in, (creating emplacements), as conventional practice.
51 The First Battle of Ypres established the lines which would remain for four years. See map page 41.

On the morning of the 20th October, the full weight of the German Fourth Army fell on the British 3rd and 5th Divisions of II Corps. *'We have been hard up against them'* i.e. falling back *'for several days, hanging on till something happens somewhere else to relieve the pressure. The infantry have had a dreadful time.'*

'I have just come back from the trenches. Our shells were bursting only 500 yards in front of us. The poor fellows there are in rather a bad way.' The Germans had more and heavier guns. *'Some of the Seaforths[52] had an uncomfortable time on the way up. The big German guns got wind of their position and they got in close on a dozen heavy (5.9) 'krumps'. A lot of the Indian troops are also up here and they are seeing a terrible lot they do not understand; what with the almost continual shelling by the high explosive shells of the heavy German howitzers, and with aeroplanes.'*

The British were not equipped for an artillery battle of attrition. They needed help. *'I wish we had as much heavy artillery as the Germans have. We have three French batteries helping us here. Thank goodness we are not fighting them.'*

'We have really had a fairly hard time of it,' he says. But his stoicism and understatement make it difficult to interpret what is going on. The brigade diary is not very informative either. Only on the 29th October did he write fully.

'I am in a farm house and three old women are making a dreadful noise, milking their cows as if nothing is happening. I am just about a mile from our front line within range of German rifle fire.' The wagon lines for his battery were at this farm house, where they were very vulnerable.[53] One night in late October, they kept the horses there harnessed all night, fearing a German breakthrough. Unsurprisingly in every

---

52 The 1st Battalion, Seaforth Highlanders had been stationed in India, part of the 7th (Meerut) Division, and arrived in France with the rest of that division and the 3rd Lahore division, on the 30th September.

53 His howitzer brigade with a range of over four miles is situated with all their horses less than a mile from the German front line, in very flat terrain, in full view of German snipers. They were up almost with the infantry in open battle, conventional tactics at the time. But in retrospect it does not seem sensible.

subsequent campaign through the war, the wagon lines moved slightly further back, speed of mobility being sacrificed for security.

Two days later on the 1st November 1914, Colin was wounded in the calf by a rifle bullet. *'The brutes hit me an hour ago, it has gone through the calf of my left leg. It is really nothing at all. It is getting a little stiff now and will probably prevent me from undertaking any active operations for perhaps 10 days.'*

He was sent to England and was still in hospital in London on the 5th November. The Times recorded that "2nd Lieutenant Hutchison, a well-known rugby football half back, who has played for the army in representative matches is among the wounded." *'Only a scratch,'* he said, *'have been interned here. Am kicking up a fuss and might get home tomorrow. Leg only a bit stiff.'* He was passed as fit on the 26th November.

★

So Colin was now a veteran. He had fought through five major battles in three months: Mons, Le Cateau, the Marne, the Aisne and 1st Ypres.

He was actually reported as killed in the Times of 18th November. With him on the list that day were five colonels, four majors, thirteen captains and thirty-one lieutenants, all listed as killed. Three quarters of all regular army officers had been incapacitated by the end of the year. His corps of 37,000 men had sustained 25,000 casualties. The First Battle of Ypres effectively destroyed the British regular army.

Part of the reason for these devastating casualties is rooted in the optimism and offensive spirit which characterised the army. Colin embraced this spirit, but even in 1914 he thought that the offensive defence which served them well at Mons and Le Cateau should have been continued into the campaign in Flanders which was the First Battle of Ypres. He knew that infantry attacking positions supported by heavy artillery and machine guns would, in his words, *'have a terrible time'*. But like everybody he did not envisage the war lasting past Christmas. It was there to be won.

But this was simply unrealistic, given the number of German armies and their huge size. Perhaps if the British army had arrived in Belgium before the Germans, the battle would have been a defensive one from the start. But they didn't, and in any way, the British army was trained for decisive offence in colonial war. Nobody had any experience of a continental war, and one moreover which turned seamlessly into a siege. The war on the Western Front, from late 1914 onwards, was a double siege. Two lines of men, both in fortified positions, absurdly close in places, defending and attacking, not cities, as in conventional siege warfare, but whole countries.

France and Germany had last fought in 1870 and Germany had been victorious within 10 months. Both countries expected a return match and maintained huge standing armies, based on their own territory. Both had invested in heavy artillery. England in contrast had an Empire to control and protect. The navy was the senior service with the heavy guns. Much of the relatively small British army was in India or scattered in the colonies, on garrison duty, equipped to deal with incursion or small scale rebellion.

Continental wars were different. They were won by pushing back a huge opposing army in battle, and then capturing vital cities or fortresses by successful siege. Each of these two tasks required different resources. A battle is won by infantry advancing and forcing the enemy to retreat in disarray. It helps if that enemy has been softened up by artillery and if cavalry have destabilised the enemy line, but the infantry are the primary force. A siege is won by pounding a large hole in enemy fortifications. The artillery are central to this process and are the primary force. This is obviously simplistic, but the requirements of these two military options are quite different. The battle requires mobility and the ability to hit vulnerable targets. The siege needs weight of fire and the ability to destroy fortifications.

Both Germany and France had learned from the 1870 war. They had balanced armies with a good supply of heavy guns for static or siege warfare. The Germans had won by capturing Paris. The French were determined not to let that happen again. The British Expeditionary Force, in contrast, was equipped only for open war and was expecting a quick victory. What is more these expectations were shared by the public and the press in England. Facing up to this lack of realism in 1914 had been beyond General French and the high command. But now it was a new year. Would they have learned from their mistakes?

Colin did not impress his mother with his literary efforts during this first campaign. She now had all three of her sons in uniform. Young Donald had enlisted in an infantry regiment in London, older Alec was in France and she wanted to know in detail how the war was progressing. She demanded better letters from Colin in future and he complied. And he found solace in his writing; to help him cope with the petty, and often not so petty, stresses of life at war.

In December 1914, returning to work, those stresses were that of a junior regular army officer trying to find a foothold in the shifting sands that was the formation of Kitchener's New Army.

CHAPTER THREE

1915 The Canadian 1st Division

458th Howitzer Battery, 27th Division

'We haven't the ghost of an idea where we are going.'

In December 1914, Colin was posted to Woolwich to join the 27th London Division in a new howitzer battery for the New Army. He was keen to get back to war and chafed at the delays. But in practice he was missing little. The war was fought as a series of summer campaigns. Winters on the Western Front were to be endured rather than a time for action. The time he spent in getting to know his men, and learning from his new major, Major Lambarde, stood him in good stead once they got into action.

Before embarkation in early 1915. Major Lambarde is in the centre, with Colin on his right. Lieutenants Tyler and Schooling are on the major's left.

Attached to the 27th London Division, the new 458th battery expected to be sent into action almost immediately, but they were not even allocated to a brigade until mid-February 1915. Until then, nobody really knew what to do with them.

So Colin's complaints about the 'staff' start early. The 'staff' feature very heavily in his letters for much of the rest of the war. The 'staff' can be loosely defined as that group of officers who direct and organise the actions of the front line troops. They were not necessarily particularly senior officers, though many of them were. Every officer from a colonel upwards had an element of staff support. The colonel of an artillery brigade had an adjutant and a brigade orderly officer, who under his direction, ran the brigade office and dealt with the routine administration and liaison. The colonel would rotate his orderly officer to get to know his new and junior officers.

A brigadier general commanded the four artillery brigades of a division[54] and he had a divisional artillery office[55]. And then there were staff attached to divisions, to corps, to armies and to the commander in chief.

The disposition of troops in England was controlled by the War Office, and orders would filter down this chain of command. Given the huge size of the armies involved in the war, it follows that a huge

---

54 A brigade in the infantry is a larger and more senior formation than a brigade in the artillery. An infantry brigade of four battalions (each of 1000 men) was commanded by a brigadier general, but an artillery brigade of usually three, (later in the war four) batteries was commanded by a colonel, like a battalion.

The infantry brigadier had a brigade office, while the artillery brigadier, commanding the four brigades of artillery in the division, had an artillery office at divisional headquarters. The division, with four infantry and four artillery brigades, was commanded by a major general. There were four, or often less, divisions to a corps, which was commanded by a lieutenant general, and four, or often less, corps to an army, commanded by a full general.

55 The divisional artillery office, commanded by the brigadier, was run by a brigade major, helped by a staff captain. Other more junior officers were attached to the office with responsibility for intelligence, signals, liaison, etc., up to 10 officers in all.

army staff was required to coordinate the movements of army units and to plan any military action. There was almost no precedent to the scale of the task, and it is no surprise that there were problems, which were instantly apparent to the front line soldier.

So in mid-December, there was all sorts of order and counter-order from his headquarters. *'They have played an awfully shabby trick on us. They sent us (the whole battery, mind you) 220 horses, 230 men, with six guns and 24 wagons, and made us load up in the transport. Then a telegram arrived ordering us to disembark at once and get back to Woolwich, which of course had to be done.'⁵⁶*

Only two days before, they had *'had a full dress rehearsal and it was really rather a fine show. Considering it was the first time the horses had really been together in teams, it was quite a success. We have been so busy getting equipment and issuing it that we have had no time to exercise the horses and they are all dreadfully fresh. We shall have an awful business getting them into a train I expect.'* It was clearly somewhat early days to be going into action, and in truth it was not too much of a hardship to be home in England for Christmas.

And a few days later, they were moved into billets in Charing in Kent. He and 48 men of his battery were billeted with a Mrs Pitt of Pett House, whose husband was serving in Egypt. As a consequence, she adopted the battery for most of the next year, sending out parcels of supplies, which contained among other things, gingerbread, shirts, socks, soap, books, magazines and sugar for the horses. Her generosity was extraordinary.

Colin speculated that they were destined for the Dardanelles and perhaps on the 15ᵗʰ February they were, but once again a move was cancelled at the last minute. They were still an independent battery. But the next day, on the 16ᵗʰ, the new small 118ᵗʰ Artillery Brigade

---

56 The 27ᵗʰ London Division, to which 458 Battery was attached, was based in Winchester and sailed to France from Southampton on the 22ⁿᵈ December. 458 was at Woolwich, and had not even been allocated to a brigade by that time, so presumably whoever initially ordered their embarkation had second thoughts.

was formed, with two howitzer batteries of six guns, numbered 458 and 459, and they met their new colonel. It was a few days more before they acquired an ammunition column[57] and another ten days before the necessary 12 signallers[58] joined the brigade.

They embarked for France on the 10th March. *'The battery is very elated over our move. Even the horses seem to be pricking up their ears.'* Colin's love for his horses is a recurring theme. *'I have a splendid new horse. She has been a ladies' hunter and is a beautifully made compact little black. But I am a bit worried about her today as I cannot get her to eat anything at all. I have coaxed her with carrots and all sorts of things. It is due to a sore throat I think.'* She was better by the time they moved.

The move itself was not without incident. *'The doctor's[59] horse took charge of him, and was eventually stopped by our sergeant major and a policeman. I will exchange his horse for a slow old thing in my section. The doctor's horse is a good one.'* So much for the poor doctor.

And neither did Colin's journey start well. He had acquired a number of envelopes that had been pre-stamped 'Passed by Censor'. *'I have had a rotten piece of luck. You remember those censored envelopes. Well I left them in the sitting room at the Old Kent Arms in Ashford, and I'm jiggered if they weren't found by Major General Doran[60]. He has burnt all the envelopes and given the major a talking to about it.'* Colin never took censorship as seriously as the authorities.

---

57 An ammunition column in 1914 was commanded by a Captain and 3 Lieutenants. It serviced the batteries and acted as the brigade reserve, with a Sergeant-Major, Quarter-master Sergeant and Farrier-Sergeant, 4 Shoeing Smiths, 2 Saddlers, 2 Wheelers, a Trumpeter, 9 other N.C.O.s, 5 Bombardiers, 30 Gunners and 96 Drivers. Those of 1915 were smaller than this. Ref: Chris Baker www.1914-1918.net/whatartbrig.htm.

58 The Brigade diary states that *'12 signallers joined the brigade, but that many of them posted were very inexperienced and unsuited for their duties in the field.'*

59 Lieutenant E Grey RAMC reported himself as Medical Officer on the 1st March.

60 Major General Beauchamp Doran commanded the 25th division of the New Army till June 1916.

The censor's stamp was fairly standard through the war. This from late 1915.

And then, *'I was not wakened till 5.15 this morning and consequently nearly missed the train.'* *'Got down to market place by 5.30.'* Only at Southampton was he sure they were really going to France. *'Don't think they can possibly wire us back now.'*

Worse was to come. Having arrived at Le Havre, they were posted in France to the 1ˢᵗ Canadian Division[61]. What a come-down for a regular officer! *'We are attached to the Canadian Division, I believe. Nice lookout, isn't it? I only hope they have got a little discipline, that's all.'* Colin did not trust the Colonials! *'I only hope we don't go anywhere near Neuve Chappelle. I did not get very fond of the place during my fortnight stay in its neighbourhood.'* That is where they went! [62]

---

61 The Canadian 1ˢᵗ division was the first of the colonial divisions and had arrived in England in October 1914. It was commanded by Lieutenant General E. A. H. Alderson, a British officer. They had spent some time training on Salisbury Plain, before leaving for France in February 1915.

62 The brigade reached France on the 11ᵗʰ March, and La Gorgue, a railhead 9 kilometres north-west of Neuve Chapelle, on the 14ᵗʰ. See map page 41.

They were welcomed by a Canadian staff officer. *'We arrived at La Gorgue at 10.30 pm and were told we were wanted in action that same night. We got all our vehicles and horses off the train by midnight and marched 8 miles to our present position, but the motor car leading us got bogged up to the axle line. It took us ¼ of an hour to get it out and by this time, one of the wagons was in a worse plight than the car. When we at last arrived at the position selected for us by the Canadian staff, there was no way into the field and no light allowed. We were told to park the pack wagons on a bit of waste ground, but discovered it was the site of a burnt out house and there were holes through to the cellars below.'* This inauspicious start did not give them great confidence in the capabilities of the Canadian Artillery staff.

However, they got the battery of howitzers ready for action, and the next problem was to set up a forward observation post. This meant identifying a spot with a good view of the enemy lines, strengthening it so it was safe to sit in for hours on end, and rigging up a telephone connection. The wire for this telephone had to be rolled out for a mile or so from the battery to the post.[63]

The land was very flat, and German snipers were the main danger.

'Went forward with the major at about 2 pm to look for an observing station. Got sniped at on the way back. Beggar got two shots jolly close, will take care to avoid that spot.'

---

63 Once an Observation Post had been set up, the forward observation officer (FOO) would instruct the battery to fire ranging shots at selected targets, observing the shot fall, and by telephone adjusting the range and direction till the gun was on target. The readings were recorded at the Battery, and the other guns synchronised, so that theoretically all the guns could fire later on the spot that had been 'registered'. But the guns shifted slightly with each shot, and soon lost the precision needed for an accurate bombardment. For this reason, a professional battery never fired without a FOO observing. The selection of observation posts was crucial to the effectiveness of a battery and the higher the post, the better the view of the FOO. Most of the Western Front was flat terrain, so even a low ridge gave an advantage to one side or the other. It was not till 1916 that maps of sufficient accuracy to allow estimation of range were in general use.

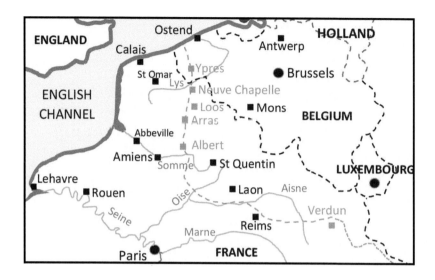

And a few days later, *'Yesterday I had to lay a mile and a half of telephone wire along the trenches. Luckily the Bavarians have just come in opposite and there is very little sniping. We had continually to show ourselves to get our wire in the air over communication trenches, and were not fired on until we started making a line on poles[64] over one particularly nasty bit, when I suppose they thought that was going a bit too far. They fired two shots and we scuttled down under cover for a bit. They were a little more active today and I don't think I would have shown myself at all.'*

The next day, *'I went forward alone to look for an observing station. I found a good one in the rafters of a farm building. The German trench was 700 yards away. The lack of tiles on the roof was rather trying and I got an occasional rifle bullet through the roof. So I spent the evening rigging up sandbags and a platform.'*

Due to the contours, their observing stations on this front had fairly limited views, so much of their forward observation work was done from the front line trenches. *'I spent a quiet day in the trenches. The German trenches were only 70 yards away in one place. My periscope was smashed by a German sniper.'*

---

64 Suspended wires were very vulnerable to enemy shell fire. All subsequent references are to wires being laid, or buried if they had time. If just laid, they could of course be easily tripped over or accidentally cut.

Trench periscopes in use, some miles north.

'*I nearly got shot by a mad Canadian shooting hares behind the trenches.*' Despite this experience, he quickly warmed to the merits of the Canadian troops. '*Met Captain Warden[65] of 1ˢᵗ British Columbian Regiment. Went round with him. The Canadians have improved the trenches they took over immensely as they are almost all handymen. Beautiful trenches now.*'

'*Another quiet day in the trenches. I had a jolly good look all along the front with the telescope. I only saw two Germans all day, but I could see their wire entanglements behind their first line trenches, all hidden with branches laced over them. My telescope was much admired by Canadian infantry officers in the trenches.*' The telescope was a present from his mother.

'*The Canadians are really a splendid lot of fellows. Captain Warden is a very nice man and I often have lunch with the officers of his company in the trench. They are all tremendously hospitable. The men are very independent and have to be treated quite differently to our own.*

When I was down there the other day, a sergeant came with two men and asked if he might go to a deserted garden just behind the trenches (exposed to

---

65 Captain J W Warden, known as 'Honest John' by his men, commanded the 1ˢᵗ Company in the 7ᵗʰ Battalion (1ˢᵗ British Columbian) of the 2ⁿᵈ Canadian Infantry Brigade. By 1917 he was a lieutenant colonel. There were three infantry brigades of four battalions in the division, a total of 12000 infantrymen.

the Germans) and fetch some onions. The major of course said "Certainly not." The sergeant went to the men and said "I'm sorry, boys, you can't go." "Very well, Sergeant," they said. But they went straight off on their own and got their onions. It's no good trying to force them to do anything, but they are splendid men where duty is concerned.

The Germans bombard here rather continuously and the shells were bursting round one of their sentries on a cross-road. I stopped and asked him why he had not taken cover behind a house while it lasted. He answered in their peculiarly slow drawl, "I reckon it's none too healthy round here sometimes, but I came out for it so I'm just going to stay right here and stick it." They really are a jolly good lot.'

It was about then that he wrote a plaintive letter home. 'We are really feeding very quietly here and have no delicacies of any kind except omelettes made with real fresh eggs. Did you once tell me you had sent Donald out a curry that only had to be heated up? The major would appreciate it awfully if you can manage it. The trouble is we would want some rice too – and instructions how to cook it.'

The advantage of family money was immediate. 'I can hardly keep count of the parcels I have to thank you for. The rice was splendid. We had a delicious curry made out of ration beef and an egg curry with the second lot. I told Major Nicholson that we had had a real Indian curry, rice and all, and treacle tart for dinner last night and he was quite upset at the thought of it. They get things sent out every fortnight, but he says they last 3 days and then they exist on rations. What with Tyler's mother who also knows what to send out, we are living like kings.' ⁶⁶

The additional spur of genteel competition between the ladies was the icing on the cake so to speak, though not everything was quite as successful. 'We had the pudding last night, but unfortunately our cook did not boil it long enough and the inside of it was not hot. We are going to have it fried tonight and I expect it will be jolly good.'

---

66 'Tubby' Tyler was his fellow subaltern in 458 and a friend from his days at Woolwich Academy. Their mothers had met at social gatherings there and knew each other. Major Nicholson commanded 459, their sister battery in the brigade. His early army career had taken him to India.

They were not exactly starving. *'The old lady of this farm is going to sell us two ducks for 6 francs. I paid 18 francs for two chickens in the last place. She keeps 24 cows and makes the most delicious butter, and her wholemeal bread is simply excellent. We have fresh laid eggs, as many as we want and she gives us a pot of cream for porridge in the morning and as much milk as we want.'* But they were at war.

'The Germans shelled the cross-roads 200 yards on our left. Black Maria' (the German 15 cm howitzer) *'landed a shell under a wagon of the 6th Canadian Battery*[67] *and threw it 12 foot over the trail of the gun, smashing the near gun wheel. Luckily there were no casualties.'* And a few days later, *'Tyler and I went over to a Canadian Battery for a visit and we saw shells bursting over our battery, so we strolled back.'* Bad decision! *A shell burst over our heads, which hurried us into a dugout. One shell registered a direct hit on a bag of horse shoes on an ammunition wagon. Several of the shoes were cut clean in two; the wagon top was torn off, exposing the explosive*[68]. *We will cover the wagons with a row of sandbags in future.'* [69] Wagon lines were still very close up.

They stayed in this position on the front for about two and a half weeks and were moved back in to rest on the 6th April.

Their time at rest was not a happy one. It started badly and got worse. Just as they had had problems getting into the line, now they had problems leaving it. Yet again the Canadian staff revealed their inexperience.

---

67 There were three brigades of artillery in the Canadian 1st division, the 1st, 2nd and 3rd, with four batteries (all field guns) in each, numbered one to twelve. The 6th battery was in the 2nd brigade. They had no howitzers.

68 Lyddite, the high explosive widely used during the First World War, was composed of molten and cast picric acid (named after Lydd in Kent where the first trials were done). It was unstable and could detonate with a sharp blow. There should have been a massive explosion.

69 *'Tyler and I found the time fuse of the shell that burst 20 feet beyond us set at 4800 metres.'* Fuse collection was an important counter battery task as it supplied the time fuse setting from which could be calculated the range to the enemy battery. It was generally the task of the junior subalterns to collect them.

First they were ordered to parade an hour earlier than necessary and then '*after the first 20 miles, the Canadians allowed us no halt at noon, to have lunch and to water and feed the horses. The colonel should simply have halted and let the Canadians go their own sweet way. Worse was to come, we arrived at the pre-arranged cross-road and our billeting party was nowhere to be seen. It was raining and very cold. The colonel[70] and the majors were all very bad tempered. After 2 ½ hours, a Canadian staff officer turned up and appeared to know where our billets were, but did not trouble to get out of his car, and kept Robertson[71] out in the rain. He made a rough sketch of our billeting area and drove off. We lost our way to the billets in a road he had not marked on the map.*'

Majors Lambarde and Nicholson were used to regular army efficiency and routines. '*I am afraid we are not very fortunate in our colonel,*' said Colin, he '*simply crumbles up when anybody senior talks to him.*' He irritated his junior officers too. '*Tyler had the elements of head cover explained to him for an hour this morning.*'

The tensions in the leadership spread through the brigade. '*The major has been rather upset by the colonel's fussiness.*' '*Captain Robertson, the adjutant,*' said '*that the colonel and majors are very trying.*' '*I would not be adjutant of this brigade for worlds,*' Colin says. Never one to keep his discontent to himself, Colin then went off and had a furious row with the sergeant major. The constant rain did not help. '*With any luck the colonel might get a bad attack of gout this dreadfully wet weather we are having.*'

The men picked up on the malaise. '*Unfortunately, somebody found a bottle of raw spirits at Nouveau Monde Inn last night. There was a disturbance and the proprietress said it had been stolen. I went and took down her evidence. The major insisted on having her round today to identify the men who had been at the inn. She identified 10, good men mostly (most of the battery had been there). The major proceeded to remand the whole batch for the colonel.*

---

70 The Colonel was clearly a sick man and there is nothing to be gained by giving his name.

71 Captain Robertson was adjutant, the Colonel's senior staff officer, responsible for the brigade office.

I had visions of losing some of my best men. We were saved a lot of bother by the proprietress telling lies and contradicting herself. The major had to drop the whole business and stop the colonel coming round. He punished the battery collectively – extra piquets etc. – this should have been done at first.'

Major Lambarde was not in a good mood. He was *'liverish and took a violent dislike to our battery director man. He wanted one of Tyler's best layers for director[72].'* Colin took Tyler's part in *'hotly opposing the idea. The major would hear of nothing else at first, but on being left to cool down, we think he has decided to accept defeat.'*

Altogether it was not a good time. *'I don't know what I would do if it wasn't for Tyler. I think I would have sent in my name for anti-aircraft work!'* But the pair of them managed to get one good day off. *'We are quite near to a small town called Cassel[73], perched on about the only hill for 50 miles around. Ypres and La Bassée can both be seen. Tyler and I rode up there yesterday and the view was simply magnificent. It was the first real fine spring day, clear all around. It was very hard to believe the noise we heard occasionally in the distance was really guns firing. We had tea in a little patisserie and came leisurely back about 6 pm'*

He had been very outspoken in his writing that fortnight, and he had a sudden thought. *'You won't publish my diary, will you? It would be distinctly unpopular.'*

But he soon had more important things to worry about. *'We are moving at last. I am going with the major and the colonel tomorrow to inspect the positions. It is a 30 mile ride from here. We are taking over the emplacement of a French 90 mm battery somewhere just north of Ypres.[74] Apparently all the roads are dominated by the German heavy artillery.'*

---

72 The battery director, knowing the direction and range of the target, adjusted the aim of each of the six guns onto the single spot, while the layer was responsible for dialling in the settings of a single gun.

73 They were in rest at Oudezeele, about 30 kilometres west of Ypres and six kilometres from Cassel.

74 The Canadian Division was to relieve the crack French 11th Division, commanded by a General Ferré.

CHAPTER FOUR

1915 Second Battle of Ypres

458th Howitzer Battery, 118th Brigade, 1st Canadian Division

'Our new position is a trifle insanitary.'

On the 18th April 1915, the whole Canadian Division moved back into the front line, to St Julien, just north and east of Ypres, relieving a French contingent. It was only days before all hell broke loose. But all Colin knew at the time was that the position they had taken over was horribly exposed to enemy fire.

On the 20th, *'I spent the morning with Captain Longchamp of the French Battery. I also looked for fresh positions because from the French position, our gun flashes were visible to the German trenches. Our right section came in that night and three French guns went out.'* [75]

From just behind their position at Pond Farm, which is clearly visible from the high ground on the horizon.

---

75 *'We replaced French 90 mm guns, very old pattern, which had to be tied down and run back again after each round.'* The De Bange field cannon from 1877 had no recoil system and had been obsolete for years, but the French had a big supply of ammunition for them and put them to use. Unlike field guns, with their flat trajectory of fire, howitzers could shoot up and over, from concealed positions.

'Left section came in last night after dark. The rest of the French guns went out. Our right section was in a dreadfully exposed position. The first time we fired they gave it to us and put two shots bang off, one in front and one behind our position, and very near the right section.' [76]

'We decided to change position and selected one at Fortuin about 300 yards to our rear. We started work on digging the gun pits in the evening and got the right section in that night.' 'We worked like Trojans until 8.30 getting our guns back and in.'

Their old position was clearly unsafe. With two shots, *'one in front and one behind'* the guns, the German Artillery had registered their battery. All they needed to do now was to align the rest of the guns of their battery with the one they had confirmed was exactly on target. When that was done, they could fire in unison and destroy the battery. A battery faced two choices if it had been registered. They either moved out fast, or they dug in deep. This was a recurring dilemma throughout the war. This time they chose to move. Probably only regular army officers, trained to initiative, would have had the courage to abandon their exposed position and pull back to a safer one at that stage of the war.

It needed only subtle dips in the contours to greatly increase their safety. Their second position at Fortuin, utilised the tiny valley of a stream, best seen as a rise in the road in this view of their new position. Pond Farm is seen in the distance across the road. They were now hidden from view from the higher ground on the horizon.

---

76 They were being registered by the Germans. See note 63 for a brief description of the registration process.

Literally hours after they had completed this move on the morning of the 21st April, the German battery which had registered their original position, opened fire in earnest. They targeted not only their old battery position, but also the farmhouse nearby which was their billets and brigade headquarters. Their old battery position and their farmhouse billet, both now well in front of their guns, were completely destroyed.

'*The Germans started shelling our billet and set fire to it. We had rather an exciting time getting our horses and kits out, as unfortunately there was a strong wind blowing, and we only managed to get everything collected about 30 yards from the house, when the bombardment made the place too hot for us.*'

'*Then the burning roof came down and landed on everything we had got outside. Knives, forks, spoons, enamel mugs etc., all 'gone west' as the Tommy puts it. They were all melted in their boxes. The knives and forks were the last thing I saved too. I packed the wretched things carefully into the box and carried it outside, only for it to burn, provisions and all. Tyler and I were very lucky – we were sleeping in the dugout and all our kit was safe. But the colonel has only his great coat left, also the doctor and Captain Robertson the adjutant.*'

Telephone contact with the divisional artillery was cut, and they lost all their brigade records. Even the brigade war diary was lost.[77]

'*Unfortunately two men were hit as we got the horses out of the house and tied them up in the barn. Then the barn caught fire. I tried to get our horses there saddled up and taken away. Bombardier Puttock and I were harnessing up two horses when a shell pitched 6 feet in front of us, hitting him badly and both horses. I did not get a scratch. We had to cut the remainder of the brigade horses loose and let them away. I am afraid one of our men has lost the sight in at least one eye.*'

---

77 This is significant, as it is impossible to cross reference Colin's following account of the battle of 2nd Ypres with a contemporaneous brigade diary. It was not written up till a week later, and then by an officer who was not present. A Canadian staff message at 9 pm on the 21st confirms that the 118th brigade headquarters had been completely destroyed, and communications not yet re-established.

Colin carried the injured man out of the burning building and then went back in, under continuing shellfire, to free the terrified horses.[78] His Military Cross came through eight months later. *We recovered all the horses during the evening. Some were brought in by Canadians. The Germans shelled our old position thoroughly.'*

This German bombardment proved to be the prelude to a major assault the next day, the 22nd April, the start of the Second Battle of Ypres. For the first time a deadly gas was used in a major attack, and it engulfed a four-mile stretch of French held trenches less than a mile to their left.

'Towards 4.30 pm, the Germans began to get lively on our left flank. At 5 o'clock, they shelled St Julien very heavily using 11 inch guns.[79] We saw a peculiar cloud of green and yellow smoke on our left flank and smelt a very unpleasant smell. It made our eyes and throat very sore. We opened fire on Passchendaele Ridge, but nothing happened to our immediate front.'

The gas was chlorine. [80] It terrified and it killed. The French

---

78 Colin's mother had to wait for a letter from Lieutenant Schooling, their junior subaltern, to get this snippet of news. Colin, home on leave, had mischievously asked her to send Schooling a cake. He was embarrassed, as his family could not afford to send out such luxuries to share in the officers' mess. So in light hearted revenge, he decided to embarrass him by telling her the story. He asked her not to show Colin the letter.

79 The main German heavy howitzer in 1915 was the 15cm (5.9 inch) schwere Feldhaubitze 13, and they had many smaller 10.5 cm Feldhaubitze 98/09 howitzers, equivalent to the British 4.5 inch. The Germans did not have 11 inch guns. It is surprising Colin says they did. Perhaps he means the approximately 11 cm howitzer.

80 The French were the first to use gas in the war, trying tear gas against the German army in August 1914, though it was not very effective. Chlorine which the Germans used at Ypres, reacts with water to form hydrochloric acid, which quickly kills when inhaled; also causing vomiting and severe eye damage. Easily seen as a green cloud, with a strong bleach smell and highly soluble so that even a damp cloth over the face confers some protection, it is not a very efficient deadly gas, particularly as it is denser than air and so settles round the knees. But it settled in the trenches, causing panic as the infantry, without masks, ducked down into it. It killed less than the initial estimates of over 5000, but enough to cause a serious problem to the defence. www.compoundchem.com

Algerian troops broke and ran. Within an hour there was a four-mile hole in the lines.

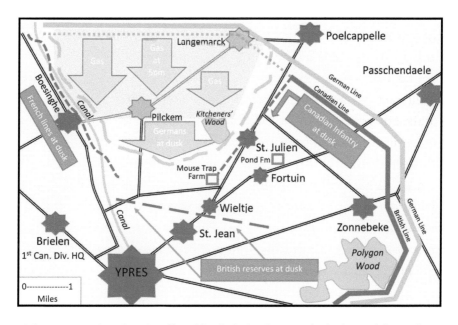

The gas was released at 5 pm[81] and by dusk the Germans had advanced four miles. The Canadians left fell back to defend the Poelcappelle to Ypres road, and the nearest British reserves were urgently mobilised to throw a screen in front of Ypres.

The German soldiers, unsurprisingly, were very unenthusiastic about attacking through it, and the assaults that advanced furthest were on either flank, i.e. very close to Colin' battery. Rifle *'bullets began coming in to the rear of the battery'* (from Kitcheners' Wood, where unfortunately the wagon line of 459 Battery had been parked). The success of the attack, which was illegal under international law, surprised even the Germans.

The Canadian infantry and artillery in front of St Julien were being attacked from in front and round behind their left flank. They had to swing their left flank back. The confusion at this stage of the battle cannot

---

81 Captain Longchamp and the French battery they relieved at Fortuin were wiped out at Langemarck, Colin recorded later.

be overstated. The French infantry who had survived the gas attack were falling back in complete disarray, some of them dying hideously as they did so. The Canadian infantry reserves at Fortuin moved through these broken troops and took up position on the Wietje to St Julian road to link up with the broken front line, and further reserves were ordered up from over the canal. On and behind the front line, wounded were being carried back, and ammunition was being brought forward. Communications were cut, and nobody had a clear picture of what was going on. It is also almost impossible to overstate the courage of the Canadian infantry on that evening and the following days.

Colin's battery opened fire at 6.30 pm and their fire, along with that of the other Canadian Artillery, was effective in reducing the intensity of the attacks on the Canadian line in the aftermath of the gas attack.[82] Probably around 9 pm, the brigade was ordered to cease fire and to retire a few hundred yards to await redeployment.

The Canadian infantry reserves launched a counterattack on Kitcheners' Wood at 11.30 pm *'The Canadians charged the wood later on, saving the situation as far as we were concerned,'* Colin says, and the battery was given just enough time to retreat at midnight[83] from just north of Wietje, less than a mile from the wood. When Colin says the Canadians charged the wood, this is exactly what they did, incurring huge losses as they fought hand to hand with bayonets in the dark. [84]

---

82 Shoestring soldiers, The 1st Canadian Division at War, by Andrew Iarocci. Ref. Kneiling and Bolsche, Reserve infanterie. (The British guns attached to the Canadian Division are not covered in detail in the book.)

83 The timings given are an educated guess. The batteries of the Canadian 3rd brigade were ordered back at 9 pm to a point just north of Wietje to await redeployment and it is probable the 118th brigade fell back at the same time to the same place. The post-dated brigade diary gives 11.30 pm as the time they received orders to re-deploy further back, and Colin's diary says midnight. The Kitcheners' Wood attack commenced at 11.30. There was little artillery support for it as most of the guns were on the move.

84 The 10th and 16th Battalions of the Canadian division, who were their front line reserves, attacked Kitcheners' Wood and fought all night. After the battle, less than 500 out of 2000 men were left standing.

458 was now falling back through St Jean. Major Lambarde probably met and took advice from British infantry officers who were trying, in front of Ypres, to put together a screen of reserves from the motley collection of units who happened to be in the area.[85] He chose to site his guns on their extreme left flank, in front of the Brielen Bridge. There were no guns to his left in front of the canal, and only 200 men of the Middlesex Regiment between the battery and the advancing Germans.

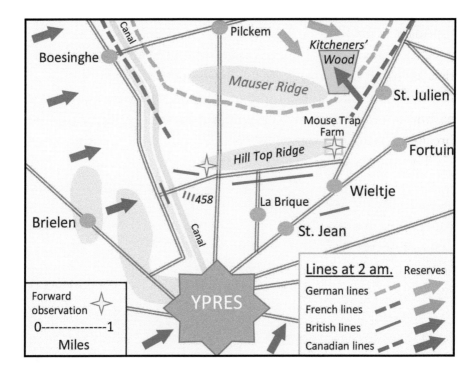

458 took up a position to defend the bridge to Brielen with good observation from Hill Top Ridge. They were not able to help the 1st Canadian Division in its desperate defence of St Julien, but were well placed to support the thin line of British reserves.

85 The British infantry reserve force was commanded by Colonel Geddes. It consisted of 28th and some 27th divisional reserves. His left flank had to cover the strategically vital bridge to Brielen, which had been left exposed by the advance of the Canadian front line reserves to attack Kitcheners' Wood.

The 118th Brigade had been ordered to La Brique. 458 was at Brielen Bridge. 459, having lost its wagon line, 35 men and 77 horses in Kitcheners' Wood earlier in the day, made its way back over the canal to Brielen to regroup. Neither battery had obeyed orders. [86]

Colin at Brielen Bridge was oblivious to this and nervous. *'Ascertained we only had a small body of the Middlesex Regiment in front of us and no other battery near us. We waited anxiously for dawn and expected the Germans at any minute.'*

And when dawn came on that 23rd April, it became clear how good their position was. East of the canal, the ground rises and falls in a series of low ridges. They were hidden in a fold of ground behind the first ridge in about the only spot where they could not be overlooked by the Germans who had advanced to the top of the higher Mauser Ridge, the second ridge back in a line level with Kitcheners' Wood.

View of Mauser Ridge and Pilckem, from the site of the observation post in a farm at the Western end of Hill Top Ridge, looking north.

---

86 It is likely Brigadier Burstall was unimpressed. The British howitzer brigade had lost its head-quarters and now gone missing. For several hours he did not know where they were. 459 fired from Brielen on the 22nd and then moved to St Jean on the 23rd. Where their colonel was or what he was up to is difficult to ascertain.

The Germans were preparing a further advance. *'I observed from the roof of a farm house on the ridge just beyond the battery and I saw the new German front line on the next ridge 2000 yards away. The German position commanded all the ground in front of us. Helmeted variety of Germans occupied the trench in strong force and were getting up and looking over, greatly excited. One man got up and waved his helmet. We gave them something to wave their helmets about – we demolished the four houses in their front line in the next forty minutes.*

We had to support belated and spasmodic attacks of our own infantry in the trenches to our immediate front. The attacks failed, losses pretty considerable.'

This diary entry does not do justice to what occurred. Two Canadian reserve battalions came over the bridge at dawn, and linked up with the five reserve battalions of British infantry (including the Middlesex Regiment) who had mobilised overnight to cover the gaping hole in the line from Kitcheners' Wood round to the canal.[87] They attacked, not just once, but again and again on that first day, supported by 458, *'the only artillery support to this portion of the front,'* according to the brigade diary.[88] The line held, and reinforcements poured in. *'The French poured across the canal during the evening,'* Colin wrote.

By now, the German infantry knew approximately where they were, and by the next day (the 24th) the artillery did too. *'The Germans put twenty-four 11 inch shells within 50 yards of our battery during the afternoon, very unpleasant. They knocked down most of our temporary billet without hitting it. The French and Canadians attacked in considerable force during the afternoon and would have succeeded, but the Germans turned the gas on again. Gas was pumped out from their trenches like a liquid which*

---

87 Colonel Geddes of the East Kent Regiment (the Buffs) commanded the so-called Geddes Detachment of British reserves, which filled the gap between the Canadian front line on his right, and the Canadian reserves on his left. He was killed on the third day of his epic leadership.

88 There were 4 field artillery batteries of the 1st Canadian brigade between Brielen and Ypres, behind the canal, but they were a mile or two back and concentrating on the defence of St Julien.

turned to a thick sulphur coloured gas, which settled over our trenches, the wind all this time being favourable to the Germans.'

On the 25th, the Canadian Division ordered the battery to support a larger and more organised attack, and specifically to arrange observation from Mouse Trap Farm (see map page 53). *'I was told we had to support an attack of our infantry on Kitcheners' Wood. We had to run out our wire to a farm house 600 yards short of the wood.'*

'It was rather perilous proceedings for the last 500 yards, as we were under heavy rifle and shrapnel fire. Running the wire out to that farm, we had to stop and mend the wire four times over a bit of ground that looked as though not a mouse could live on. Yet very few men were hit crossing it. The Germans also put several large shells near the house, but failed to hit it. Our attack progressed fairly well for the first half hour, but the German heavy guns shelled the infantry back, with very heavy losses.[89] Our telephone communications had no chance of working, as the Germans were shelling practically every inch of ground in the neighbourhood.'

Mouse Trap Farm on Hill Top Ridge – as it is now, looking north. They ran the wire across this field from the left; the Germans were on Mauser Ridge, the next visible.

'The idea of a forward observation post in that farm house was absolutely futile, with no chance of getting messages back. Had quite a warm time getting

---

89 Brigadier General Hull's 10th brigade from the 4th division attacked Kitcheners' Wood and St Julien across open ground on the 25th. His brigade was almost annihilated in the attack, with 2400 casualties.

away from same.' Tyler was inexplicably ordered back that afternoon on divisional orders despite the fact that the farm had been abandoned hours before by General Hull (and their own colonel) as a hopeless place from which to maintain communications. Having repaired the wire in *'24 places'*, Tyler arrived there only 40 minutes before it was razed to the ground. *'He and the telephone men had a very narrow shave. How anybody got out is a mystery. He had about 12 shells within about 6 feet of him. They got a lot of poor fellows in it.'* He was very lucky to survive the experience.

This is an early example of how divisional intelligence on the progress of attacks was often hours behind front line conditions, causing the general to issue an order that was plain wrong. To add insult to injury, a Canadian medical officer, Francis Scrimger, won the Victoria Cross for carrying a wounded man away from the house. Colin was not particularly impressed, and Tyler was left feeling very hard done by. *'He was there at the time and helped him get a man away, but of course got nothing for it.'* The arbitrary nature of heroism awards was a constant cause of complaint.

Their colonel, who had almost certainly been wobbly since the day his headquarters had been razed to the ground, gave way under the strain of this second heavy bombardment, and was relieved. He *'lost his nerve',* says Colin, not enlarging on this bald statement of fact, or when he in fact lost it. There was nothing further to say. He and Tyler needed all their energy to keep their own nerves.

'The situation is a little trying,' Colin says with masterly understatement, *'they are dropping about an unusual quantity of exceptionally large shell. This asphyxiating gas is the limit and no mistake. All our attacks fail because of it.'*

Brigadier Burstall had tried to involve them in the central salient battle for Kitcheners' Wood and St Julien to the north-east, but the battery was not well placed for this and it was clear that they were in a much better position to support the left of the line, north of Ypres. So he seconded them, probably with relief, (they had been nothing but trouble), first to the French and then to a series of British divisions. [90] They were so close to the infantry front line, with such good observation, that much of their firing was done on their own initiative. They hit the German lines wherever it looked as though it was needed, ignoring the enemy artillery who were targeting them. They were after all a howitzer battery. With its steep angle of descent, the howitzer shell was much more effective than field gun ordinance against trench defences.

For the first few days, they cooperated with a series of disastrous Canadian, French and British infantry assaults, which were all repulsed with heavy losses. The Germans, on higher ground, not only had good sites for their numerous heavy guns, but good observation too. And they could and did discharge chlorine gas on the attacking troops whenever the wind was favourable. Not only did the allied attacks fail to gain ground, they provided an opportunity for the Germans to counter attack.

On the 26th, the brigade diary records that the Ferozepore Brigade (of the Lahore Division[91]) and French colonial troops attacked, and that when the latter were gassed, they broke leaving a gap of 400 yards in the line. 458 Battery *'immediately turned its fire on to the German infantry they saw standing on the parapet about to advance, and prevented them from doing so.'* And the next day, *'the enemy looked like advancing, having let loose some gas. Fire was immediately turned on their trenches and no progress was made.'*

Colin's diary entries lapse. *'Allies position really quite hazardous,'* he wrote. There is only one entry for the 26th to 30th April. *'All very much*

---

90 An order dated the 26th April from Canadian Divisional Artillery allocated 458 to the Ferozepore Infantry Brigade of the Lahore division to provide close support, ordering Major Lambarde to liaise direct with its commander, not with its divisional artillery. This was an unusual but pragmatic order in the circumstances.

91 The Lahore division was the first of a series of divisions who occupied the gap between the French on their left front and the Canadians still occupied with the salient battle well to their right.

alike. *Constant shower of shells from the Germans. They have one 17 inch gun, four batteries of 11 inch and numerous 8 inch howitzers on this front. We have now got one 9.2 inch howitzer to meet the above mentioned German Artillery.*[92] *'They are bound to spot our guns sooner or later.'*

Enough said, especially when we *'appear to be the only battery supporting, and all our attacks have failed to gain any ground at all.'* But by the 30th, he was more upbeat. *'We are still in the same place and it is no more comfortable than it was before, but we are comparatively happy and cheerful, as it might be worse.'*

'I was through Ypres yesterday in a car, going back to reconnoitre emergency positions. The 17 inch they have been throwing into the town is simply wicked. It makes a smoke about the size of St Paul's Cathedral and destroys at least two houses at a time. The town is a dreadful sight, not a soul there as they shell practically all day. I can tell you the driver came through pretty fast.'

But as the days passed, the relentless shelling began to take its toll. *'They tell me that today is May 4th, which means we have now been here 14 days. I have lost all count of time. The fighting this last few days has been by far the worst I ever hope to see. The casualty lists are enormous. Fully 60 percent[93] of the Canadians are lost. The Lahore Indian Division is practically out of action as a fighting force and the losses of the 4th, 7th, 8th and 28th Divisions have all been very considerable.'*

The counter-bombardment they had to endure was unremitting. *'We fire and the Germans fire. They shell us from in front, they shell us from the side, and to crown all the dirty beggars have now begun to shell us from behind.'* *'We buried four dead horses in the crater of an 11 inch shell and there are six close to this house. The 17 inch continues to fire into Ypres and today*

---

92 The German heavy 42 cm (17 inch) howitzer, nicknamed Big Bertha, fired a shell weighing over 800 kilograms Again, possibly Colin means the 10.5 cm howitzer and 7.7 cm calibre field guns. See note 79. The British army heavy howitzer, the 9.2in BL Howitzer Mk 1, fired a shell weighing 130 kilograms.
93 In fact, about one third of the 18000 men of the Canadian division were killed, captured or incapacitated.

threw two big poplar trees the height of the church spire. There is one of its craters just behind our position and you could put our living room at home in it.'

'The noise[94] day and night really gets very trying. A French battery just on our right lost 4 guns blown up and an 18pr battery just behind us got it very hot this morning, but so far (I'm knocking wood) we have not lost anything very much.' They were hidden from direct observation. Most of the other batteries could be seen.

It was a different matter with their observing posts. These of course were in full view of the enemy. *'They put a sixty pound 5¼ inch shell through the wall of a barn I was observing from. It came through level with my feet about a yard away, displaced a lot of straw and brought me and my ladder down with a crash. It burst inside the barn and covered us with tiles and brick dust. I thought a volcano had gone off. The shrapnel in it riddled the end of the barn.'*

On the 7th May, *'I am afraid this is not going to be a long letter as I don't feel capable of writing very much. We are still in the same position and have really had enough of it.'* He did not, could not, expect their charmed lives to continue. He was overtired and overstressed. *'As Tyler was saying today, it has been the nearest approach to hell ever he wants to go through.'*

But he kept writing. He could be grimly poetic, *'Poor old Ypres is burning away and it will soon be nothing but a mass of bare walls and charred remains. It was a magnificently awful sight last night. The one remaining spire and the ruined Cathedral stood out black against the glare, a study in outlines. But the best thing that can happen to the town is to burn – inside is too dreadful for words.'*

And grimly humorous. *'In one of their attacks the other day, one lot of Germans let off their gas and the wind drifted it down along their*

---

94 Surprisingly he did not complain so much of German shells exploding, though *'when their high explosives are close, they make a rotten tearing noise that is very irritating indeed.' 'It is the noise, more of our own guns. We often had field artillery batteries immediately behind us. It is alright when you are behind a gun firing, but it is rather trying being just in front of them.'*

own trenches. *Since then strangely they have not used it. I expect one lot of Germans had something to say to another lot of Germans.'*

The next day, the 8th May, *'the Germans gave us another heavy bombardment, and the consequence is troops are being hurried in again. They put about 20 large shells round our observing station again, and one clean through the roof of it. Thank goodness I wasn't in it this time.'*

'The Canadian Artillery have had several guns knocked about and have had pretty heavy casualties. They are all going back.' And when on the 11th May, *'they have gone back to rest'*, Colin clearly felt abandoned and upset that Brigadier Burstall did not seem to want them, and he probably didn't.[95] *'We were attached to the Canadians and were just as much in it as they were, only I suppose being regulars we are able to stick it longer than they were – or rather are not worthy of the same consideration. We have now been attached to the 4th Division. The Canadians were simply magnificent. I do hope that they let us go back to their division as before.'*

They just had to keep going. *'The major'* (Lambarde) *'was rather shaken yesterday when the head of a shell went through our barn straight between his legs and the bricks displaced knocked him clean off the observing platform. He hasn't even a scratch, but he is a little old for such treatment.'* This is the first time he refers to the major with real affection. Colin, Tyler and he were a team. By this time, the battery was almost independent, acting on its own initiative to support the infantry in front of them. Their new Colonel Stewart let Major Lambarde get on with it and concentrated on 459.[96]

By the 12th, the shelling in the vicinity had tailed off a bit and

---

95 The infantry went back to rest, but in fact the artillery were redeployed, albeit to quieter sectors. But the 118th Brigade was left behind. Brigadier Burstall might not have been too sorry to lose them. On the first day, the brigade had not gone, as ordered, to La Brique to support the desperate Canadian defence of St. Julien; and then their colonel had collapsed at a crucial time a day or so later. He cannot have thought them reliable.

96 Not only had 459 lost men and horses in the gas attack, but they had also lost their Major (Nicholson) wounded on the second day. It was Colonel Stewart who wrote up the backdated brigade diary.

Colin is more relaxed. *'Our infantry have lost no ground since the 22nd immediately north of Ypres, as you may gather from our still being in the same position. But we have also had to support our infantry east of the town, and they have been very hard pressed.*[97] *It is very difficult to find battery positions this side of the canal and it is very difficult to support them adequately from the other.'*[98] *'There are now only 4 batteries left this side.*

Of course being nearest to the infantry we are called on by them to shell snipers and little gatherings of Germans they imagine they see. The Germans hold the crest of a hill which makes it possible for every one of our batteries to see and range on their front trenches. Consequently, when we start to bombard them they have a distinctly bad time. The Major gave me one gun to play along one particular bit of trench. It was shooting beautifully and I knew the range to a yard. We did not waste a round, bang in to the trenches every time and you cannot drop a 35lb shell into a trench without causing a certain amount of consternation.' Sometimes the understatement is glorious. *'At the request of infantry brigades,'* their targets *'were chiefly observation posts or lairs used by snipers and machine guns.'*

Colin had experienced independent command in 1914 and he was given it again now. He learned again the effectiveness of providing close support to the infantry in front of them by informal front line liaison, such as was still routine in the regular army.

On the 6th May, *'the infantry report gas being let loose and our trenches shelled. Enemy trenches filling up. 458 was turned on these trenches. The expected attack did not develop.'* And on the 8th May, *'very heavy bombardment of 28th Division front on our right. Both batteries turned on to enemy trenches in front of Mouse Trap Farm. Infantry reported our shells falling in enemy's trenches full of Germans.'*

---

97 *'Hard pressed'* means 'pushed back'. By the 3rd May, General Plumer had completed his withdrawal from the very exposed salient north-east of Ypres. This had had no effect on the sector north of Ypres.

98 The steep west bank of the Yser Canal and the contours behind, severely restricted the field of fire possible from Brielen. It was almost impossible to defend Brielen Bridge and the lines in front of it from the west side.

Their defensive battle at Brielen Bridge went on. On the 11ᵗʰ, the battery site was again registered by the German Artillery. *'They put some big shells very unpleasantly close. The major's dugout was ruined by a direct hit.*[99] *We took all our men away and put them in a deserted support trench about 200 yards in front of us.'* And on the 15ᵗʰ, so was their forward observation post. *'Just going up with Tyler to choose a site for a new dugout. The Germans have got a very good line on our old one and landed half a dozen shells within 20 yards of it, so we think it is time we dug another one.'* The battery could not move. But their forward dugout could, so they moved it.

Then finally on the 18ᵗʰ May, *'we got orders to leave Ypres that night. The wagon line teams arrived at 9.30. We drew out of position all night, but one gun and limber was forced into a ditch by an infantry transport. The thing looked a picture for good and all at the bottom of the ditch, but we got all the battery on to it and took 1 ¼ strenuous hours to get it out. Unfortunately, we weren't clear of the danger area and were continually worried by a beastly German field gun which fired nearly all night.'*

Their sister battery, 459, following behind, continued with its bad luck. *'459 was delayed by a pole breaking on the pontoon bridge and then by dropping in to the same ditch we did. Brigade eventually collected.'*

★

'That was the battery which saved the situation at Ypres,' said an infantry officer a year later on learning that Colin served with 458. It is obviously unfair to credit any one small unit with such an accolade. It was the Canadian 1ˢᵗ Division who prevented Ypres falling on the first day, holding up the German attacks. The Germans had not expected such success with their gas and had insufficient reserves to exploit their early gains. The Canadians held and absorbed the few fresh troops they had.

But holding Brielen Bridge was pivotal. It was the supply

---

99 By a *'Jack Johnson'* he says, the name given to the smoky explosion of a 15-cm shell; after the black American who was world heavyweight boxing champion from 1908 to 1915.

route over the canal north of Ypres. 458 was the only battery in a position to defend the bridge and they were part of the Canadian 1st Division. Like the infantry further east, their heroic resistance sent a message to friend and foe alike. Ypres would be held. It would not be encircled. On the morning of the 23rd April, and for several days thereafter, it was a giant bluff. With minimal reserves, and against gas and massed artillery, the allied infantry assaulted with reckless courage, their only effective artillery support in that sector being 458.[100] The German lines were held at Mauser Ridge.

The whole line in front of Ypres had to be held thereafter, of course. But in that crucial sector, with the contours in their favour and with intelligent artillery support, the infantry held their ground. If they had not, and as in all battles, there were so many ifs, Ypres would have been lost.

And 458 was lucky. Troops like luck. It is catching! The infantry of six divisions rotating in and out of the line would have seen 458, still there, just off the road by the bridge, surrounded by shell craters, still firing, Colin, Tyler and the major all still alive, all unwounded, still helping them out, on call 24 hours a day for 26 days. Other batteries were knocked out, 458 wasn't. Other batteries moved, 458 didn't. Even through all the horrors to come, the troops who had been there, remembered them with affection, admiration and gratitude.

Perhaps the last word should go to Major Lambarde who won the DSO for his part in the battle. Colonel Lambarde *'is quite certain that his 458 Battery quite alone saved the whole of the Ypres salient on April 23rd 1915,'* Colin wrote in 1917, only half tongue in cheek and in reminiscent mood. He may have been right.

---

100 One has to commend Brigadier Burstall, commanding the Canadian artillery, who had ordered the 118th Brigade into sensible positions, and seen them ignore his orders. When he eventually discovered where they were, he did not over-react. He recognised the strategic importance of the position that 458 had taken up, and he left the battery where it was. He saw that they would be of no help to his division after the second day, and authorised their secondment to other divisions, possibly without regret, but entirely logically.

Colin never forgot the lessons of defensive artillery warfare he learned at Second Ypres. It was common sense really. Site the guns well, using initiative; find good observation posts; dig in deep; don't be afraid to move; and shoot at what you can see, liaising with the infantry, to cause the maximum discomfort to the enemy.

Colin spent a lot of his time in contact with the infantry only yards in front of them. He discussed tactics with many young infantry officers. He thought about what he was witnessing and doing. As he said at the time *'the best we can hope for is that they will attack us. It makes it all the easier for us to slay them in the quantities we want to, and much less cost to us. Their gas will not now succeed I think.'* Defence was so much easier than attack.

But in May 1915, he takes these thoughts forward from September 1914, when he had said much the same thing, leaving aside the gas. They were no longer outnumbered. They had to attack. *'We shall never beat the Germans until we can keep up a simply colossal shower of shells on them. The poor infantry simply exist to go through the places made for them by the artillery.'*

He was saying that planning for offensives must start with an artillery plan, not, as was current practice, preparing an infantry attack and adding artillery support. Until that lesson was learned, the infantry would pay with their lives. It took a long time.

★

It is reasonable to ask why Ypres was so important. There were battles for Ypres in 1914, 1915, 1917 and two in 1918. The map overleaf helps provide the answer. As can be seen it is protected by canals north and south; it has good roads, especially from the east; it had an east-west railway connection; and it is on low ground dominated by a half moon of higher ground to the south and east.

The British as a general rule held the low ground and were trying to capture the high ground, so as to provide a springboard for further advances. Conversely the Germans generally held the high ground and tried to convert this advantage into territorial gain, symbolised by the town of Ypres itself.

This symbolisation was important in its own right. The British press had celebrated the fact that the town had been held (at great cost) in 1914, and it would have been a public relations disaster if the town had subsequently fallen.

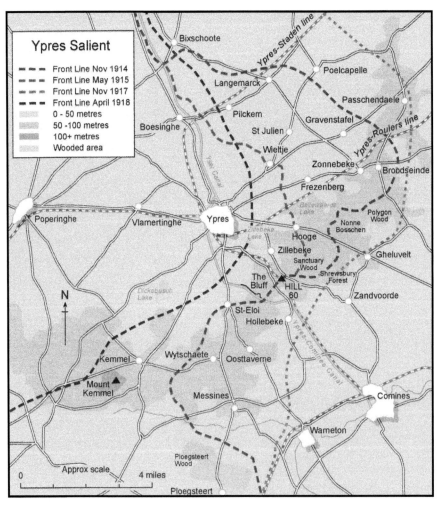

Ypres became the focus point for the war in Flanders.
Colin was between St Julien and Ploegsteert for much of the war.

CHAPTER FIVE

1915 Festubert and Givenchy

458th Howitzer Battery, 118th Brigade, 1st Canadian Division

'Thank goodness, still with the Canadian 1st Division!'

For most of their time at Ypres, the 118th Brigade had been temporarily attached to British divisions and Colin was worried. *'The Canadians were really magnificent, both their infantry and their gunners, and deserve every bit of the credit they are getting.'* They had been cheered off the battlefield. *'I do hope that they let us go back to them as before.'*

But the Canadians had been pulled out on the 10th May and were enjoying, if that is the right word, their fortnight at rest. So on the 19th May, as the battery was marching the 25 miles to their rest billets, the Canadian Division was already being allocated a new sector to occupy. Colin and Major Lambarde spent the next day reconnoitring a new battery site, riding a round trip of 20 miles. *'Seat a little sore!'* Colin recorded ruefully, and *'then the same night we had counter orders cancelling everything.'* They did another round trip of 20 miles to another site the next day. *'The staff work of our army[101] is really too absolutely childish for worlds. But I really believe we have at last got fixed and we are going back in to action tonight.'*

And they moved with the 1st Canadian Division back into action

---

101 Their first day reconnoitring (on the 21st) was under orders from the 7th division, who obviously tried to keep them, having recognised their professionalism at Ypres. The 1st Canadian Division ordered them to reconnoitre another position on the 22nd. On the same day, the Canadian artillery diary says that *'the locality of 2nd Artillery Brigade could not be ascertained.'* The Canadian staff were not in total control of their brief.

on the 23rd, allowing them almost no rest at all. They all so badly needed it. But every artillery general wanted howitzers, and back in to action they went. The battery they were relieving had already moved out when they arrived at Festubert, forty kilometres south of Ypres on the 23rd, and the battle of that name was ongoing.[102] *They have had 8 days in action. I would like to put them in action for 26 days at Ypres and see what being in action really means.* So they had to start from scratch in searching out observation posts and running out telephone wire for their guns. The brigade was ordered to support an attack the next day requiring pinpoint accuracy in targeting the German trenches.

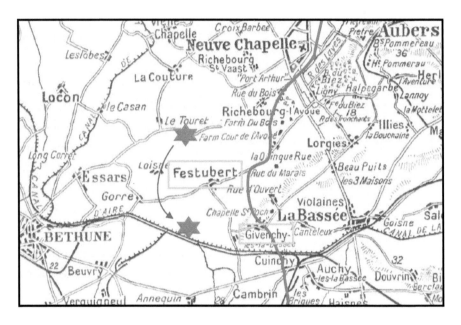

They are back just south of Neuve Chapelle. Brigade positions starred.
Approximate front line shown, but the trenches and area of devastation
extended for a mile either side of the lines.

---

102 The Battle of Festubert started on the 15th May and the British had advanced about one kilometre beyond the village for the loss of about 16,000 men. By the 23rd May, the ground from the guns to the front was devastated. The brigade took over positions just north of the village of Festubert and they had to observe either from a brewery on the northern edge of the village, or from the forward trenches.

With no handover to prepared observation posts, the brigade was temporarily blind. *'The divisional orders were to open fire at 5 pm, giving us ½ an hour to get out 2 miles of wire and locate an unknown house. Our batteries had to bombard a portion of trench which was only 40 yards from our own. Littlejohn*[103] *and I went down to the trenches as FOOs to observe fire. We got out to the required trench at 7 pm. It was a German redoubt, just recently captured, dead still unburied. Of course we could not get through'* to direct the guns *'because the wire had already been cut by German shells. Sent 3 signallers back along the line to try and get through. Came back at dark at 9.30 pm.'* [104]

The divisional artillery staff had not insisted on an organised handover, and were giving them orders which were impossible to carry out. A pattern is emerging. Colin was in no doubt who to blame. *'The men are really splendid, but some of those on the staff are too trying and incompetent for worlds.'*

The situation on the day they arrived at Festubert was far from clear. *'The Canadian infantry has already distinguished itself here and we are continually gaining a little at a time. There is a terrible mix-up though. We are behind the German trench line in many places, and in parts they still hold their trenches with our fellows in the same trench 20 yards away.'* It was very difficult to keep track of the battle situation.

On the 26th May, they had to support another local assault. *'The Territorial 47th Division and the Cavalry Brigade under General Seely delivered an attack on 'L8' redoubt. Ferguson*[105] *equipped with an electric signalling lamp accompanied the bombing parties along a trench supposed*

---

103 Lieutenant Littlejohn was a subaltern with 459 battery.

104 This attack was probably that of the Canadian 3rd Battalion on a trench line at the Rue d'Ouvert. There is no mention in the 118th Brigade diary, presumably because they failed to deliver. The attack itself failed. The howitzers were used to destroy trench parapets prior to an infantry assault. The field guns were generally used to cut the barbed wire, landing shrapnel shells just in front to blast through it. An excellent account (with maps) of the attacks on different sections of the line is given in Shoestring Soldiers, the 1st Canadian Division at War, 1914-1915, by Andrew Iarocci. Applicable also to notes 106 and 116.

105 Lieutenant S Ferguson was another subaltern with 459, their sister battery.

to be occupied by the Germans. A green rocket was the signal for the attack having succeeded. The rocket went up at 11.30.'

'Ferguson reported back that they had worked along the wrong trench in the dark, but the territorials would not be convinced and he got into dreadful hot water.' The staff initially believed the infantry battalion commander rather than the artillery lieutenant. But they did act reasonably when they learned the facts. *'He had a full personal apology from divisional headquarters as his information proved absolutely correct.'* But Colin, loyal to his friend, overtired and hot headed, was again confirmed in his perception of staff incompetence.

So when *'we got a message to shell a house 300 yards from our trench supposed to contain German snipers,'* he was in no mood to keep his discontent to himself. *'We could see every scrap of ground and reported that the house did not exist. Staff of 3rd Infantry Brigade insisted it existed, so I was sent out to find it. It took 1 ½ hours to get out, ground simply foul, no dead buried, dead still lying in trenches, mostly Huns. The infantry in the trenches knew nothing of the house or sniping. Another 4 hours walk for nothing, I'm getting tired of doing useless things to amuse the staff. Besides which the trenches are very unhealthy to get in and out of in daylight.'*

He decided to provoke a confrontation. *'I went back and personally reported to infantry brigade HQ to ask if the pencilled house could be removed off their maps. I am afraid I am not very popular with the staff captain. I suppose I must have been a little sarcastic. I am glad I got some of my own back on him.'*

'Whilst up in our trenches, I took the opportunity to look along another trench the Germans had just left. No officer's patrol had been up and it was uncertain whether the Germans had really left it or not. It was important we should know, as we had to shell the part the Germans were in. Things are very mixed up here.[106] *No-one knew how far anybody else had got, as most of these trenches have been taken by parties of bomb throwers going along them*

---

106 This was on the 27th May. He was at K5, a strongpoint very recently captured, and explored along L8, a trench-line which had been reported captured the day before, though there was still doubt it was free from Germans. The German positions at Festubert and Givenchy were designated by letters and numbers.

with bombs[107] *and when they exhaust their supply, a barricade is made until another supply can be brought up. I got the sergeant of our advance barricade to come along with me. We went along till we came to a gap exposed at 60 yards to the Germans, and dodged across the gap to find no cover on the other side. So we bolted back and came away. Enough for one day.'*

'The trench work that we have been doing has been anything but pleasant as the trenches have all been taken lately from the Germans, and there has been no burying of the dead as yet. Some of the sights and smells are ghastly, and there is no getting away from them as they are in narrow trenches and you cannot show your head above the parapet.'

Of course, normal life went on as well. He was not writing much more than a diary from the front, but his mother tried to be chatty. *'It is funny you asking about my watch. Father's nice alarm watch went in the fire at our billet. I hope to get compensation out of the Government of about £12 in all. I wonder if you could get me a real good time keeping stop watch. I want one for timing the difference between the flashes of German guns and their reports, by which knowing the velocity of sound, we are able to locate German batteries. If you could also get me a Stewards floating compass, I should be very pleased.'[108]*

Then at the beginning of June, they were moved a few miles further south to Givenchy[109], still without a break to rest and

---

107 Bombs were handheld grenades, almost always with a safety pin and a four second delay. A British trench bombing team conventionally had nine men: an NCO, two throwers, two carriers, two bayonet-men for defence and two 'spare' men for use if casualties were incurred. www.firstworldwar.com

108 Part of a subaltern's duties each day was to localise any enemy formations in sight and to report findings back to the intelligence officer at the divisional headquarters. Simple observation was not very accurate and a lot of research went in to improving techniques through the war. Where they could see the enemy gun flashes, usually at night, they could at least make an estimate of range by the method Colin describes, and this was the principle tool in early 1915. They could also examine the fuses from enemy ordinance (note 69).

109 See maps on pages 68 and 41. They moved about three miles south to behind the village of Givenchy. The brigade headquarters was at Gorré, and their battery was on the edge of a wood just south of a curiously shaped road junction known as the Tuning Fork. They had several observation posts in and behind Givenchy.

recover. *'We have moved to another position now, right down opposite La Bassée at the extreme south-east of the British line.'*

Again, they had to get themselves set. *'We have a beautiful observation post we call Artillery House.*[110] *It is what remains of a house, you have to get up two very shaky ladders, crawl along on your stomach and get through a shell hole through a dividing wall, worm your way across the floor of a room with practically no walls standing to half of what was once a window built up with sandbags. You have to look through a slit of a sandbag loophole on our trenches which are 200 yards away. The German trenches are some 80 yards beyond.'* Beautiful maybe, but it sounds like a death-trap!

'Things are pretty busy here all the time as we are continually worrying the Germans everywhere. The worrying process is rather a tiring business for the worrier too. Tyler and I are forced to do all the observing work between us. The major is really too old for the hard physical exercise necessary for climbing into the sort of observation stations we have to observe from nowadays.'

A view from a front line observation post further north (taken by brother Donald).

110 This observation post was in the village of Givenchy itself.

He took time out to write a good letter on the 6ᵗʰ June. *'I have got a lot of things to thank you for. Webbing equipment, watch and the drawers. The watch is splendid, just exactly what I wanted. I have been without a watch of any kind now for the last three weeks and it is a blessing to know the time again.* (And a few days later, *'Stop watch and compass are both much above what I expected. Compass is a beauty.'*)

I literally have not had an hour to myself for the last three weeks. Tyler and I do all the observing and communication work, run the shooting of the Battery, manage all ammunition supply, and when we get back we are asked why we haven't got notes of battery registrations. I am ashamed to confess it but I am frightfully rude to the Major on occasions. Poor Schooling is frightened of him, and Tyler does things he is told without grumbling, so he gets put upon. I have to sort of act as buffer between them.'

The arrogance of youth! Poor Major Lambarde must have been exhausted too. Later letters tell how he becomes terse and irritable under pressure. He must have felt a heavy paternal responsibility for his young officers.

'Today has been a glorious day. A piper is at work somewhere in the distance, and but for one shell which has just this minute landed 20 yards short of our dugout, it is a beautiful peaceful evening. As I have had about 6 day's strenuous work by night as well as by day, I am getting a rest staying with the guns. Tyler and Schooling have gone up to the observing station. It is very trying work up there under our present conditions and with our present targets. We have to go to most unhealthy places about 200 yards behind our own trenches to get a view of the German front trenches. They shell the place very regularly, and very heavily when there is any show on.'

There were new dangers. *'The Germans have been troubling us with a new trench mortar.*[111] *You cannot hear it coming, and it makes very little noise in the air, dropping with a beastly crack. I am afraid we ran away from*

---

111 7.58 cm leichter Minenwerfer (LMW; 'light mine launcher'), was a wheeled muzzle loading trench mortar, which had been developed just before the war. It was light enough to be moved by one horse or four men and had a maximum range of about 1400 yards.

it the other day. The major and I were going down into the trenches when one burst just in the next traverse very close to us. We both agreed on the spot that there was no violent necessity to pass that way, and made a hurried and undignified retreat.'

And the same old ones. *'The 'subalterns' happy home"* (another observation post) *'was vulgarly treated by a German heavy howitzer this morning. Ferguson[112] and I were up there and several shells came pretty near us, about 80 yards away, but as they were off our line, we continued with our work. We had just finished and had got down from the top to come away, when they landed another one just short of the house. We and all the other officers in there thought it was time to clear out, so we bolted to the communication trench. We could not see a yard for the brick dust, but managed to find the trench. We had no sooner reached the trench when they landed another shell almost on top of us and covered us with turf. I got my foot caught in a telephone wire in the trench and blocked the way with about 20 officers and telephonists pushing behind me. When we heard the next one coming, I fell into a dugout just off the trench and all the rest prostrated themselves flat in the trench, collapsing like a pack of cards on their faces. One Canadian captain passed me with a huge bit of turf on his head. It made me roar with laughter. Of course it's all right now, but the wretched shell landed within 10 yards of us. You will notice I said others behind me – I fancy I was just about the first out of that house with Ferguson, who once played wing 3 for the army. I won by fully a yard, not bad eh. The house is sandbagged up, so I was very frightened of it coming down and burying us, which would have happened had the shell hit the place.'*

Colin's hysterical laughter suggests that the continuous strain is starting to tell. As he put it, with glorious understatement, *'I am afraid my wrist watch has had a rotten time, and like its master really, wants a clean-up and a little oiling.'*

The orders coming from divisional artillery did not help. *'Our*

---

112 Lieutenant S Ferguson was with 459 till late June and then promoted to captain and transferred to the 7th division. He was with Colin at the Somme in 1916, and survived the war.

zone[113] *of front has just been changed for the third time since we came into this position a week ago, and so we are once again registering points in another area. We had to run out yet another wire, and Tyler and I got very hot doing it this morning.'* Then a few days later, *'carried out registration in front of Givenchy, but zone changed. Laid out wire to the factory, very hot'* (i.e. dangerous), *'work, never used this observation post, told to come back again, zone changed. Laid wire out to Brewery for new zone. Did a few registrations from there. Came back at night to find zone changed again, Givenchy again necessary.'*

A few days later, on June 15th, they supported a strong attack at Givenchy. On the day, Colin was proud to write *'have spent the last four days laying double fresh wire, laddered in 10 places.[114] It kept through beautifully for registrations notwithstanding several shelling's. We registered trenches H2–H6[115], being under the impression that these were the allotted targets for our battery. Artillery House, Givenchy was the only good observing station for these targets.'*

'On the morning of attack we received orders to bombard trench line I3– I9. The bombardment zone was changed at the last minute and we had to use an observing station, which was not prepared. Notwithstanding our bombardment from 3 o'clock till 6, the Germans were ready and they had

---

113 The guns were all lined up on a registered target. They could fairly easily adjust to targets which were a few degrees either side of this line, in a zone. This zone was much less than the total arc of fire from the position. If a different zone was required, centred on another target in the arc of fire, all the guns had to be moved, lined up on each other, and re-registered, a process which took some time.

114 Wire communications from observation post to battery and from battery to brigade were vulnerable due to shelling of the front line areas cutting the wires. The partial solution was to bury the wires deeper and to create ladders in the wiring so that it had to be cut several times before the connection was broken.

115 The German J trenches, so named by the British, were north of Givenchy, H trenches east and south, with I trenches between the two and extending round behind the H trenches. The terrain was such that there were three different observation posts, two in Givenchy and one at Windy Corner, a crossroad behind Givenchy, with different views of the German lines. This last observation post was the one they had to use to see I3–I9.

their trenches full. Out of 200 Yorkshires in the attack, only about 90 reached the German front trench. They had machine guns laid and swept down our men. All leaders were put out of action in the first rush.' That evening they changed to shell J13–J14.

And the next day' *'Tyler had to go out at 3.30 pm at very short notice to observe fire on German front trenches H2–H3. The wire to Givenchy had been cut by enemy fire and it was impossible with 30 minutes warning to get wire laid to take on this target. Target had been properly registered so bombardment was carried on from previous registration which had been done very accurately.' 'Divisional Artillery told us we did not hit trench H2–H3 during bombardment. They ordered us to lay out wire at once. Tyler started to lay fresh wire out to Givenchy which was being so heavily shelled as to make movement there almost impossible. He was recalled just before reaching worst part by a fresh message from divisional artillery changing our zone again, making Givenchy useless as an observing station.'*

This attack was a total failure.[116] Colin wrote summing up the battle. *'We have been having a hard time round here, and what is more sickening is that we have little to show for it. The Germans are holding very tenaciously to a redoubt we have been trying to take for a week. Our casualties are perfectly appalling and all we can hope is that the German casualties are as bad if not worse.'*

Colin's brigade had come away from Second Ypres with relief, but with pride as well. They had done the job they were there to do, and done it very well.

But the situation completely changed on the offensive battlefields

---

116 The brigade diary records the targets requested with no comment. The Canadian Divisional Artillery diary says only that 'three forward guns did good work smashing the parapets,' thereby implying that the other batteries involved did not do much 'good work'. Andrew Iarocci (see note 104) suggests that the confusion during the battle was partly caused by an overlap of responsibility between the Canadian division and the 7th division artillery staff. He also notes that the infantry staff often informed the artillery staff of operations so late that it was impossible for them to make the necessary arrangements to support the attacks.

of Givenchy and Festubert, with them now firmly under divisional artillery orders. Infantry assaults were hastily arranged with inadequate artillery support. They uniformly failed. There were no artillery attacks with infantry exploiting the results.

The artillery generally failed to destroy the barbed wire and strongpoints in the enemy lines. Lack of ammunition was a factor, though Colin's comments on the 9th June, are ambivalent on the subject. *'Great talk everywhere about a lack of ammunition. We are rather inclined to believe this slightly untrue, but the ammunition column also reports a shortage,'* and later *'unfortunately, our ammunition being limited, we are not allowed to make ourselves as objectionable as we would like, but the French appear to have all the ammunition they require.'*

In forward observation, Colin would have met many junior officers before and after assaults. He would have been ashamed at the ineffective support the artillery generally was giving them, especially after their good work at Ypres. None of the remaining junior officers would have had faith in the staff process by which attacks were coordinated and planned.[117] Their casualties, as Colin says, were appalling.

And as for himself, *'I hope they will soon give us a bit of a rest, as sleep has been particularly scarce just lately. I was up all night the night before last, and again last night. The major has had very little sleep and Tyler was up here at the observing station for the night, when the blighters put a shell through the top of the roof.'*

By the 21st June, the intensity of battle had settled, but *'they have a nasty habit of throwing their shells about unpleasantly close to our billet about 6 o'clock every evening. They put about 30 or 40 just 100 yards over the billet the other night, which I came back in the middle of. Everybody had cleared out. I was very frightened myself sitting with my back to a wall while the shell fire only just cleared the roof of our billet, but I was too tired to move. Besides which I fancied I was safer where I was.'*

---

117 Andrew Iarocci suggests that the Canadian sometimes 'modified' their orders to avoid suicidal casualties.

Colin walked in to a barrage[118] and then just sat down, and waited for a shell to fall on his head, almost wanting to be hit. He needed a rest and he needed it very badly. And he knew it. He wrote to a girl-friend that week. *A minor ailment would really be very acceptable under the circumstances. My last effort was just about the best anyone can hope for, a flesh wound through the calf incapacitates just for a nice period, 4 or 5 weeks, and has no evil effects.'*

They moved on the 25th June, to the quietest sector of the line, Ploegsteert Wood south of Ypres and Messines Ridge, where the British held the high ground.[119] It was the sector given to those units which had been most damaged in action and which needed time to regroup.

But Colonel Stewart[120] did not take the quiet for granted. He put the brigade to work. They were regular army. *'We have had to make ourselves a gun position and dugouts and consequently have been very busy getting in.'* Colin was put to further work. He reconnoitred forward. *'I talked with infantry officers in the first line trenches,'* and he reconnoitred back. *'I went for a long ride this afternoon to have a look at our second line of defence position, just in case we have to use it. This is a wise precaution which I think was probably learned as a result of the German breakthrough at Ypres.'*

Two days later, *'I went for a ramble on my own amongst our support trenches, chiefly discovering where there weren't any. I had to bolt for cover twice, with Germans sniping at about 1400 yards.'* The next day, he went back with Tyler and telephonists, *'looking for new observation*

---

118 Neither the brigade diary nor the divisional diary had anything to report that day. It was quiet!

119 The battery was situated on the northern edge of Ploegsteert Wood, just west of St Yves, south of the high ground of La Rossignol Hill (hill 63). There was *'an observing station from which we can see for miles only ten minutes' walk from the battery position.'* The map on page 66 shows their rough location.

120 Nor it is fair to say did the division generally. General Alderson who commanded the 1st Canadian division co-ordinated very considerable strengthening of the British lines in this sector over the next month or so.

stations, and laid wire to 'Fort Brandon' and 'Gas trench'. Our present observation station is none too healthy and we are much afraid we shall have it knocked down very soon. This won't be a new experience for us if it does happen. I am going up this evening to arrange the exits a little better, so that in case of necessity we shall have a clear run to a trench. I don't believe in sitting in a house that the Germans are trying to knock down with high explosive.'

And over the next few days, he continued his assessments of the brigade's position. 'I reconnoitred roads to GHQ position for the brigade. It took the whole morning. We found many roads marked in maps as red (i.e. metalled) only existed as tracks hardly traceable on the ground. GHQ is right on the Franco Belgian frontier. Difference remarkable, French roads excellent, Belgian very bad.'

The professionalism with which the major, and probably the colonel, guided their young protégé officer is impressive. Colin was learning the military skills required for effective command. He was thoroughly assessing their defensive positions, checking morale and anticipating eventualities, working to improve both the gun line and their observation posts. Major Lambarde must have watched on approvingly.

They did have a bit of fun on the 24th July. 'A deserter had told us that the German soup kitchens in Messines distributed the men's dinners between 9.15 and 9.45 pm when all the cooks of different regiments collected for their daily rations. At 9.30 pm, about 20 batteries (including us) opened a violent cannonade on Messines for two minutes with the object of spoiling German dinners. The bombardment looked most effective. It was a dark night and the bursting shrapnel looked very pretty indeed.'

There was a downside to their quiet sector. 'This place is a training ground for raw troops, and we have got three officers from the 37th Division attached to us for instruction', not that he minded that too much. But 'the staff are trying to make us send in all sorts of useless reports, trying to teach us (regimental officers) our own job. They *give us no end of trouble, and as the Tommies say, "we aren't having any."*[121]

They became entitled to home leave back to England and for all of them it was badly needed. The major went first, and Colin, not Tyler, was left in command of the battery in his absence. The war had been going on for less than a year, and Lieutenant Hutchison, Royal Field Artillery, who had only that month been routinely promoted from second lieutenant, found himself at the tender age of 22, doing a senior captain's job. Not only was he not yet ready for the added responsibility, he was not fit for it. And small wonder.

The wonder is not that he should show some signs of stress, but that he did not break entirely. For two months now both he and Tyler had been continuously at risk of death or worse, continuously sleep deprived, continuously deafened by concussions, continuously worried for their men, and continuously witnessing scenes of horrific carnage. The stress had been unrelenting.

Colin's letters to his mother are of course very understated. He was a confident (and fairly unimaginative) young man who made friends easily. He would have met a lot of junior officers his age in the line. How many of these brief, probably quite intense friendships, ended quickly in the death or worse of his new acquaintances? He does not say. He has briefly described some of the horrific sights he has seen. And he has described loss of emotional control under bombardment on two occasions, deep tiredness, and difficulty in controlling his anger. These are the symptoms of traumatic stress. There must have been other symptoms. He was quite damaged.

Before he left on his leave, Colin boiled over with anger when

---

121 This is not good. Relations between the divisional staff and front line officers were now at a new low. Major Lambarde and Colonel Stewart must have allowed Colin to see their irritation and disdain. Regular army officers, as has been mentioned in 1914, did not do written reports and were much more comfortable with verbal communication. But disengagement and acrimony could only impede tactical development.

he saw the number of staff officers in the honours list for the end of June. *'God help England if we have to depend on the staff. The generals are mostly all right, but they have officers on their staff who have never been near the fighting, and have no practical experience of regimental work <u>during this war</u>. Unless they turn all their pampered pets out and take advice from regimental officers who have practical knowledge as regimental officers, we shall have continual repetition of Festubert shows.*

I have spoken to a great many infantry officers and there is a nasty undercurrent of feeling among the infantry that all our shows are organised by people looking at maps miles inland, and by people who have no regimental experience at all. Such a terrible lot of officers are so afraid of authority that they dare not do anything at all without permission, by when of course it is too late.

The chopping and changing of zones which we experienced was all inefficiency, and the infantry are far worse treated than us. Inefficiency is a crime and ought to be treated as such. Artillery plays such a great part in this war that artillery officers who know the lie of the land on any particular front ought to be consulted before any part of the German line is attacked. Them's my sentiments. And I can see myself being hung for them soon. It would make some of my CO's before the war go purple in the face with rage if I spoke to them as I sometimes talk to senior officers now.

I shall get court martialled if this letter is censored, I expect. Don't criticise this letter, only acknowledge it. I shall like to hear it has arrived safely.'

With Colin on leave, it is worth considering this letter in more detail. He reiterates once again his conviction that this is an artillery war, a siege and not a battle; that assaults should be planned by the artillery first and the infantry second.

But he aims his disdain at the staff and not the generals. Slightly unfair, one might think, but it was 'they' he saw as incompetent. The orders came from the general through them. It was 'they' who had not reconnoitred their initial position at Neuve Chapelle, telling them to park in the dark on a plot with holes down to abandoned cellars; who had mismanaged their move in to rest and their allocation of billets; who had left their brigade behind at 2nd Ypres; who had sent them on useless reconnaissance and then failed to arrange a professional handover at Festubert; who had given orders that were impossible to obey on their first day there; who had mismanaged them in the subsequent battles; who had ordered Tyler to Mouse Trap Farm, and Colin to K5 on the basis of information that was at best out of date, and at worst plain wrong.

This disdain was completely conventional thinking. Generals in 1914 relied on their junior staff to put them right. They had to. Communications were such that they were often hours behind the action. Their junior staff had to bring them up-to-date, and brief them on regimental reports in a way that influenced future tactics. So if the staff were unable to perform this service for the generals, it was 'they' who were at fault.

The inexperience and incompetence of the staff, particularly in the new divisions, was a damaging sick joke, both in England and in the army in France. The fact that the joke existed, and the reasons for its existence, were simply not being addressed, and it was therefore perpetuated. As a generalisation, the generals did not understand that they were not being properly serviced. The new staff thought they were doing the job well. And the politicians listened to their professionals and left well alone. This in a nutshell is the tragedy of 1915.

Colin saw the problem, but saw no solution. He treated the staff appallingly. Small wonder if this disdain between staff and regimental officers became mutual. The staff officers who Colin was rude to at Festubert and Givenchy, or the ones he refused to cooperate with at Ploegsteert, would have been reluctant to learn from him. Disdain works both ways. But more on this subject in later chapters.

CHAPTER SIX

1915 Saved by the two colonels

118th Brigade 1st Canadian Division to 113th Brigade 25th Division.

'If ever I get away from here honourably,
it will take a deal to get me out again.'

On return from leave in late July, Colin wrote to a family friend. *'It was very nice getting away for that leave. That seven days makes things feel fresh again.'* It does not sound convincing. He needed more time, but seven days was the ration in 1915.

Back at the front, he kept himself busy, checking out new and existing observing posts. He ordered 4000 cigarettes from his father, and sold them at cost to the men of his battery, a service he kept up for the rest of the war. He used the local currency thus earned to cash cheques for the other officers, payable to his father.

And with more time to himself, he muses on their tactical options. *'The brutes have just been peppering our nice comfortable position. No damage done, but we are saving up our weeks supply of ammunition to give them a really healthy dose somewhere. Personally I don't agree with this. I think we ought to use it in little bits for the benefit of the infantry. The infantry here are rather sick of things, and the new drafts coming out are not as steady as they might be under really nothing at all in the way of shellfire. Perhaps some of the officers are to blame. I don't know.'*

Even in their quiet sector, it was still dangerous. *'I had to crawl with a telephonist into an open field just behind the trenches to mend a wire. We were perhaps a little long over our job, and a German sniper located us in the long grass. Of course it was very long range, but they were too close to be pleasant. We had to bolt for it.'*

On the 30th July, *'I heard a violent bombardment at 3 am, realised it was out of our zone, so slept on. The major was greatly excited, waking up the telephonists and they went up to the observation station. Thankful to say they did not disturb Tyler and myself. I think they just managed to catch sight of some shells bursting about 10 miles away. Tyler slept through it all. The noise was the Germans attacking and taking some of our trenches well to the north of here,'* a surprise attack on the trenches at Hooge, east of Ypres[122]. Planning started immediately to retake them.

Colin's younger brother Donald, aged only 19, was coincidentally rotating in and out of these same trenches behind Hooge, not far away. Donald had volunteered in London, been commissioned into the Westminster Rifles and had been out in Flanders since Christmas 1914. The two brothers had met only once in that time, being some miles apart, and their free time rarely coinciding. Donald was not a very regular correspondent and Colin worried every time he heard the noise of battle further north. But all was well. He was not in the line for this attack.

On the 9th August, Colin wrote to his mother. *'Things have been quiet on our immediate front, but I am waiting to hear from Donald. His 6th Division today retook the trenches the 14th Division lost at Hooge without much loss, for which thank goodness. We were up very early this morning as the racket up at Hooge started practically the whole line off. I think our division was the only one not to join in the general hullaballoo. It started at 2 am and I was idiot enough to dash up to the observation station, followed about half an hour later by the major, who stayed until 5 am, so of course I had to stay too.'* You probably will have heard from him by the time this reaches you if he has managed to get through all right.

On the 14th August 1915; *'My dear Father, your note just knocked me all in a heap this morning. I knew poor D. was in for the attack on the 9th, but I was for some unknown reason perfectly certain he had got through it*

---

122 The first time that flamethrowers were used against the British. The portable 'Flammenwerfer' had fuel gas cylinders strapped to the back of the man using it, with a lit nozzle attached to each cylinder. They caused a degree of panic, but the men using them were very vulnerable.

all right. And so he did, and then taking up orders on the 10th. Poor Mother must be dreadfully upset, and I must try and write her a line tonight. Can't write any more just now.' The 10th August was his young brother's 20th birthday.

Colin wrote to his mother too. *'Father's letter has just about knocked all the stuffing out of me. And I know how poor Father and you must feel at home, because it is so much worse for you. It does not seem fair that some should get off with slight wounds and others should get no chance at all. I cannot write any more just now, in fact I don't feel capable of anything at all. I only wish I could help you and Father at home. Things have to go on the same out here. It's difficult, but very much easier.'*

Donald's death was a devastating blow. The brothers were close and Colin had encouraged his sibling to join the army. Inevitably he felt irrational guilt. His mother, of course, was prostrated and he found her letters very hard to handle.

'I am afraid I have been very slack lately. I have not been up to the observing station all day. There is a constant noise of heavy shelling from the direction of Hooge. It is almost a comfort to know that Donald is free of it all now. Don't forget to write every day for a bit.'

'Do ask Father to write a line when he has time. I hope to feel more like letter writing in a day or two.'

By early September, he was coming to terms with the first raw grief. *'You really must try and think of what Donald has done for you, and try and cheer up a little. You know Donald does not want to be mourned beyond a certain extent, no-one out here does. He has died for his country, he was not a coward and he has left a very fine record. No man can do more, very few have done as much. He is proud of it, and wants us to be proud too.'*

His best friend Tyler had lost his older brother killed in April. Now Colin had lost his brother. They were both grieving, both hardly capable of coherent thought. And to make matters worse, Major Lambarde left them. He was promoted colonel and posted to England to command a new artillery brigade in the 21st Division at Aldershot. Schooling[123] their junior subaltern managed to break a rib and also went home.

All that year Colin had had a lot of post[124], and this correspondence supported him and kept him in touch. But his mother was getting worried. She broached the subject of nervous collapse. Colin did not evade the issue; *'I wonder what caused Jack Ambler's nervous breakdown. I am not surprised at it. Quite a few people get dreadfully jumpy out here. What division was he in?'*

Colin had taken over temporary command of the battery, pending the arrival of a new captain and he did try to keep his letters upbeat. But when their new captain did arrive, his worst fears were realised. *'Our new captain is a regular soldier, full of regulations. He has never seen a howitzer before and has not seen much service.'* Neither Colin nor Tyler were in the mood to cooperate with their new commander. And when Colin set out to be awkward, he was awkward.

So their Colonel Stewart, whom Colin both liked and trusted, saw a problem developing. He had already allowed them to choose their new junior subaltern, and he now arranged for both of them to be relieved of some of their front line duties.

'I am spending three days down with the horses at the wagon line. First time for more than five months I have slept where I cannot hear the rifle shots in the trenches. We have rigged up a tent and are taking it in turns to spend three days down here. Rather lonely but extremely peaceful.'[125]

---

123 Major, now Colonel Lambarde promptly organised for Lieutenant Schooling to join his new brigade.

124 *'I have received so many letters from people to whom I have not been writing regularly, that I have got very behind in answering them.'* Completely integral to this book is the post. And it is worth making the point that its efficiency, and it was unbelievably efficient even in 1914, was crucial to morale throughout the war. Colin received some letters in 1916 only 36 hours after they had been posted in England. Three or four days was the norm – to the front line. Not only letters but parcels arrived in huge numbers, and Colin is constantly thanking his mother for food and other essentials like soap and razor blades.

125 The wagon lines at Ploegsteert were back out of range of all but the largest German guns.

The young officers of their sister battery also tried to help. *'I went and dined with 459 battery yesterday and we had a frightfully noisy evening. Their interpreter, who is a very famous cello player indeed, got hold of a rotten old violin getting remarkably good results. Harboard has a mandolin, Maxwell plays the flute and Captain Browne ran the show with a couple of sticks on a biscuit tin. The finishing chorus of 'God Save the King' was particularly effective, though the whole performance was somewhat marred by an irate old Frenchman who came and bawled out something about wanting to sleep. 459 had no compassion for him as he wakes them up at 4.30 am every morning and ought not to be living so near to the firing line.'*

Even the Padre got involved. *'There is a padre, one Cannon Scott, who comes in and sees us every day now. I don't know whether he thinks we need reforming. Perhaps on the other hand it may be the cup of tea that draws him, he always turns up about that time.'* Colin's stiff upper lip state of denial at his fragile state goes on for weeks.

He did enjoy having another go at the poor staff of the division. *'I have been carefully preparing an observation station in a tree in a very exposed position right on the top of the hill. We had been very careful not to leave any tracks and I had been up there for three weeks training the tree by tying down the branches one by one, and had commenced to dig a dugout.'* The dugout, sheltered by the branches, was for the telephone and signallers. He would have been up the tree. *'Then this week somebody sent a working party by night to our tree and made a huge track burying a cable up to it. They ruined all my work by breaking down the branches.*

I had the satisfaction of telling the divisional staff officer responsible for the whole business exactly what I thought of him this afternoon. He eventually apologised. I have seldom had such an enjoyable half hour. These poor staff officers have never done any forward observation work in their lives. They have no idea how to hide them from the Germans.'

He continued to be unimpressed by Major Lambarde's replacement. Their new captain was heavy handed imposing his authority, and criticised routines that had served them all well under the old regime.

Then in late September, 'Poor old Tubby' (Tyler) 'is rather unwell for the moment. He has been sent to bed and reduced to a milk diet.[126] He cannot eat anything and cannot keep anything down. I hope to goodness he is not going to break up. I don't know what I would do without him. The trouble is that he is very much in love with a girl at home. He is thoroughly sick of this business.

There are times especially when it is fairly quiet and I am by myself when the mere sound of a single German shell coming through the air makes me bolt to the nearest imaginary bit of cover, even though the beastly thing does not come within half a mile of me. It is not as though I cannot judge where it is going, it is sheer cold feet, funk.'

Crisis! This in the middle of a routine letter! Shell-shock, traumatic stress, call it what one will. Days after he wrote this letter, Colonel Stewart offered him a temporary job as adjutant for a few weeks, allowing him to sleep comfortably and eat well, slightly back from the front line.

Colin never enlarges on the anatomy of courage, but he knew only too well of collapse under the strain of warfare. It was not to be condemned; it was a fact of life. He was only 22 years old. A few weeks later, his mother brought up the subject again. 'I don't wonder Musgrave funks coming back. If ever I get away from here honourably again, it will take a deal to get me out again.'

As for Tyler, he was quite unwell. 'He expects to get off on leave tomorrow and that is cheering him up a bit. I have been trying to get him to go before a medical board when he gets home. He has had quite a lot of trouble with his stomach again.'

And when Tyler did get home, his mother was horrified. She wrote in distress to Colin's mother. 'I received your letter enclosing Mrs Tyler's. The latter has been destroyed, but I don't know what there is to be troubled about. Of course I shan't talk about it. Mrs Tyler is quite right to take Tubby to a doctor. He is not fit to stand a winter out here.' The doctors disagreed. He came straight back out again.

---

126 This was the treatment for a presumed stomach ulcer.

'*This wretched adjutant's work keeps me in practically all day, and I can hardly ever get away.*' He was now experiencing staff work himself, albeit at its most junior level. Some of it was mundane. '*We got a note from Division Artillery Command saying our telephone wires were bad. So I went out with the battery commanders and colonel to see. We thought our wires rather good. I sent in a report to that effect.*'

'*There is a new scheme for testing our stock of ammunition*[127] *devised by some worry somewhere in some office. The batteries now have to count their ammunition at 8 pm, when it is pitch dark, when it was at 2 pm. It is simply extraordinary how difficult it is to count ammunition. I managed to get correct statements through from the batteries and I have been at divisional office all morning trying to explain to them that my figures were correct and theirs were wrong. I succeeded in the end.*' If ever consulted, a regimental officer could have pointed out the practical difficulties.

But he did enjoy getting to see and understand the wider picture. '*Did you notice in the papers how the Germans claimed to have repulsed an attack of ours north of Armentieres with supposed great loss to us? Well, that's us. We were given a very stingy allowance of ammunition and told to make the Huns believe we were coming for them. We did it too, made them jolly jumpy, they fired away with rifles and machine guns, and with as many guns as they were able to wake the gunners up to serve. We made a pretence of bombarding them, and the infantry lit some smoke flares down in the trenches, blew a few charges on the bugle and shouted a bit, and the Bosche fired back wildly, not hurting anybody at all. It was rather amusing. We sat tight and noted where all the machine gun emplacements were.*' This was a ploy partly to divert attention from a new assault further south.

The next day, the 25th September, was the opening day of the

---

127 About 100 rounds per gun were kept up at the battery, with approximately another 50 rounds per gun in the Brigade Ammunition Column. According to www.1914-1918.net/whatartbrig.htm these were minimum figures and would have been rather greater for 18 pounder batteries. The divisional artillery also had an ammunition column and an ammunition park with reserves of at least 120 rounds per gun. Army reserves were kept even further back behind the lines.

battle of Loos[128]. His brigade and the 1st Canadian Division sat it out and Colin's diary entry on that day is telling. *'I am particularly anxious to hear a little more about the French doings. The real thing must come from them. I don't think we have the organisation to carry it through like them. You can't make an army like a machine in one year, or even two.'* He thought the British army was not capable of winning the battle. And by that autumn, Colin was arguably unfit for active service. But was his mental state typical of the army as a whole in late 1915? Lieutenant Price, Donald's best friend, who was corresponding, was *'war weary'*, Tyler was ill and Robertson their adjutant was on sick leave. Colin's brother Alec, a sapper, was unfit straight after Loos, and probably before. *'The infantry here are rather sick of things,'* Colin had written earlier. If defeatist sentiments were common throughout the British army, this would have been another reason why the battle of Loos was such a costly failure.

Colin's spell as adjutant was not itself an unqualified success, though he was probably being somewhat self-deprecating. *'Colonel Stewart was jolly good to me while I was doing adjutant, as I made one or two howlers and merited a dressing down which he did not administer in a bad way at all. Robertson[129] turned back up at headquarters just before lunch and I told him about all the messes I had got into and that he would have to get out of. This took a long time.' 'And I arranged an exchange for the colonel of two draft horses for two cobs which headquarters wanted for riders. I am back at the battery again, and I'm not quite sure whether I'm pleased or not.'*

Then providentially Colonel Lambarde returned to this sector from England with his new 113th Brigade. *'In the evening, I paid*

---

128 The battle of Loos was a major British attack which cost over 50,000 casualties. Gas was used for the first time, fairly disastrously. The plan was for the infantry, supported subserviently by artillery as at Festubert, to exploit the gas, and engineer a cavalry break through. The artillery did not, could not, lead the planning. It is no surprise that the attack failed badly. The generals blamed the fiasco partly on a shortage of ammunition.

129 Captain Robertson was still the adjutant of the brigade. He was shortly to be invalided home.

Colonel Lambarde a visit. He has got a very sickly subaltern for an adjutant and asked me to go to him in that capacity. I said I would.' Instantly! It was probably just as well. It sounds as though Colin was being thoroughly tiresome at the battery and picking fights with his captain. *'I got a wigging today, but have been getting my own back with interest all the evening.'* Another letter details his plans to upset the captain even more.

Colonel Lambarde talked with Colonel Stewart and the two colonels sorted out a deal. Colonel Lambarde would take Colin as his adjutant and Colonel Stewart would take Tyler to be his brigade orderly officer, with a view to becoming his adjutant. Both the boys would be taken off battery duties for a time. Neither was fit for front line service. And as Colin said *'This means another half-crown a day, £48 a year, not to be sniffed at, but it means leaving the most efficient 4.5 battery in France.'* He started work with Colonel Lambarde[130] on the 21st October, 1915.

Colin's mother was happy that he was away from his dangerous observation duties. *'As you mentioned very nicely in your last letter, this job is less hazardous than battery work.'* Becoming an adjutant was also, of course, an important career move. *'It will do me a lot of good to have a couple of month's adjutant work, as it probably leads to other things.'* However, the fact that he had entered the job *'dreadfully jumpy'* as he put it, meant that he regarded this most junior of staff jobs primarily as a route to recovery. *'I have had 8 months' forward observation work pretty well on end, so deserve a short respite.'* But he still felt guilty about it. *'I have one of the softest jobs available here,'* he said, and in another letter, *'It's scrimshanking really.'*

Those in the army, and many back in England as well, had a

---

130 Colonel Lambarde now commanded the 113th howitzer brigade, 25th division, of 4 batteries of four guns each (dropping to 3 batteries in November 1915). The division was established in September 1914, as part of Kitchener's Third New Army, and was made up of volunteers. Due to a shortage of equipment and military instructors it was not ready to move to France until September 1915.

very clear idea of the relative risk of different areas of service, a significant issue at the time. A junior officer was on almost a death sentence in the infantry. It was marginally less dangerous in quiet sectors or in the artillery, but much safer further back behind the lines where the staff up to divisional level resided. Safest of all were the administrative back areas out of range of even the heaviest artillery, where the army and corps staff were situated, along with the numerous supply corps and other units.

The front line officers were intensely aware of this. Medal ribbons were worn at all times, and there was a hierarchy of 'honour', often unspoken. But this hierarchy of 'honour' was mildly noxious, and contributed to the disdain with which Colin treated those staff who had never been in the front line. Some on the staff would have been intimidated by officers like Colin, with medals and the tired knowledgeable scruffiness of prolonged warfare. Can we be surprised if they reacted by polishing their boots and acting their rank? The best would have sought front line duty, because how else could they learn and earn respect? The worst would have fought hard to stay where they were. This is a generalisation of course. But it resulted in many of the best and bravest choosing to serve inappropriately. Brilliant administrators and politicians were killed at the front, while many dunderheads languished in staff roles beyond their capacity.

But Colin for the time being was very happy with the paternal Colonel Lambarde, and probably vice versa. They were veterans together in a brigade of novices. They had done great things together at Ypres. A bond had been forged between them that would carry them both through the next two and a half years. The colonel could handle Colin, and Colin could handle the colonel.

And they both relished the challenge of their new brigade in its new division. *'The division is dreadfully green and really does not know anything at all. But they seem fairly keen which makes up for a certain amount. We have not one officer on the staff of our divisional artillery who has been out here before.'* This statement is difficult to believe. But he repeats it a few weeks later, and goes on; *'of course, they are very keen and confident, so much so they are a public menace. However, they will tone down under careful treatment I expect. If they try and make us do anything we don't like, we will get written orders.'* This was an insult, and meant as such. *'And then they will have to face the music if there is any to face. The ADC and staff captain are two brothers, temporary captains before the war. I believe they had political aspirations. Let's hope this war stops them ever getting to parliament.'*

A few weeks later, *'the great importance of artillery work means that capable gunner officers seldom have staff jobs. The result is that the poor gunner has infantry officers to look after him at headquarters. This is an impossible state of affairs.'* The expansion of the artillery was such that anybody with practical experience in handling guns was required to do just that. The failure at Loos becomes even less surprising.

Even the brigade battery commanders were new to the front. *'I have been trying to get Colonel Lambarde an efficient battery commander. Well I asked Captain Smith, a fellow I know well in the 3rd Division if he would come. He jumped at it, and everything was sent through but jammed at Smith's brigadier general, a General Sandilands.'* The regular divisions wanted to keep their best officers.

'Yesterday the colonel wrote a note and the general went out of his way in his car to deposit me at 3rd Division headquarters. I had to wait over an hour to see the general. When he heard that I had come to try and make him change his mind, my reception was anything but pleasant. When I had got my courage back, I told him what a d----d shame it was that in the new divisions such awfully inexperienced people were allowed to have batteries. This I fancy rather surprised him. But he would not let Smith come, and I had to come away with a comparatively polite note for the colonel.'

This early winter was a relatively quiet time on the front and they were in one of the quieter sectors. So Colin, still wobbly, had time to look for help and support. He contacted Alec, his older brother. Their meeting was not a great success. *'I went over two days ago to Armentieres and found Alec quite easily. He is not really looking very fit and is complaining about the effects of the gas at Loos[131].'* Not much help there then. And indeed Alec, when he got home on leave, went in front of a medical board and was given prolonged leave, then a job in England.

So he tried elsewhere. *'I had a fit of writing the other day, and wrote about eight letters. As yet I have had no replies to any of them. If you see Miss Ferguson, you might remind her that she owes me a letter.'* This writing paid dividends. In mid-October, *'I had a highly satisfactory mail. Two parcels, cakes from Mr Strachan, some gingerbread from Mrs Pitt, two letters from you, one from Dr Hunter, one from Miss Ferguson, and one from the postmistress sister of Germaine Antoine.'*

Germaine Antoine, and perhaps more importantly, her two daughters, lived close by in Armentieres, and had looked after Donald's excess kit, among others. Both the daughters were upset by his death and wanted his photograph. Colin visited, to collect Donald's belongings. He enjoyed their company and visited the family perhaps more often than was required to fulfil his fraternal duties.

The Canadians, in November 1915, were still alongside his 25th Division. *'The colonel and I called on the Canadian Division and saw Tyler who is now adjutant. He did not look up to much, but he is happy with Colonel Stewart which is a blessing.'*

'Colonel Stewart told me I was getting fat, but I can't see it. I'm sure I have not been putting on much lately.' Colin was still prickly and prone to sense of humour failure. Colonel Stewart, his old colonel, tried in a jocular way, to tell him he was looking better! But Colin missed the point entirely.

Some divisions adopted a live and let live policy, hunkering down for the winter. Not the Canadians. *'The Canadians next door had a splendid show the night before last. It started with a subaltern asking permission for himself and three men to creep out and in the night throw a lot of*

---

131 He like many British soldiers at Loos was caught in 'friendly' gas when the wind changed.

bombs at a particular bit of the German trench. The company commander said 'let's make it a company show' and went and asked his battalion commander's permission. The battalion commander said 'good idea, let's make it a battalion show' and went to ask his brigade commander's permission, who said 'no, we will have a brigade show' and asked the divisional commander's permission who said 'excellent plan, we will make it a divisional show', and permission was asked of the corps. They approved of it, and arranged for the divisions on either side to cooperate.

So two nights ago the Canadians shelled the German front trenches about 1 am.[132] They then lifted off the front trench to allow two bombing parties of 20 men apiece who bombed with the greatest of ease into the trench selected, killed 30 to 40 Germans and took 12 prisoners. They then quickly evacuated the trenches again, taking the prisoners with them and losing only one man.

Then they waited while the Germans organised their bombing parties and proceeded to retake their own empty trenches by bombing them in force. When they had done this and had again crowded into their front trenches, a very heavy fire was again opened on them – with good effect we hope.

Last night German wireless reported that 'an attack on our trenches on the Messines Armentieres road was repulsed'. However, the night's amusement must have puzzled and worried them very much indeed. They were very indignant the next day, and had the impertinence to throw a few shells about our way.'

Colin settled into his new job. 'This brigade office is an awful mess and for the time being I am absolutely full up with work. This adjutant job is very tiring. It consists of sitting at Head Quarters answering all sorts of questions about ration returns etc.' 'I have got a lot of little things I must attend to. Somebody has issued some special cartridges he should not have issued and somebody else has run out of primers and has got to be blown up about it.'

---

132 On the 17th November. Even in this carefully pre-planned raid, the Canadian artillery staff (by now far more experienced than the staff of the 25th division) nearly ruined the attack. They ordered 'A' battery, Royal Canadian Horse Artillery, to cut barbed wire, where *'a line of trees blocked the target from the gunners' view.'* The wire was cut by hand. Andrew Iarocci, Shoestring Soldiers.

He was lucky to be in an office. *'It is an awful day[133], blowing a gale and raining. Both sides are at present too busy patching up trenches to do much else. If there was any accurate sniping going on there would be a lot of casualties as all of the communication trenches are under water and the front trenches, though better than the communication trenches, are in an awful state. The mud here is something terrible and the road past our headquarters is about 14 inches deep in slush and mud in places and the ground is saturated. I fell into a hole last night trying to find my way in the dark, and was a pretty sight when I got in.'*

The weather stayed foul. On the 3rd December, *'it is raining hard again. Most of the battery and wagon positions are under water or mud. One man back at the ammunition column yesterday carrying a bundle of hay to his horses went up to his waist in the mud in the road and stuck there for about half an hour before they found him and pulled him out with ropes. This was on the road they have to go along every time the horses are watered.'*

The war was still going on. The intermittent bombardments they suffered did not usually cause inconvenience. But sometimes they did. *'A German 15 cm gun shelled the road just short of Nieppe at 5.30 pm today.[134] The first two or three shells fell harmlessly but it suddenly changed its line and range and put the first of four shells into one of the huts where the drivers of 'C' battery were having their tea. The shell upset the brazier and set the hut on fire killing two men outright. 5 died later in hospital and 8 others were wounded.'* Death could happen any time, any place. The wagon line was moved.

But he had enough leisure to give sage advice to his maternal uncle, Duke Marshall who had sold his business in Japan and returned to England to enlist. Colin worked hard to get him a commission in the artillery, using Colonel Lambarde's contacts in London. *'I enclose a note from Colonel Lambarde to Colonel Biscoe who is at Woolwich. I think if you got him to sign that blue form you would get*

---

133 13th November 1915. The brigade were situated near Ploegsteert, 3 miles north of Armentieres.

134 4th December 1915. He and the colonel inspected the carnage.

your commission within a week. He is a field artillery colonel if you fancy field artillery work. But I will tell you why I recommend garrison artillery work to you.

The training is less strenuous[135] *than with Field and though with the heavier guns the observing officers run exactly the same risks, you have a great deal more freedom to get about behind the lines. The heavy guns are kept further back where more comfortable billets are to be found, and yet you have to go up into the trenches to observe just as much, and can see what is going on.'*

He goes on to muse on the field artillery. *'The real field artillery officer, and I admit there are very few left now, looks with scorn upon anything mechanical. He claims to be able to hit targets without calculation for temperature, pressure and wind, and looks upon anything drawn by other means than horses as beneath contempt.'* He leaves unsaid that they were also likely to look with contempt on New Army officers.

'It is extraordinary how some men can shoot batteries well, and others never get good results though you cannot detect the mistakes they make,' Colin had said earlier in the year. As a first class rugby player, he understood that instinct as well as rigorous training, constant practice and team-work were required for success. The real field artillery officers could shoot batteries well.

And by this time, he was getting impatient with his office work. *'I know jolly well I could run a battery as well as these battery commanders, & shoot it, which is more than some of them can do. I have one of the softest jobs imaginable as adjutant here, but really it could be filled by somebody who knows nothing about artillery work whatever, and the colonel ought to give me a battery. He's damned obstinate unfortunately.'*

But with the selfish impetuosity of youth, and that is a statement, not a criticism (he was only 22), he underestimated, or rather ignored, his talents. *'I am at liberty to move about and see things on a wider zone, as I have to take an interest in four batteries instead of one.'* He knew what he was seeing, as few staff officers in the Division did. Would that more had done so.

---

135 Duke was 41, used to his comforts, and somewhat stout. See Chapter 8.

'*These battery commanders really do not do things properly. One never knows what is going to happen next with some of them. The other day, one battery was quite content and pleased to let an officer of another battery do its observing. A true gunner never fires a round without sending one of his own officers to report.*' This statement was the golden rule of the regular army artillery.[136]

'*We were looking at one of their observing stations yesterday, which was in the first story of a house. The divisional cyclist company had got an observing station in the roof above them!*' Colonel Lambarde would have been severely unimpressed. The higher the observer, the better the view.

He and Colonel Lambarde made a good team. '*Of course I know the colonel's ways. I wonder he stands me sometimes, as I always put him off any of his pet schemes. He was jolly funny the other day. I came back sooner than he had expected, and he had just had a brainwave which was going to be sent in to division. He swore when I brought it back to him, he had meant it to go off at once. As a matter of fact it did go, as it couldn't possibly do any harm and they want keeping occupied at headquarters.*' One has to like the colonel! Colin records his dislike of formal dinners and of making a fuss; and that he was particularly partial to creamy Gruyere cheese having it sent out from England in '*wholesale quantities*'. Colin must have been quite a strain to him at times!

And they both had a hard time adjusting to the new style of army life. '*There are things that happen that make a regular officer squirm. The only thing that can save us in the army is to kick everybody out of a command who has not had a training at Woolwich or Sandhurst. One learns things at these places without realising it. There is such a deuce of a lot in the upkeep of tradition which these new fellows know nothing about. They have not the slightest concept of their responsibilities.*'

There was, of course, an element of self-interest in this opinion. '*It is high time all my term at the shop had batteries. We at any rate understand what is required of a soldier.*' But it was also a genuine lament for the

---

136 Easier said than done of course. The officer in forward observation had to pick a good camouflaged spot, maintain communications, and he had to interpret what he was seeing correctly. All highly professional skills.

passing of the certainties of regular army life and tradition. The army had lost a whole generation of officers whose professionalism and code of conduct, had made it such an effective force in 1914. They had had a rigorous elitist training and an almost chivalric upbringing to create archetypal, and very competent British regimental officers. Many of the new recruits, even to senior posts, had none of this ethos.

'Their responsibilities' did not need definition by Colin. Part of it was the professionalism of building an effective fighting team. But more than that, an officer never asked a man to do something he was not prepared to do himself. He looked after his men and his horses before himself. At every opportunity, he made a military assessment to identify risk and possible openings. He accepted verbal orders, liaised with local units and used his initiative.

Colin had many times commanded detachments or controlled the guns of the battery himself. Neither he nor the colonel was afraid to make adjustments to their positions, or to stand up to senior officers. They went beyond the letter of their orders. Their men were constantly at work improving their dugouts and protection. Colin, at least, did some of this manual labour himself. They regularly scouted back and forward. Much of their luck in surviving thus far was due to professionalism and hard work. Both Colin and the Colonel knew the meaning of, and insisted on both. It was their 'responsibility' so to do.

But for now, in December 1915, survival was the main aim. '*The floods round us now are dreadful. It is impossible to go anywhere without getting into mud over one's jackboots. The communication trenches leading to the front line trenches are simply awful, falling in on all sides and well up to one's middle.*'

That week, '*General Plumer, commanding Second Army, inspected our wagon lines. I must say he showed the right spirit in refusing to be done in by the mud. There was a procession of about 15 'red hats' or 'shiny legs' according to how you designate staff officers, and we had just about the best thing in mud walks waiting for them. They were to have gone round the brigade ammunition column, but they had had enough for one day as it was 3.30 and they started their rounds at 10. It was a pity because the ammunition column had made great preparations. There was one place where a narrow and slippery board had been laid down with 2 feet of mud on either side. The general was to have been helped across, but the rest would have been watched with great interest.'*

General Plumer   Flooded trenches in early 1915

Yet again, the staff officers were the butt of the joke. *'I was very disappointed with General Plumer really. He is a very old man with a double chin and very white hair. He is really too old to walk around in the filth and mud he had to walk in. But for his chin he might have been quite a presentable looking soldier.'* He was only 58, and though his appearance was described as unprepossessing, this seems a bit harsh.

A divisional attack was organised for the 9th December, but was cancelled due to the ghastly weather. *'The next day, the Germans shelled Armentieres again rather vigorously, but apparently only in retaliation for a bombardment by a corps on our right. The division on our right replied with something like 2000 rounds to their 500 or so. I don't think it is a good thing our firing off all those rounds. I don't think the damage justifies the expenditure.'* Yet again, Colin criticises the mindless use of ammunition. Never once during this time does Colin refer to any policy plan to guide the artillery in their selection of targets.

His adjutant work went on. *'I got an order this morning on 6 pages of foolscap, referring me to 3 previous orders and asking for a report mentioned in one paragraph to be rendered to the divisional office by 4 pm today. I had to wade through those orders, extract the required paragraph, decipher it and try and make out what they really require. It was simply this; 'are all our alarms for gas attack in order?' It took me three quarters of an hour to discover this. I do all the work of this sort by telephone, and just ask straight for what is required. The divisional staff simply do not understand the difficulties of regimental work. None of them have had any experience of it. It is enough to drive a saint mad, and I make no pretensions of being a saint.'*

This anecdote illustrates beautifully the difference in culture between the office based staff and the fighting soldier's conditions on the front line. All the brigade paperwork had to be loaded onto a horse drawn wagon every few weeks and transported to a new 'office', which could be a damp dugout. Their filing system was probably somewhat disorganised (*'this brigade office is an awful mess'*), but the difficulties in maintaining comprehensive brigade records are clear.

With Christmas approaching, Colin took on the responsibility of ensuring the men got a good dinner that day. *'By the way I wonder if you would have the time to send us out enough turkey galantine and perhaps a ham for Xmas dinners for the men at headquarters, 40 men. I will send you a cheque for the amount out of Funds. Also plum puddings if you can procure them.'* If his mother was daunted by this request, there is no evidence in his letters. She also sent out game pies, sausage rolls, mince pies and Christmas cake.

'The puddings, hams and mince pies have arrived. One or two of the latter were a little bit broken, so of course we had to finish them up. They were rated excellent!' Two days later, *'The cake, treacle tart and sausage rolls have arrived. The game pie is also to hand and by Jove it looks and smells good.'*

'The men managed to borrow beautifully clean white table cloths from the inhabitants and really had a splendid spread. They had fresh pork, turkey and ham galantine, ham and just about as much plum pudding as they could eat. We gave them a bottle of champagne of the country between four of them and what with a fine Christmas cake and some slabs of gingerbread Mrs Pitt sent, they did not do so badly.'

'We had one of your plum puddings, and it was the first time I have seen the colonel really tuck in. He said it really cost him two nightmares, but he could not resist it. We had the other today – for New Year's Day, and he partook of it, even though he knew the same fate was in store for him.'

And on that same New Year's Day, Colin summed up England's task with grim poeticism – *'The wind is blowing from the south and there is a terrible continuous rumbling of guns, all the guns firing from La Bassée up to here. Everybody has got to make terrible sacrifices before the business is to be successfully put through. We can't be beaten, but it is going to take a long time. It is a beastly day outside.'* Paraphrased, but the sentiment is clear.

And for himself, even by early December *'I am beginning to think that I have recovered some of my nerve. I shall probably find I am mistaken the next time I run into shellfire. But I am a jolly sight better than I was 3 months ago, of that I am certain.'* And over Christmas, *'I have been having a little recreation building an observing station. It has been very much battered by shell fire but still offers very fair protection and one gets a very useful view from there.'* Not everybody's idea of recreation, building an observation post in deep mid-winter, 250 yards from German trenches with snipers and enemy batteries watching vigilantly. I think we can safely say that his nerve was back!

He was 'Mentioned in Dispatches' in the New Year List. And on the 16th January, *'learnt for the first time of getting the M.C.[137] from your letter. Many thanks for letters and congratulations,'* this to his father.

Colin as adjutant was writing up the brigade diary. Often in his letters he commentates on what he has written up officially, and

---

137 This Military Cross, his first, pertained to the incident at the beginning of the Battle of 2nd Ypres.

sometimes his personal journal style transfers to the official report. It is almost unprecedented for critical analysis to be written in a brigade diary. But Colin did it and Colonel Lambarde signed it off.

For instance, he is critical of the planning for a trench mortar attack supported by the brigade on December 27th. The brigade were to bombard behind a German forward trench with the aim of cutting the telephone connections to their artillery, thus preventing counter fire on the trench mortars as they took up positions.

'*Trench mortars were ordered to bomb the German trenches. 'A' battery cooperated and fired 40 rounds. Operations timed for 2.50 pm and carried out as ordered. The day was very clear, so the trench mortars came in for considerable accurate retaliation from German heavy artillery.*' So far, factual, but he continues; '*The Germans never observe from front trenches on clear days. Misty days should be selected for attacks, when the chances are in favour of our breaking their lines of communication. Also the trench mortars were unable to fire effectively, as they were not given time to prepare the necessary platforms for their guns.*' Colin knew the German Artillery observers were further back, and that their batteries only relied on observers in the front trenches (whose communications they had hopefully cut) on misty days. And not only was the site selected for the trench mortars in full view from German occupied high ground, but it was also a swamp of soft mud where the trench mortars could not be stabilised. The operation was rendered a total failure by divisional staff planning which did not use local knowledge.

Similarly, he offers a two-point critique, this time prior to an assault on the Le Touquet salient (opposite the south-eastern corner of Ploegsteert Wood) on the 19th January. '*No provision seems to have been made for dealing with hostile observing stations which are better than ours for the locality.*' Colin knew that enemy artillery, with good observation, could quickly neutralise an infantry attack. After the attack, '*unfortunately we lost rather heavily ourselves as they did not take long to shell us back, and of course we had concentrated troops forward for the attack,*' a bland statement describing carnage.

His second critique was equally prophetic. *'Communications for 'A' and 'D' batteries are very long and the disadvantage of having batteries so far apart noted. It is considered'* (presumably by Colin) *'that effort will be made to concentrate howitzers in future. Sufficient telephone wire is never obtainable.'* He was arguing that artillery brigades should be closed up, shortening communications, and thus allowing greater duplication of wiring to important points. A single enemy shell landing on a buried telephone wire could negate a whole offensive battery, cutting off its communications, either forward to the observing officer or back to the brigade headquarters.

'Wire cutting bombardment commenced at 12 noon and soon afterwards German retaliation began to seriously interfere with all communications. A wire buried three feet deep from Le Touquet was one of the first to be cut. 'A' and 'C' batteries, cutting wire, lost communication. Communication from one observing station was maintained, but none of the front trench lines survived. Messages had to be taken back by orderlies.'

The disruption caused by the enemy fire to their communications that day was so significant that the battery commanders were asked to provide written reports. 'D' battery's report was the most succinct. *'Wires to allow communication from our forward observation at Le Touquet, through Le Gheer, to the battery were established. They were unable to communicate their observations to the battery owing to the wire being cut. Between Le Gheer and Reserve Farm alone the wire was cut in 4 places. Repeated and unsuccessful attempts were made to repair the wire.'*

The commanders of 'A' and 'C' batteries prepared similar reports and the latter appended a helpful hand drawn map (see overleaf) documenting the cuts that had been made by enemy fire on his communications, and showing the single line to Le Gheer on which 'D' battery, and incidentally brigade headquarters, were relying.

Needless to say the incursion was not a success. The object was to destroy mine workings which were thought to be threatening the British positions. German counter attacks, supported by artillery, prevented the British infantry, unsupported by their own artillery, from advancing far enough.[138] Colin, with local knowledge, had foreseen the flaws in the plan and forecast the result.

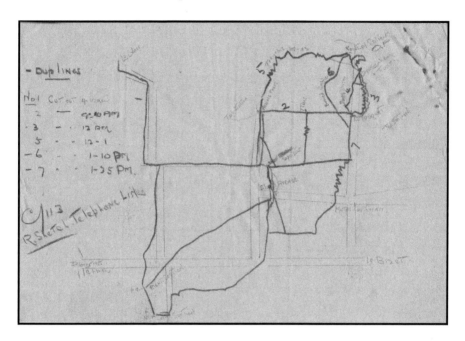

Sketch of Telephone Links – 'C' battery. The Ploegsteert to Le Bizet road runs north south. The battery is in two sections, bottom left; the 'point of salient' observation post at Le Touquet is top right, about two kilometres from the guns. The cuts in the wire at 1 cut communication to the brigade at Le Gheer, those at 3, 4, 5 and 6 to the front observation points.

These accounts show that the lack of front line knowledge and experience in the staff not only impinged on matters such as when to count ammunition reserves, or how to ask a brigade a simple

---

138 The 2nd Battalion Royal Irish Rifles, together with a contingent from the Royal Engineers, executed the raid. The Irish lost 3 officers killed and 4 wounded out of 9; 48 other ranks being incapacitated out of 210. The two surviving officers would have had words with Colin when he visited the front line. The fact that Colonel Lambarde commissioned an enquiry into the lost communication and poor artillery support speaks for itself.

question about alarm protocols; it also had a serious effect on the infantry being told off for attacks. In short they died.

But why at the end of 1915 was this happening? After all, Colin as a 22-year-old lieutenant, in and out of the front line, was able to see local tactical problems clearly. He lived there, and he talked on a daily basis with other young officers where the angle of a trench, or the siting of an enemy sniper, was a matter of life and death. To him then, each quarter mile of trench line was different; different observation points, different strong points and different artillery possibilities on both sides. He could identify the critical points that needed to be attacked, or for that matter defended.

But the divisional staff officers couldn't. They did not have the front line experience, and they did not have the familiarity with the local topography that the front line soldiers had. Colin has said several times that none of the artillery staff had artillery experience and none had been out to the front before.[139] In Colin's divisions, most of the junior artillery staff did not have the ability to make meaningful military assessments, and many of them did not even understand the capabilities and limitations of their own guns.

The problems of the artillery staff were compounded by the fact that the infantry staff led the planning, arranging attacks on strong points which had not been sufficiently degraded by the artillery. And this planning process did not have a mechanism for intelligent challenge by their own front line officers. The boundary between cowardice and constructive criticism was fatally blurred. Far too often, intelligent officers accepted orders they knew were suicidal and died without feeling able to challenge them. Worse than this,

---

139 As late as April 1916, Duke Marshall, Colin's uncle, arrived in France with 5 other officers, all newly trained as artillery subalterns. One of his colleagues *'was very fed up at the ammunition column, but says he has 'struck oil' and is now temporary A.D.C. to General Brock of the 36*[th]*. He hopes to stay on in the office if only as office boy. Just suit him I should think. He likes travelling about in a motor better than our horses.'* He had had no military experience at all.

attacks, which on objective analysis had failed, were either not properly recorded, as at Festubert and Givenchy, or publicised as successful.[140]

Almost the only example of failure explicitly acknowledged in the 113th Brigade diary was a purely artillery debacle. *Aeroplane shoot on German battery failed to come off owing to confusion in registration. Our 18 pounder battery shot on the same target as a Canadian heavy battery. Division had given both the same call.'* This is a pretty elementary planning failure. [141]

This incompetence of the staff, reported home in letters, allied with the bad press alleging that they lived in comfort and safety, was very damaging. There was simply not enough learning going on – in both directions. Colin has made it clear how he dealt with the staff – confrontational and disdainful, frankly obnoxious. Not a recipe for harmonious development and planning.

An anecdote from just after Christmas illustrates the point. The brigade were moving out to their rest billets (with the colonel on leave), and Colin had a completely unnecessary row with the divisional staff captain, because they had been allocated last place in the rota for pulling out. *'I have been having a little scrapping with the staff captain. I have to contain myself when the colonel's here, but he took advantage of the colonel's absence to be rude, so it's not my fault.'* In fact, when the move happened, it was *'carried out without difficulty or trouble. Units managed to get to billets before dark.'* It is difficult to avoid the conclusion that it was his fault, and the fact that he said it wasn't

---

140 The raid at Le Touquet was written up as a success by the 2nd Royal Irish Battalion with many medals awarded. Almost all the evidence on failed attacks comes from private diaries or letters. There is no evidence in the official records of any robust feedback process.

141 Aerial observation work was very dangerous and to risk a mission with sloppy planning was near criminal. An aeroplane observed a target, and by wireless directed a designated battery's fire onto the target. It was obviously crucial to have only one battery firing on the target. The targets were those that could not be easily seen from front line observation posts.

seems to imply that he suspected it was. So when a few days later, and he was socialising with the staff at rest, *'I have had a distinctly frosty time just lately but met them today and the storm seems to have passed for the time being.'* He was of course still very young.

Colin had watched failed offensives all through 1915. *'The poor infantry simply exist to go through the places made for them by the artillery,'* he had said. The infantry generals, if they recognised this truth in 1915, did not act on it. They sent their infantry forward, regardless of whether the artillery had done their job.[142]

The senior generals, almost exclusively from infantry or cavalry backgrounds, led the planning, the detail being filled in by their staff. With a subservient and inadequately staffed brigadier, the artillery could not dominate the planning as they needed to. In addition, it took much longer to prepare artillery for a focused attack than it did the infantry. They had to lay out wire, prepare observation posts and register the guns. Both front line infantry and artillery officers knew what was needed.

But the only way that this information could get through to the generals was via their staff. As a generalisation, the best junior officers did not want to join the staff. And in the artillery, they were almost

---

142 It is easy to forget that there were practical difficulties in planning attacks. In early 1915, shortages of ammunition were common, but this should not have been a problem by late 1915. Also the maps used were small and not necessarily uniform in 1915, so that two or more maps might have to be used in the same attack. Some were inaccurate or did not show important topographical features clearly. The map produced by 'C' battery commander for Colin is a very amateur affair, and many of the infantry maps were not much better than this. In late 1914, fairly accurate large scale maps of Belgium were being produced, the originals having been evacuated from Antwerp, but maps of French territory were generally smaller scale and less useful. After a period of piecemeal development and much use of litho-printed hand drawn maps, it was not till late 1915, that good trench maps based on aerial photography and topographic surveying were coming on stream, and their use was not general till mid to late 1916. It was 1917 before large scale maps were available for the entire front. Reference – *www. library.mcmaster.ca*

barred from the staff, being needed to officer the many new batteries being formed. So the planning for battles was fatally flawed.

Just occasionally of course, intelligent attacks firmly rooted in the local tactical position did occur. A splendid example is the Canadian attack described on page 95. It is significant that this was an attack where the plan originated in the trenches, and even that was nearly ruined by artillery staff incompetence.

Kitchener and the senior generals must take responsibility for this damaging state of affairs in their own armies. They did not recognise that their infantry and cavalry backgrounds were disastrously side-lining the artillery. They did not recognise that their roles as senior soldiers embedded in a massed army had changed to that of senior administrators of a thin line of trenches, and that they and their staff had lost essential feedback. They did not recognise and forcefully address the poor quality of their junior staff. And, most significantly, they did not recognise that this combination of factors was stifling tactical innovation.

So the British army was not in good shape to plan the campaigns for 1916. The generals and their staff could see that their major attacks were failing. They received rose tinted reports with all the expletives deleted, without any robust analysis of the generic cause of failure. They could see that the Germans were using their artillery effectively to defend and counterattack, as indeed were the British. The failures were in attack and they looked for solutions.

Their main conclusion was not earth shaking. If the enemy lines were not being breached, then the problem must be inadequate resources. The obvious answer was to increase the number of men, the number of guns and the ammunition supply. It was much easier to blame the quality and quantity of their resources than the quality of their own tactics and execution.

It is true that in mid-1915, there was a general shortage of ammunition, though the only time Colin refers to this is at Givenchy (see page 77). He complains much more of misuse of ammunition than shortage. There was a shortage of bombs during an assault by his division at Givenchy, and it caused a problem, but *'the Canadians just next door had a tremendous store.'* That was a logistical problem, not a supply one.

In late 1915, he did however say that *'4.5 howitzers are scarce and are invariably all required for 'close' shooting in every scheme,'* and that *'sufficient telephone wire is never obtainable.'* So the front line soldier did perceive problems, but there is little evidence in Colin's account that attacks failed solely for this reason. The Germans had shortages too. *'The Germans are not retaliating much and seem to be on rather a short ammunition allowance,'* he said at Ploegsteert.

Certainly by late 1915 he records no shortage of ammunition at Ploegsteert. Rather the reverse. He complains about the policy of storing up ammunition and then using it all at once on soft targets. In November, he says that *'the Germans started being aggressive and we at once turned all batteries onto their batteries. I fancy we gave them back about five for their one. We had a number of very heavy guns available whereas the Germans return their fire with nothing bigger than a 5.9 howitzer.'* Later *'they will be almighty sick of their lines round here by the end of the winter, as we are letting them have about three to one of theirs and we have much heavier stuff about.'*

In an assault at the end of the year, one of the brigade batteries reported that 5 out of the 278 rounds they fired had exploded prematurely, an occurrence potentially lethal to the gun crew. In another assault at Christmas, Colin says that *'some of our big shells are failing to explode. 6 out of 10 blinds is a terrible waste and apt to hearten the enemy.'* He only mentions this latter problem twice, the first time about their own ammunition when a new detonator was introduced in June[143], but munition problems were addressed with

---

143 *'They have now given us a new detonator for our Lyddite shell.'* 9th June 1915. *'They are a great improvement and have about as much effect as the German 5.9" howitzer which throws a shell about twice the weight of ours. Unfortunately we now have an occasional blind; however the detonation of the others easily makes up for this. The difference now is that our Lyddite is detonated, where before it was only exploded. It gives the ear-splitting crack which the German shells have and which demoralises our infantry more than anything.'*

some vigour over the year from mid-1915, and there were almost monthly improvements in the design of much of their equipment, ranging from respirators for gas protection through communication technology to bombs and shells.

The real question was how long he would have to wait for the tactical and staffing problems to be tackled.

CHAPTER SEVEN

1916 A battery command

Moving to 105th Battery, 22nd Brigade, 7th Division

'April is the month to be out here by, not before. Nothing doing till then, nothing but mud and slush and mist, day after day with little to relieve the monotony, the dangers are frostbite and pneumonia and colds. These are just as easily obtained at home.'

Colin had long wanted the command of a battery himself. In September 1915, Colonel Lambarde had suggested the possibility of giving him command of one of his new four gun batteries in England, but that plan had been quietly shelved and quite rightly. Colin was not then fit for it. But by December 1915, he was feeling ready for the challenge. *'I know jolly well I could run a battery as well as these battery commanders, & shoot it, which is more than some of them can do,'* he had said. Colin did not do modesty in letters to his mother. It was clearly a bit of a joke between them. *'It's no use saying I know how to blow my own trumpet etc.'* he responded. *'I keep telling the colonel, if he would only give me a battery, I will kill 10 times more Germans than his present commanders.'*

But for the moment, Colonel Lambarde wanted him better, and he wanted an adjutant who could do the job. Colin did not push the issue too hard. *'It is a beastly day outside now, but an adjutant's job need not take him out unless there is some great necessity for it. Consequently, I don't go out. Things are very quiet, and as long as I can get back to a certain amount of activity later on, I am quite content with my lot just now.'* And besides, he was still learning.

It was a time of rapid technical development. He writes to his father about a new flare invented by a Canadian friend; he comments on experiments with shell casing design and he observes German shell explosions to work out the killing zone.

He even tried out a typewriter that was used in the adjutant's office. *'this is not much of a typewriter is it but it is extraordinarily useful for copying orders as it will make 5 coppies easily through carbon paper I am improving wonderfully with it all these apparent mistakes are really the fault of the machine it does not seem to able to keep up with me as it is only one of thse little Blick machines which are not meant for really fast work.'*

In early February, the brigade was withdrawn from the line and went into rest.[144] *'We are now a very long way back, in fact further back than I have ever been since being out here. This is a quaint little village and the country is a distinct improvement to the usual flat Flanders.'*

But the world at war was a darker and more sombre place. Colin's mood reflected this. *'I am wanting some Germans to shoot, one gets a sort of fever for killing Germans. I can feel it coming on again.'* Eighteen months of war and he had lost his innocence, and perhaps was in danger of losing his humanity.[145] War was a greater reality than peace. Colin himself recognised the change, *'rather bloodthirsty tonight, perhaps be saner tomorrow.'*

And this emotional darkness is not confined to him. *'The doctor and I went into St Omer yesterday. We found it terribly oppressive and did not know what to do with ourselves. There was a terrible atmosphere of suspicion about the place and as we had got in without the necessary passes we felt a little guilty. We killed time by going to have dinner at the Restaurant Vincent. And when we got back to Hazebrouck, there was no means of transport to Caestre so we had to walk back along the railway track. There was a French sentry at every crossing, but they did not seem to mind us at all.'*

---

144 At Volckerinckhove, (five miles north of St Omer) in Watten training area.
145 He expressed similar sentiments at Christmas 1915. *'We are living in a house with a child whose mother and baby sister were murdered by the Germans and whose father was taken away to Germany by them.'* It is of course impossible to verify this, but it is clear he was not full of seasonal goodwill. British propaganda by this stage of the war was brutal and effective.

There was a paranoia about spies. One wonders what the poor doctor was thinking. He would have been far less comfortable, more aware of the restrictions, of which Colin seems oblivious. But Colin, at least, was happy to wander around restricted areas without a pass, and to greet, in fluent French, sentries who should have arrested him. After all, he was a British officer and minor celebrity. Normal rules did not apply.

And, in part, Colin's ability to completely ignore inconvenient rules was one of the factors which made him such a brave fighting soldier. Sustained courage requires it. Think too much of the possible consequences of exposing oneself to enemy fire and to do so becomes near impossible.

So the two colonels could be pleased with themselves. Colin was recovered in nerve, his self-esteem regained, much more aware now of strategy and tactics, rewarded and ready for the next stage of his army life. And perhaps most importantly he had retained the essential essence of his pre-war training, his ethos of hard work and willingness to take *'responsibility'*. He was hardly aware that he had been nurtured for this moment.

But on the negative side, he was prickly and overconfident with authority, and somewhat arrogant. He was still young and had picked up colonial attitudes from the Canadians to merge with his army and upper class upbringing. Not to put too fine a point on it, he was mouthy. *'I have got into the habit of saying just exactly what I think.'* Colonel Lambarde had had words. *'The colonel expects me to be temperate for at least a month.'*

But Colonel Lambarde must have sighed as he read almost his last entry as adjutant in the brigade diary, as they came out of rest. The brigade is *'to move at 6.15 am tomorrow. The commander in chief is to inspect us on our way through.'* And the next day, *'Started 6.15 am. Snow and freezing. Commander in chief did not inspect us.'* Colonel Lambarde let the entry stand and signed it off at the end of the month.

But it was time for Colin to move on! And preferably to a regular army division.

On the 14th March 1916, he was ordered to join the 105th Battery, 22nd Brigade, 7th Division. Why that battery or that division is unknown. The 7th Division had been at Ypres and Colin had said that *'there are a lot of fellows I know in this division.'* Probably Colonel Lambarde, if he had any say in the matter and it is likely he did, would have recommended him to the post.

'Got orders yesterday to join the 7th Division to 'act as captain pending promotion'. This means acting as captain in a six-gun 18 pounder field battery. The rotten part of it is I shall have to leave Colonel Lambarde and we were rather thinking of working this war out together. But it is a regular division, one of the best.'

His first job was to find them. *'I left the 113th Brigade on the march, and took a goods train from close to Heuchin where we were at rest. The railway transport officer knew nothing of the whereabouts of the 7th Division, so I decided to go to St Pol'* (-sur-Ternoise) *'and from there to Abbeville. Arriving there, I found my destination was Mericourt and that the train left at 9.27 the following morning. I found rooms and had a good dinner. The next morning, I came on to Mericourt and walked the ¾ of a mile to 7th Division headquarters. I had lunch with a Major Wynter. The general was out,[146] but he came in soon after and I was posted to this battery – the 105th.'* He was on the Somme, just south of Albert.

Colin had travelled only 50 miles, (see map page 35) but *'this country is a simply splendid change from Flanders which was a sort of nightmare; here we have a fine ridge to observe from.'*

An *'extremely nice'* Captain Selby at the battery, spent four days showing him the ropes, and went off on leave. *'I hope nothing happens*

---

146 Major Wynter was brigade major (see note 154) to 7th division artillery. Brigadier General J.G. Rotton commanded the 7th division artillery. The next day, Colin *'met General Watts'* (Major General Herbert Watts KCB, KCMG, 7th division) *'going along the trenches. I believe he is extraordinarily good.'* He had a good reputation, but had always been a regimental officer, never attending staff college.

while he is away, as it's absolutely new. The subalterns seem all very nice fellows and our Colonel' (A.S Buckle) *'is really a most delightful man, but just a little bit of the worrying type.'*

In fact, Captain Selby hardly came back. His leave was prolonged by the sinking of S.S. Sussex[147] in the Channel, which delayed all the leave boats, and then he was promoted to brigade major[148], leaving Colin in command of the battery in early May.

'I can't quite realise yet, that I am in charge of this battery. Think of it, one of the old regular batteries, and in one of the best divisions. A regular battery of six guns was a major's command before the war.' The New Army batteries of Colonel Lambarde's brigade had only four guns, and it was a considerable compliment to be promoted so young to a six-gun battery.

But before he got the command, he had to relearn the downsides of front line action. *'My dugout is a poor substitute for the sort of habitation I have been finding for the colonel.'* The weather was foul. *'Had a misfortune yesterday, my dugout collapsed – and it poured all day today while they were building it up again. Getting wet has not put me in the best frame of mind.'* And a few days later, still in March, *'we had a heavy fall of snow last night, 3 inches, and it was bitterly cold this morning, as we had run out of coal.'*

And perhaps worse. *'The rats in this part of the world are really a pest. They make life very hard in the trenches, though rumour has it that they have their uses. A sentry was found the other day with a piece of cheese on the end*

11477   The S.S. Sussex, out of Folkestone, was torpedoed by a U-boat on the 24th March on the way to Dieppe. At least 50 on board were killed, including a famous Spanish composer, a Persian prince, and a well-known British tennis player. The ship remained afloat, without its bows, and was towed stern-first into Boulogne, providing a priceless photo-opportunity. The resultant international furore led to a modification in instructions to German U-boat captains.

148 A brigade major was the second in command of the divisional artillery office, under the brigadier. Experienced artillery officers were now moving into staff roles. With first-hand experience of the artillery failures of 1915, they would hopefully help address some of the issues that led to those failures.

of his bayonet and when asked what he was doing, said he was waiting for a rat to come and eat it, when he just pulled the trigger of his rifle. So ended the rat.'

His uncle, 42-year-old Duke Marshall meanwhile had arrived in France[149] as a junior lieutenant with a Royal Field Artillery unit in the 35th Division, so Colin's mother was now getting a double dose of artillery news from the front. *'It's a good story of Colin's about the rats but not really very much exaggerated, judging from the numbers round this place. Last night one of our officers killed one with a brick. I was standing talking to him at the time.'*

Colin made friends quickly, meeting up with contemporaries from Woolwich, and perhaps one of them gave him a word of warning. *'I have got into the awful habit in Kitchener's army of saying just exactly what I think. That sort of thing is not encouraged here. I shall have to try and contain myself.'*

His move had caused his mail to be misdirected. *'I have received a colossal mail which could not be carried by an orderly. I had to send down a cart for it.'* History does not relate what the 7th Division thought of this. But it is worth mentioning again the extraordinary efficiency of the postal service to the front line. Letters and parcels arrived like clockwork and were clearly a great boost to morale. On the 24th April 1916, Colin records his fastest ever receipt of a letter. *'Yours of the 22nd to hand. Many thanks. Pretty quick getting it by 11.30 am today.'* That's about thirty-six hours door to door from Hatch End in Middlesex, across the Channel and across France to his front line unit close to the Somme. Letters back to England or between units in France generally took longer, being censored on route. *'I received your letter of the 28th today and you have not yet received my letter of the 24th. What a beastly nuisance these d-----d censoring authorities are. They*

---

149 Duke arrived at the front on the 29th March, a mature man but a very callow artillery subaltern. He had worried about getting lost on the way. *'At Rouen, we found trains leaving for their destinations at intervals, the carriages being chalked off for the different divisions, so that all was made very simple,'* he says with relief.

hold up the letters for such a long time needlessly, they have no right to hold them up so they take seven days longer than ordinary.' Bit of exaggeration here, but he was trying to sort out some fishing in Scotland on the assumption his leave dates in May would be kind. (They weren't.)

He got to work, first at the wagon line. *'Am off now to try and find somewhere to water the horses. We are using a well, but it won't last very much longer, which means we will have to trek down to the river. This wagon line work doesn't suit me at all.' 'I can hear the train puffing away up. It is extraordinary, isn't it, the train goes to within 2600 yards of the German front line trenches with materials etc.'* [150]

Then up at the guns. *'Last night our trenches were attacked by a German raiding expedition, but they were unable to get into our trenches. Our infantry were very pleased with us and apparently we dealt pretty well with their effort.'*

This was despite the fact that *'the guns of this battery are getting a little tired, having been out here since the beginning. Rounds are falling short and no end of trouble is being caused all round. Naturally the infantry object to being shelled in the back by at least 1 round per day. Luckily we have done no damage so far, but things might of course be very nasty. We have also had several instances of rounds being too small in diameter. One of ours fell 3000 yards short of the target the other day, and tickled up a battery just in front of us. They howled like anything and accused us of putting the wrong range on. We are thinking of giving them one ranged accurately and letting them judge the difference. With a bad round the shell comes very slowly and can be heard coming, but a good round would reach them before they heard the report of the gun.'*

He was only 23 years old, commanding about 200 men, many of them old enough to be his father. Small wonder if he felt a bit

---

150 'The brigade were ordered to use this train for ammunition supply each night. *'Those who took part in unloading that beastly train and loading the ammunition into the 50 assembled wagons, often under shell fire, will not forget it in a hurry.'* Derisively known as 'Rawlinsons folly, this obviously dangerous practice was soon discontinued.

insecure at first. *'I am very junior to have command of a six-gun battery. I have not got the experience and added authority of years, and these count for a great deal, as everybody knows. I am signing myself captain now, though I haven't been gazetted yet and am not really a captain.'* But with surprising maturity, he observes in passing, *'things have to be organised according to my methods as gradually and imperceptibly as possible.'*

There speaks the rugby fly half, taking over a new team and moulding them to his strengths. So much of his confidence must have emanated from his sporting talent. His efforts to develop his musical talents were less successful. His mother sent him out a piccolo, presumably at his request. *'Do you know what the silly idiots have done? They have sent a mouthpiece too big for the playing part of the instrument. It is a beautiful thing and I am dying to try it. I am returning the mouthpiece.'* But a week later, *'just discovered I have been such an idiot over the piccolo. I had been trying to play it upside down. Please send mouth piece back as soon as possible. Awfully keen to try it!'* But not before his mother had dutifully returned to the shop. *'I don't wonder that poor instrument maker was bewildered. I can't think how I can have been so stupid over it.'*

So one hopes he got on better with his 18 pounder field guns, rather different from the howitzers he was used to. He did know about communication equipment, and wanted something better than the routine issue. *'I wonder if Father could send me out 6 Obach dry cells, manufactured by Siemens of London. We are in very urgent need of these for the telephone instruments owned by the battery. I will pay for them out of the account.'* His father had many such commissions over the next few months.

But he soon had real work to do. On the 8th May, *'we are getting ready gradually for a big effort. If we can only break them somewhere, I believe Hilaire Beloc's idea of the cracked pitcher letting all the water out will come true. They surely cannot afford to man all their lines continuously like they do now, and we shall be able to slip through the gaps. However, there is a good deal to be done before that state of affairs can be attained. The Germans certainly show no inclination at all of being short of men or munitions round here at present.'*

The preparations for a great attack on the Somme were under way.

Over the winter of 1915, the generals had identified a lack of artillery as being the main reason why their offensives in 1915 had failed. And a titanic effort was made on the home front to increase the number of guns and to build up a huge reserve of ammunition.

More guns allowed wire communications within artillery brigades to shorten, as batteries were forced closer together, addressing one of Colin's complaints from 1915. But the lack of experienced NCOs and junior officers to man the guns became critical, though not quite so much of a problem in the regular army divisions, who had held on to their best men. All the army now had to plan, as professionally as possible, for the coming battle.

Their first job was to select gun positions. In the January of 1916, Colin, as adjutant, had been instructed to reconnoitre new and safer battery positions for the brigades in his sector at Ploegsteert. His brief was to find sites which were supportive of the infantry, but at the same time not visible from the German lines. Gun flashes were easily seen at night and attracted counter fire. This was tiresome at a time when no major attack by either side was anticipated and they were in a phase of what Colin called peace warfare. The army wanted to conserve its resources.

His notes survive, and he records a professional and systematic assessment of twenty-four different sites under seven headings. The first necessity was for his chosen spots to be out of sight of German positions. He had to consider not only direct observation from the German front lines, but also observation from any high ground further back, and from balloons or aeroplanes. The contours of the ground were the main protection, but woods, hedges and buildings could all help hide the guns from view.

When in position the guns needed to be able to hit enemy targets.

So he records the compass line and arc of fire available from each position to attack the enemy lines. Restriction by trees or houses might lessen the arc, but too large an arc made it difficult to cover and protect the guns. He is searching out sites for both howitzers and 18 pounders. Some of the sites he surveyed for the field guns, he notes as unsuitable for front line wire cutting. The features which conferred protection blocked their line of fire to this very forward area. In addition, some of the sites were as much as 4000 yards back from the front line, too far for really accurate work, with their maximum range of about 7500 yards. But these constraints were not too significant in mid-winter with no attack planned.

The elevation of the guns at each site was also important. At some, the guns could be dug in to 3 feet and covered over with turf. In others, it was necessary to build raised emplacements before covering them with sandbagged huts. In addition, he had to consider access roads and billeting requirements, as well as any specific work required, such as cutting down trees, bridging ditches or building huts for the men.

Colin had been selecting battery positions and observation posts since the beginning of the war. It was second nature to him and he only wrote down his findings on this occasion because he was assessing so many sites.

The crucial point was to know one's target arc and ensure that everything that was likely to be a target within that arc could be hit from the position. Elevation, contours and trajectory all had to be right. Colin was an expert at the task.

In late spring, when Colin moved to the 7th Division, he found that they too had pulled their guns back during the winter.[151] *'We are far too far back for our poor old'* (worn out) *'guns to do any decent shooting.'* He complains of the long walk to the trenches and is not overly impressed with what he is instructed to do when he first arrives. *'We sort of take it in turns to have a violent five minutes' outburst on some poor*

---

151 The withdrawal of guns had been a general army directive.

particular spot, but I don't think very much damage is done. It only means more working parties to build up what has been knocked down.'

And then the Somme. The 7th Division, a regular division, was positioned in the centre of the southern half of the planned offensive front and on the 15th June they were briefed for the battle. *'Haven't been so happy as I was last night for a long time. The trouble is of course this letter would never reach you if I gave any details of any sort.'*

The bombardment prior to the battle would last for a week, which forfeited any chance of surprise. So the bombardment, and the preparation for it, had to be good. They had long since selected positions. On the 17th June, *'we are in the middle of a move at present as we are going up into positions that we have been working on for ages.'* *'My suitcase had a sad accident on our move up. It was caught by a passing train and knocked to pieces, most of the contents were in more or less intact condition, but my beautiful jaeger sleeping bag has been cut clear across.'* In fact, his suitcase did survive, and came up to the forward position with him.

The guns were moved into forward positions from which they could cut the enemy front line wire prior to attack. These positions had to be close, to ensure the pinpoint accuracy required; they had to be hidden to survive counter fire; and they had to have a field of fire sufficient to hit the necessary targets. On this battery site selection, and on the accuracy of their fire, depended the result of the first day of the battle. It really was as simple as that.

Colin's battery was well sited, and his observation post too was good. *'I am at the mouth of our observing station dugout'* and can see *'shell fire in no-mans' land'* and *'a hawk perched on the barbed wire.'*

The 7th Division were regular army and they knew what to do and how to do it. Their corps commander, General Horne[152], was himself from the artillery. He would have known what he was seeing as he inspected the preparations.

---

152 General Sir Henry Horne KCB KCMG (later Baron Horne) commanded XV corps, which comprised the 7th, 17th, 21st 33rd and 38th divisions. The 7th and 21st attacked on the 1st day of the Somme, with the 17th in support.

The 7th division's artillery plan for the attack is logical, concise and thorough. In the pre-assault bombardment, there were four main objectives. The first was comprehensive destruction of the barbed wire defences. The second was destruction, so far as that was possible, of enemy front line trenches, strong points and observation posts. The third was destruction of enemy artillery positions and the fourth was disruption of the back area roads, supplies and command posts (the latter two objectives being met mainly by heavier guns).

On the 24th June, the brigade diary records that '*all batteries began wire cutting.*' The defences had been thoroughly reconnoitred. '*The wire tasked for 105th and 106th is very strong and deep and mounted on iron 'knife rests'.*' Cutting this wire thoroughly took the full week. Shrapnel shells had to be pitched just short of the barbed wire and the resulting blast flattened and cut the wire.[153] It required close observation and pinpoint accuracy.

He describes the process. '*Wire cutting cannot be done efficiently at a quicker rate than four rounds a minute. Due to the care we have to take of our guns, it is impossible to fire more than 40 rounds on end at this rate without some slight adjustments taking place. So the hours of firing are divided into 40 rounds per gun, 5 guns only taking part, the 6th gun resting, then half an hour so called rest, during which time the men have to do a hundred and one odd things, and the guns had time to cool. We fire continuously for ten hours without a break, and then firing goes on at a continuous slow rate all night.*' But it was even more complicated than this.

'*Guns often started shooting badly, though this was generally unaccountably rectified by the armament artificer making small insignificant adjustments. Also a very marked improvement in the shooting of the guns was obtained by getting the layers to turn back the elevating and range drum wheels a considerable distance each time before re-setting the range and angle*

---

153 '*High explosive shells burst after ricochet and are absolutely useless for dealing with the wire. The iron knife rests referred to would have been much easier to deal with if we had had a good percussion fuse for the high explosive shell.*'

for each round. It is difficult to do this conscientiously every round, but the men played up splendidly and the shooting of the battery has been excellent.' They also had to allow for the vagaries of both propellant and fuse. *'Cordite MD shoots a full 75 yards shorter than other propellants,'* and *'to burst shrapnel 2 foot off the ground, the 85 fuse is markedly superior to the 80 fuse and also shoots much more accurately.'*

This demanding and technical work required years of collective training and experience – which only the regular divisions had.

The 7th division diaries makes it clear that their bombardment was sustained and effective. They were hitting observation points to hamper counter artillery fire from day 1 and other strong points later in the week. Flexibility was built in. If one battery fell behind schedule in its tasks, another battery was ordered to help out.

Meanwhile the Germans responded by sending a lot of troops into the front line, where they were most likely to be incapacitated by the bombardment, despite their very deep dugouts. But they also arranged defence in depth, duplicating their strong heavily wired front trench line three miles back, and again at about five miles back. If these lines were sufficiently manned, then the attacking armies would have to start all over again to breach these defences. They also reinforced their reserves in the area and prepared counter attacks.

Colin had to work hard, and life was not easy. *'I have been up till 4 am for the last two nights; I have an awful cold in the head, a beastly sore throat and my left eye absolutely refuses to see clearly. I have a bruised hand through tripping over a telephone wire and taking a header into a 5-foot trench with trench tramway rails in it, and a fly stung me this morning.'*

The coming battle was supposed to be secret, but Colin does not do secrecy, and his letters home drop heavy hints that an attack is pending. *'There's nothing to say today that can be said without causing the censor to tear this up, however I will try to record events for future perusal. Keep me supplied with parcels; it is so difficult to get back to any shops in this rotten country.'*

The bombardment was heavy and continuous. *'Things are deuced noisy and probably you will read about things in the paper long before this reaches you. I cannot possibly tell you anything just now.'*

The brigade diary says on the 25th that *'wire cutting continues. 106th battery's task very difficult,'* Colin's *'105th battery ordered to extend its zone to the north to assist.'* Something that day made him moan and it was probably this. *'Things are going fine at present, barring one or two small things. I have grumbled horribly, it makes me more annoyed than anything I know to have extra work put on me unnecessarily through poor organisation and lack of forethought.'*

It seems that yet again, in his tiredness, mouth was getting ahead of brain. He says in a later letter that he had a number of run-ins with his colonel that month, and this was probably the first. But he soon calms down.

'I am just having a rest from shooting the battery. There is the very devil's own music going on, and I am writing this at the mouth of our observing station dugout.[154] *It really is a very pleasant day. It seems such a pity to disturb the quietness of the country. It is simply marvellous how the birds take so little notice of the shell fire. Several have made their nests in no-mans' land. When a shell falls, they just hover in the air until the smoke has cleared and then go back to their nests. Early this morning there was a hawk perched on the barbed wire, and he did not mind the shells in the very least.'*

No mention of the danger, of course. If he could see the enemy lines that clearly, then enemy snipers could certainly see him. He would have been somewhat safer back with his guns, certainly safer than in the trenches, but it was not particularly safe, even in the battery. There was of course enemy counter fire. But all guns of that era had a nasty habit of exploding. His guns were older and less reliable than most. Very early in the battle, *'a very unfortunate accident deprived us of a whole gun detachment.'* *'This disaster occurred on*

---

154 His battery was firing on the wire at a range of 2550 yards, and his observation post for the battle was in Durham Trench, just over 1000 yards from the front line, due south of the eastern edge of Mametz.

the 30th, the day prior to the attack and caused us the loss (killed) of 3 of our best gunners and one wounded. The fuse of a shell was struck against the extractor in loading, and owing to faulty workings of safety arrangements, the shell exploded before the breech was closed, killing and wounding every man in the gun pit and blowing the breach ring in two. Only the No 1 who was just outside receiving orders escaped. The gun was sent down that night, and arrived back re-fitted at 6.50 am, in time to take part in the second half of the preliminary bombardment and all the work of the first day.'

On the 29th, the brigade diary records that their tasks were close to being completed. *'Wire by now almost entirely removed on our front and batteries enabled to devote more attention to strong points.'* The last entry on the evening of the 30th June is *'wire completely cut'*.

As will be seen, this was a slight exaggeration, but not so far from the truth. On other divisional fronts, without the necessary training and experience, it would have been very far from the truth.

Colin knew that other divisions had not done the necessary job. On the 28th June, he wrote, *'It is up to us now, and I hope to goodness we manage something worthwhile. I'm an absolute pessimist I am afraid. There's nothing wrong with the 7th Division but if only we had a stiffening of regulars in the others, there would be great possibilities.'*

It is likely that Colin was receiving at least some news from his Uncle Duke in his new division. What Duke had to say about his experiences, as documented in the following chapter, would not have inspired Colin with any confidence at all.

But time was waiting for no man. The infantry battle would open in the early hours of the 1st July 1916.

CHAPTER EIGHT

1916 The 35ᵗʰ Division in France

'A' Battery, 159ᵗʰ Brigade, 35ᵗʰ Division

'Fancy Uncle Duke turning up like that. Don't let him do anything rash.'

In mid-1915, Duke Marshall, Colin's uncle on his mother's side, was in Japan working as a property developer. He was 41, and despite knowing that men over 35 without military experience were not wanted in the army, he sold his house and business, and took the Trans-Siberian railway through Mongolia to Moscow, and then on by rail to Bergen in Norway. From here he sailed to Newcastle, arriving in London in November. He immediately applied for a commission in the artillery.

'For a month after I arrived in England, I was kicking my heels about in London.' Finally, he lost patience. *'I enlisted as a gunner in the Royal Horse Artillery. I had two months of hard work,*[155] *from 5.30 am to 8.30 pm at barracks in St Johns Wood.'*

His persistence paid off. *'They gave me a commission in the Royal Field Artillery. I had immediately to give up Public Houses, transfer to a more expensive brand of cigarette, receive salutes from my old companions, rig myself out in a brand new kit and go off to Colchester for further training, this time as an officer. In comparison with what had gone before, it was a shame to take the money. Then they moved the brigade to Stansted, and shortly afterwards, orders came to go off to France.'*

---

155 He had a tough time. *'The roughest part was the riding school. I had several spills.'* *'We took the horses out in Regents Park, with saddle and without.'* *'Fatigue duty was loading two wagons with manure, driving to Paddington on top of the load, and putting it into railway trucks, all in the pouring rain.'*

Once in France, Duke was totally reliant on his sister, Colin's mother Emma, to support him in his wants and to provide him with home news. She took on the role with enthusiasm, but demanded in return that he write fully of his front line experiences. Since both were inveterate letter writers, it was a hardship to neither.

After a very brief induction in France, the somewhat portly and middle aged 2nd Lieutenant Duke Marshall was posted to 'A' battery (of four guns) of the 159th Brigade in the 35th Division, which had been raised in 1915 as part of the New Army. They had arrived in France on the 1st February, and he joined them on the 29th March 1916, just ten days after Colin had moved from his adequately officered 25th Division to the first rate 7th Division. By contrast the 35th Division were third rate novices to warfare.[156]

'When I arrived here[157] the battery had been in action for a week. The staff consisted of Captain Pinney and four subalterns, but two were away, one on a course and one on leave. I was only temporarily attached but nevertheless chucked into the work; that is battery work[158] for 2 days and 2 nights; then observation post work 2 days and 2 nights, and then 2 days more or less easy on odd jobs, with a bit of riding for exercise.'

Duke soon realised he was not with a crack division. Their

---

156 The 35th division infantry were the "Bantams", men under the normal regulation minimum height of 5 feet 3 inches. They had recruited in Glasgow. The 35th divisional artillery was commanded by Acting Brigadier W.C. Staveley, who had been colonel of the 30th brigade with which Colin had served in 1914. 'Training has been severely handicapped by a total lack of experienced officers and N.C.O.s.' he wrote on embarkation.

157 Neuve Chapelle, 20 miles south of Ypres and 40 miles north of Albert on the Somme. (See map page 41.) *'I can only say it's marked in past history by little wooden crosses.'* There was heavy fighting there in 1914 and 1915. Duke took censorship seriously.

158 Captain G Pinney M.C., with 7th division experience, wanted officers willing to learn. *'Battery duty means early parade, inspection of billets etc. and gun drill, and attending to anything that might crop up. Without the telephone, we should be lost. Both on battery work and at the observation post we sleep in the dug-out with the telephonist who is always on the job. The observing officer does the shooting through the phones.'*

brigadier had said on embarkation that his brigades had had no experienced tuition, and must have had doubts about the competence of his officers. Captain Pinney, new to the command of 'A' battery, had even more. He had *'managed to change all of his original officers,'* when the last was sent off disconsolately to join the trench mortars in mid-April.

Duke was taken on a visit to the front trenches. *'The trenches are not trenches at all, but breastworks made of sandbags. We were taken by a much excited infantry officer into 'no man's land' to spot a possible sniper's post. One of our own 4.5 howitzer shells fell in the trench immediately behind us. Had it dropped 2 minutes earlier, we should all have been blown to blazes – my first experience of shell fire.'* An unfortunate infantry man was killed.

'A few days later, Captain Pinney came down and told me to shoot the battery, partly for tuition and partly to see what I knew. I chose a trench target and sent my orders up the phone. Several rounds we did not observe. Shooting was difficult owing to the high wind. Finally, I got registered.' This was his first experience of shooting.

'Next morning early, under exactly similar weather conditions, I saw a large working party of 40 or 50 men, on the exact same spot, perhaps repairing some damage we had done. I sent up through the phone "Battery action. Target 30 degrees R of zero line. Concentrate 15' on no 2. Correlates 15b 4750, Salvo!"[159] *This the officer at the battery repeated and reported down the phone line, which gives ample time to observe. I have to admit to a curious feeling when I gave that order to destroy human life, the first time, of course but I hope it will not be the last.'*

He learned to sustain enemy as well as friendly fire. *'I think everyone feels the same when the shells come. You hear them in the air and instinctively look up to see them. They simply whistle, then the crash. The bullets sound like the breaking of a violin string. It's so foolish but you can't*

---

159 Number 2 gun was the one zeroed at registration, so the other guns concentrated, or adjusted to it. 15b 47 50 is the exact map reference. (See footnote 200 for how this is calculated.)

help ducking although you know they are miles past you. The machine gun barrages are rotten, they sound like hail in the trees and hedges, and one wonders how anything can live in the neighbourhood.'

Less than a month later, in late April, he was sent with a detachment to build a new position for two guns. *'Our left section of 2 guns marched 12 miles to a derelict farm to make a position very close to the line.'* The 2nd lieutenant, commanding the party, was wounded before they started work. *'This has left me on my own. I duly reported and got a reply just to carry on.' 'I wish I had half a dozen japs here. I have sent six of my 24 Scotchmen back to base, and have been going faster as a result.'* But by the next day, *'I have got one gun pit finished, could get the other done tonight if we get the material down in time.'* He had had no supervision and no previous experience.[160]

Duke was proud of his *'fortress'*. So he was not pleased when the gunners who moved in a few days later complained of the poor access. He had incorporated such elaborate camouflage that they could not easily get one of the guns into its pit.

Shortly after this, the battery was moved into rest. Through April, he had kept his sister busy with requests and by the beginning of May, he had received the essentials he had asked for, including a trench telescope, a map case, calibrated measure, notebook, coloured pencils, a collapsible wash-stand, waterproof trousers and boots, a further supply of shirts and socks, and of course tobacco, soap and cakes.

In early May 1916, his battery was sent on a week's training course on mobility which took place in beautiful open countryside. This was their training for the battle on the Somme, where a breakthrough to open warfare was confidently (by the generals)

---

160 Captain Pinney was off running gunnery courses for the division. The colonel did visit when they had nearly finished the work, but had no suggestions to make. The skills required to select and design good positions were described in the last chapter. Colin wrote of digging new positions later in the war, *'I dare not leave it to any of the subalterns yet.'* They had been with him nine months.

expected. There were four batteries from four different divisions on the course.

'*One of the batteries that came to drill with us was under a major who when asked to take over two subalterns to be attached for instruction said "no thanks. I like the officers of the New Army less than I do the men." He was sent away and his battery left in the hands of a lieutenant for the week.*' '*The colonel of another battery here will on no account have rankers,*' officers promoted from the ranks, '*no matter how good, in his command.*' Duke could not believe what he was hearing. '*Our army is not what they would have us believe. Truly there are some very curious soldiers amongst our regulars who are now in command; men must be archaic to take up attitudes such as these.*'

Captain Pinney was again away instructing, trying to raise standards in the rest of the division. But despite his absence, the battery's '*glorified picnic*' went well, and they were congratulated by the colonel in charge, and more importantly by their own sergeant major, the only other regular in the battery.[161]

The battery now moved back into action in the Neuve Chapelle sector. '*I was sent up in advance to get particulars of the country and take over their maps etc., only to find that the amateur outfit we were relieving hadn't a thing worth the paper it was printed on. I've spent all my spare time in making maps.*' And Captain Pinney was equally unimpressed ensuring that Duke '*had an awful lot of work to do to straighten up the position.*' '*We are making a telephone and orderly officer shelter which will make things much more comfortable*' (and much safer) '*when complete.*'

Duke was learning fast from his commanding officer, and revealed his own misgivings in response to news from home. '*I got a letter from Colonel Somerville yesterday. He says he is getting optimistic news, and talks of an end to the war by the close of the year.*' But '*what suggests these optimistic reports I don't know; nothing that I have seen anyhow, quite the*

---

161 '*The unfortunate part of this 'dud' division are the N.C.O.'s. We haven't a man in the battery to compare with the corporals at Colchester,*' Duke wrote.

reverse. I could never have imagined such a dud outfit as we relieved, and the infantry too in front of us, well the less said the better.'

Duke was further dismayed by his colonel, who 'is a sick man, I fancy,' and who bizarrely circulated a list naming him and another new officer as the senior subalterns of the brigade. [162] A howl of protest was sent up to the general who 'has rescinded the whole thing. It was very unfair, and not a right thing to do.' To Duke's considerable relief, the colonel then left. 'And I doubt he will come back to the front.'

But if his peacetime experience helped him to cope with the bad man management and basic incompetence he found in battery positions, nothing could prepare him for the sheer terror of observing from the front trenches on the absolutely flat plains of the Neuve Chapelle sector in a time of active warfare. 'A few nights ago, I was doing observation when a lot of artillery work went on, and it was a bit like a noisy firework show, at night of course. I'm writing this from the OP dugout. You have no idea of the row the machine gun bullets are making on the ruined walls around this dugout.'

And a few days later, a German attack on the front trenches was supported by a bombardment of his position. At dusk the shells came over in shoals. To me in my small tower it sounded as if it was all aimed at our observation post. For two solid hours it continued, and it was a perfect inferno round where I was. I cannot now understand why they never got a direct hit on the place I was in. I couldn't move; I did not even know our guns were firing, for I could see nothing for smoke; and could hear nothing outside for the noise of bursting shells so close. During the shelling the Huns got into our first line, only to be driven out by our artillery, though I knew nothing of it at the time. They left rifles, bombs and spades behind, but it is feared they took some of our men.[163]

---

162 Perhaps the colonel disapproved of the backgrounds of some of his own officers, or perhaps he felt that age and maturity counted. But the officers he had put lower down on the list had been commissioned for up to a year, and seniority by date of appointment was a firmly established principle in the British army.

163 'I see by the paper on the 1st, they claim to have taken 38 of our little men, and one officer.'

Our casualties were heavy, and no doubt you will see the affair written up in the news of the day. [164] *Of the state of the trenches, the less said the better.'*

Duke had no illusions as to the war he was in; he knew he was lucky to have survived the experience. When a friend was wounded, he wrote that *'as 50% of us are being done in, on the average, it's not to be wondered at. It will come to us all in the end.'*

But by late May, the earnest, portly, and unquestionably heroic Uncle Duke could nearly be called a veteran. He records his amusement when a new fellow officer dives into a flooded drainage ditch when a random shell pitches 15 yards from the pair of them, and the terrible injuries of another officer of his battery struck in the eye by a shell splinter on observation duty. But he does not, as Colin would surely have done, construct a new observation post and abandon their old one.

A battle was coming. His battery had already practised mobility. Now they were tested on accuracy. *'We were told to fire on a certain house which all the other batteries had blazed at from time to time. We were given 100 shots, but knocked it down completely in 39 shots, not bad, eh?'* But was this degree of accuracy going to be good enough to cut barbed wire? And what of the other batteries?

By the 15th June, *'the Huns have very little strength on our front now. That attack they made on us a fortnight ago was a blind so as to be able to move away troops and guns'* presumably this confident assertion coming via Captain Pinney. They were of course spotting German battery positions as part of their observation work. *'Yesterday we dug out some time fuses and found them to be Russian, so they have Russian guns on this front.'* And a few days later, *'any number of the shells they send over fail to explode. Of course a lot of ours are the same, but certainly not in the*

---

164 The record keeping in the 159th brigade war diary is very unimpressive, the worst of any of those used as reference in this book. There is no mention of this attack, and no references to battery positions at any time. The 35th divisional artillery diary for May is missing in its entirety, although the entries for other months are generally very good, often filling the gaps left by the brigade diary.

same proportion.' The conclusions were inescapable. The Germans were aware of the preparations for a major British attack, and were concentrating their troops and modern guns in readiness.

Four days later, and the whole brigade, indeed the whole division, was on the move. They went first into rest, but were kept moving, edging ever southwards towards the battlefield that would come to be known as the Somme.

On the 25th June, *'we have been officially told that the great offensive has commenced. Thank goodness something is likely to happen soon. This inaction is simply awful.'* On the 28th, they moved again – further south to the town of Arras, and the 35th Division stopped there, held in reserve, a few miles north of the left flank of the new battlefield. On the evening of the 30th June, they were 'awaiting orders'.[165]

Colin mused just before the battle opened on the competence of the new divisions. *'If only our new divisions can get a grip on how to do things on their own, we shall manage it. Anyone who has experienced it knows that the staff cannot do more than prepare the thing. When it really comes to business, it is absolutely dependant on the regimental officer whether the thing is a success or not. Now, I am afraid, we do not possess officers with spirit and experience in our regiments.'*

Duke's comments confirm his division's lack of experience at every level. His description of inappropriate training and poor leadership is chilling. They were simply not capable of doing the job that was going to be asked of them.

Colin knew that if the front line officers were not capable of executing the plans for their own attacks[166], then *'interference of staff will probably be necessary, and I fear a repetition of Givenchy last June and*

---

165 The 35th division had come out to France in February 1916. Of their sister divisions in Kitchener's New Army, the 32nd and 34th, had come out November 1915 and January 1916 respectively, and both were in the front line at the Somme. Their training and experience would have been only slightly greater.

166 The 7th division had shown it could be done. Few other divisions at that stage of the war had the necessary expertise.

Ypres in April.' Colin feared the ghastly casualties that he had seen in 1915, not this time through poor planning by the senior officers, but through poor execution by the junior ones.

A week later, *'I notice in the papers today they say artillery preparation in some parts was not what it was in others.'*

But it was too late now. The battle would start the next day.

CHAPTER NINE

1916 The Somme

105th Battery, 22nd Brigade, 7th Division

'Please send a treacle tart or two. They are splendid for this sort of work.'

On the 1st July, the infantry battle started.

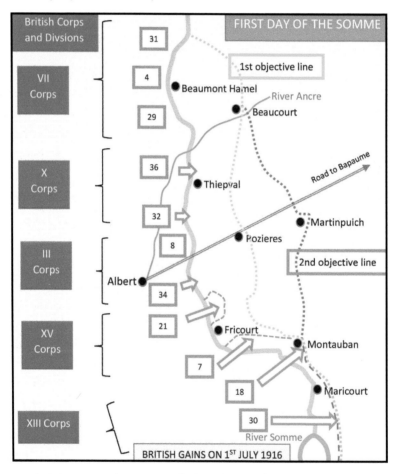

At 7.30 am, 11 divisions attacked. Only 4 made significant progress.

The 22nd Brigade diary claimed that the wire was completely cut in their sector. Certainly most of it was.

'At 7.30 am, the division moved to the assault. On the right, the 22nd Battalion Manchester Regiment with the 1st Battalion South Staffordshire Regiment had little difficulty in passing over the first line of German trenches. In the centre the 2nd Battalion Gordon Highlanders and the 1st Battalion South Staffordshire Regiment came under very heavy machine gun fire after crossing no man's land, but succeeded in advancing with the exception of their left company which was held up by uncut wire. On the left however the 9th Battalion Devonshire Regiment failed to advance and suffered very heavily from machine gun and artillery fire, the leading companies losing all their officers.'[167]

So the initial attack in Colin's centre sector was relatively successful, though the attack was unsuccessful on their left, see map overleaf. The forward observation officers for all the batteries of the brigade went up just behind the infantry, moving forward only forty minutes after the first rush, to direct fire onto resistance points. Considerable planning had gone in to making sure that these forward observation officers had good communication back to their batteries.[168] And as early as 8.55 am, all the batteries in the brigade were turned onto a German counter attack at Danzig Alley, which was on the far side of Mametz village and nearly 1000 yards forward.

---

167 Quoted from a **Narrative of Operations from 1st July to 5th July 1916, 7th division,** copied out in full by Colin. The artillery support given to the infantry is mentioned only once, so as a text for tactical analysis, it is almost valueless. The fact that it was so written serves to show how the artillery were taken for granted, even by the divisional staff of a regular division. The only time the artillery are mentioned was on the 4th July, when 'adverse conditions' are cited as the reason for the failure of the guns to cut wire successfully in the prelude to an infantry attack. No explanation of what this means is given.

168 On the 30th June, the brigade diary – *'telephone lines for FOOs laid in an artillery trench, and by tunnel to beneath the enemy's front line.'* The tunnel was opened during the infantry attack and wires run forward by the forward observers from there. Wires back were thus protected from enemy counter fire.

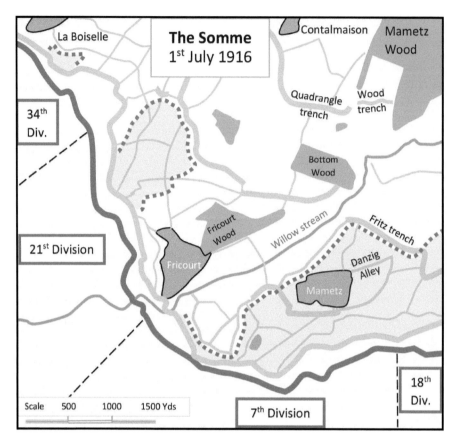

The lines south of Albert on the first day, British gains shown.
The 7th division were unable to advance up Willow Stream, which was dominated
by Fricourt on higher ground. It fell by encirclement the next day.
Not all German communication trenches are shown.

Colin's 105th battery is specifically mentioned for a series of further successful assists at Mametz in the brigade diary on the first day. '*9.36 am Fire of 105th on the east end of Mametz proved very effective. 11.07 am Our troops moved north-east into Danzig Alley out of Mametz as a burst of fire was delivered by 105th. 1.25pm Advance consolidated as 105th put on its final barrage. 7.10 pm 105th covering centre of Fritz Trench, supporting 2nd Queen's Surrey and 22nd Manchester's.*'

These assists were not pre-planned barrages.[169] They took place as a consequence of close observation and liaison at battery and brigade level. The guns, on their own initiative, fired on local targets, ignoring the 'battle' barrages being coordinated from corps and army.

This initiative was not necessarily encouraged at battery level. *'The Manchester's were held up at their first objective, by about 100 German reserves, who took up position on a crest, soon after our artillery barrage, moving strictly to time, had got beyond them. I could see this party opening a heavy fire on our attacking troops. I stopped the fire of the battery and had all guns put onto this target, at the same time informing brigade headquarters. But, before fire could be opened, I was ordered to keep up the barrage fire as per programme. I switched the guns back onto the barrage away beyond, and hurried personally to the colonel. I got permission to fire on the Germans, and the battery did some very pretty shooting. The Col. told us the General was very pleased with the battery's work, but the delay cost us many casualties.'*

The next day, *'we could see very clearly that our men were badly held up attacking Fricourt. So I got two guns shooting exactly where they were wanted. Then the colonel arrived, hot and tired, and wanted to know what I was shooting at and told me to stop. I have not been court-martialled, but fancy may have run it close. He did let me proceed when I told him the General had told us to shoot, (but not that this was some time after we had started).'*

General Haig had hoped for an advance of at least 3000 yards on the first day and his second objective was about 7000 yards away. But the normal maximum range[170] for Colin's 18 pounder guns was just over 6000 yards. The guns were 2550 yards behind the front line,

---

169 M349 in Nat. Arch. WO 95-1639-2. Documented in a report by Colonel Buckle, 22nd brigade R.F.A., 12 pm 1st July. This is the only report on the artillery tactics in the divisional records of that week. It is possible that he was being asked to justify deviations from the pre-planned barrage, but he was promoted brigadier a few weeks later.

170 Around 6500 yards, but this could be increased to about 7500 yards by digging in the rear of the gun. Increasing range meant decreasing accuracy.

and there was no provision in the plan for the artillery to advance until achievement of the first day objective, the green line on the map on page 158.[171] The close artillery support on the first day had been achieved by good forward observation and close liaison. More specifically it had been *'by request of the generals commanding the infantry brigades'*. These infantry brigades were likely to want close artillery support still more as they advanced closer to the first day objective, which was the strong German 'second line'.[172]

In the first week of the battle, Colin was up in forward observation several times. He was almost certainly forward on the second day. The divisional artillery diary says, somewhat stuffily, that evening that *'the FOO of the 105th reports that in his opinion enough fire had been brought to bear on Quadrangle Trench.'* That sounds like Colin. He was certainly doing his best to upset the colonel. The brigade was ordered to cease fire.

The infantry advance over the next few days was desperately slow. The Germans had been pushed back closer to their own guns which were supporting heavy counter attacks. On the 4th July, the 7th division's report records a failure to clear wire *'in front of Wood Trench,'* which runs between Quadrangle Trench, still uncaptured, and the bottom corner of Mametz Wood (see map). Apparently *'the 35th Brigade RFA under very adverse conditions worked at the highest pressure*

---

171 The infantry did not reach this green line for a week. Colonel Buckle did move his 22nd brigade headquarters forward on the 2nd July, but not his guns. That same day, the 7th divisional artillery diary ordered the 35th brigade R.F.A. to move forward, but a track had not been made across the front lines. It seems the order was premature; one battery fell back to its original position; the second stayed forward just behind the original front line; the third was stopped from moving. The 14th brigade R.F.A. and the heavy guns moved forward that day, because they were further back and already out of range.

172 From the divisional front line, there was a wire defended trench about 2000 yards back, in front of Bottom Wood, with another line 1000 yards behind that in front of Mametz Wood. Behind them, the 'second line', strongly fortified, ran in front of Bazentin, behind Mametz Wood, about 5000 yards back.

to clear the wire.' [173] The range for most of the batteries was now well over 5000 yards. Not only accuracy, but forward observation and liaison as well, became more difficult with increasing range.

The 7th Division Artillery had still not advanced on the 7th and by this time they were much too far back for accurate supporting fire. *'At present we are left behind, but hope to be pushed up again soon. We are firing continuously, but at very extreme range,'* Colin wrote that day, a week in to the battle.[174] The 38th Welsh Division[175] had been ordered to attack Mametz Wood that very morning, supported by 7th division guns. Colin kept only a very few orders from the Somme battle, but he kept those for this day.

The first order on the morning of the 6th July says that 'no details of the attack are yet received.' The infantry movements necessary to the attack are described, which enabled the 17th Northern Division

---

173 No problem is recorded in the artillery diaries. Both the 22nd and 35th brigade fired on German activity at Quadrangle and Wood Trenches all that day, but no wire cutting operation is recorded. The 22nd brigade barraged Wood Trench from 7.30 to 8 pm and again at midnight. The 35th brigade fired on Wood Trench from 'about 8 pm' NB★★

174 The 7th division infantry had pulled out by this time. The 7th division artillery were now supporting the 38th Welsh division infantry, who had relieved the 7th division infantry. The latter had moved back to rest after five days fighting, and had lost 151 officers and 3673 other ranks according to their report.

175 The 38th Welsh division was in the same XV corps, commanded by General Horne, as the 7th, along with the 17th, 21st and 33rd divisions. At 10 pm on the 5th, Colin's brigade was transferred from covering the 22nd infantry brigade of the 7th division, to covering the 113th brigade, 38th Welsh division. But 7th division artillery retained the responsibility for directing the artillery brigades of their own division. On a fluid battle field, requests for pre-planned support had to go from 113th infantry brigade to the 38th divisional headquarters, across to 7th division artillery headquarters, and down to Colin's artillery brigade, and responses back by the same pathway. Meanwhile, orders from XV corps were coming in to both divisional artillery offices which might override local requests. Brigadier Price-Davis VC of the Welsh infantry brigade did not have the authority to order his supporting artillery any closer.

to attack Mametz Wood from the west, and the Welsh Division to attack from the east. The enemy position to the east was a strong one, with wire in front and machine guns enfilading, (meaning off to one side and able to fire all along the length of an attacking line). Colin's hand-written instructions order a series of barrages throughout the night on positions south of the wood, terminating in a general bombardment of the 'south-east portion' of Mametz Wood from 8 am on the 7th with a lift at 8.30 am presumably in support of the attack. This was a major assault, but battery commanders were forbidden to be forward observers, due to uncertainty as to where the front line was; and their batteries were, in any way, far too far back for accurate targeting of enemy positions.

In short, we are right back to the tactics of 1915. Plan an infantry assault, let the artillery know the details at the last minute and allow them to blaze away on an area in the hope that some wire might be cut and some strongholds hit. No planned targeting.

With hopelessly inadequate artillery support, the assault was an unmitigated disaster. The attacking infantry[176] of the Welsh division were totally depending on the artillery to at least partially neutralise the enemy defences. They didn't. They couldn't. They did not know where the front line was; the range was extreme; and their guns worn out, with dud shells falling short. Colin said before the battle started that his guns were worn out.[177]

The brigade diary is unusually vague and moves on quickly to further operations later in the day. The divisional artillery diary is

---

176 The attacking infantry on the 7th were from the 115th brigade of the Welsh division, and Colin's artillery brigade was now firing in support of the 114th brigade to their left. The 113th and 114th infantry brigades were used in the assault on the 10th. Mike McCormac – www.mikemccormac.com gives a good account of these battles from the Welsh division's perspective.

177 This problem was not confined to Colin's battery. Lt. Col. O. Du Port of the 14th brigade reported on the 7th July, that 'his guns are in a very bad state. They are unable to do a heavy day's work,' (7th division artillery diary). Two guns of the 106th battery had been sent out of action on the 27th June due to excessive wear.

studiedly factual, but reports that XV Corps did not know infantry positions in the front line at 8 am; that at least one of the 18 pounder batteries shelled the poor infantry so hard they had to fall back; and that certainly Colin's 22nd Brigade, and probably both the 14th and 35th as well, had to rely on runners, as their wire communications had been cut. Orders were given and countermanded. Barrages were repeated with more friendly fire casualties. Nobody knew what was happening in the battle. The futile attacks went on all day.

It later emerged that the Welsh division had wanted an assault at dawn on a narrow front, preceded by wire cutting and covered by artillery smoke, but that they were ordered by army command to attack at 8.30 am on a broad front without smoke or adequate artillery support. The advancing men were cut down by enfilading machine gun fire, and three battalions lost over 400 men. They never even reached the wood.

The disaster is commemorated today by a Welsh dragon memorial sculpture at the scene. It was made a notable failure, because Haig, frustrated at the poor progress of his infantry attacks, chose to use this one to make an example of General Phillips, the Welsh divisional commander[178], sending him home on the 9th, on the grounds that the Welsh troops had lacked zeal in the attack. The insult lead to considerable ill feeling and recriminations.

On the 10th July, an only slightly better planned attack was made on Mametz Wood. The artillery brigade diary records the difficulty they had in supporting the attack at such extreme range. At 4.15 am, the infantry assaulted, but at 5.35 am the infantry were reported to be ahead of the barrage and so the guns stopped firing. However, at 5.45 am they recommenced ('in default of more definite information'), sticking to the schedule. *'The attack was one where our infantry suffered heavy casualties from our own artillery fire,'* says Colin. *'They captured their first and second objectives within 10 minutes of each other whereas the second objective should not have been reached for about 20 minutes.'* The

---

178 General Watts (7th Div.) took over for a few days, leading the attack of the 10th.

infantry were again reported in front of the barrage at 6.05 and later that morning *'the situation not being clear, no fire was bought forward into the wood.'* Forward observers could not see into the wood, and with wires cut, reports got back to the brigade by runners.

The divisional diary also reports fire on friendly troops throughout the day and struggles to advise its brigades on the line of fire necessary. At 1.40 pm and again at 3.54 pm, the infantry were *'still being worried'* by friendly fire. *'Situation in front obscure'* is the entry which really sums up the battle.

The infantry, advancing fast with little resistance, had the choice of following up success into their own barrage, or waiting for the barrage to lift, while the enemy regrouped. If held up, (as happened on the left of the line,) they could only watch the barrage moving forward away from where it was needed. Their losses were appalling.[179] Nobody in the artillery was happy, those in the affected infantry even less so.

That evening, the brigade diary reported that *'fighting in Mametz Wood still continues, but our advances have now progressed so far that our batteries are out of range.'* The wood was approximately 2000 yards square and the supporting artillery could not even reach the far side of it. The Welsh battalions had advanced beyond the range of their nominated artillery support.

It had been clear for many days that the guns were too far back. [180] The infantry generals wanted closer and more effective support.

---

179 The 38th Welsh Division lost 4000 casualties in the fighting for Mametz Wood. There is no record as to how many of these were victims of friendly fire. Five of the seven welsh colonels involved on the 10th were incapacitated on that day alone.

180 The only direct reference to increasing range in the divisional artillery war diary that week was on the 2nd. See note 176. Two batteries of the 35th brigade moved, probably in response to an optimistic report that the infantry were getting close to the Second Line. When this proved untrue, one battery was moved back to its original position. It seems that the artillery had orders to move forward only when the infantry were in a position to attack the Second Line. In view of the fact that one battery had moved forward on the 2nd, it is very difficult to understand why others did not move earlier.

But the guns were not moved forward. There seem to have been two main reasons. First, the 'army' plan was for the guns to move forward when the infantry reached a specific line, and they had yet to reach it. Second, there was no effective mechanism for the front line artillery and infantry to inform a general with the authority to order an advance, that one was needed.

But the successful, if one can call it that, attack on the 10th reached the line which triggered the artillery advance. *'The colonel and his battery commanders reconnoitred positions'* near Bottom Wood *'for batteries, suitable for wire cutting on the German 2nd line.'* This strong well-fortified trench line was the German second line of defence. It had been built in response to the obvious British preparations in May and June. It ran behind Mametz Wood along the front of Bazentin Wood.

The speed with which the brigade moved when they were at last ordered forward is impressive. The first reconnaissance is recorded at 9.50 pm by a surprisingly junior subaltern[181] in a forward position. The colonel and his commanders inspected and agreed the site at Bottom Wood (see map page 159) and the whole brigade was in position by dawn. At least one of the batteries had still been firing at 11.45 pm that night in their old position.

So on the 11th July, they *'came into action just behind Mametz Wood, when the Germans were still in it, 900 yards away'*. Two drivers and two horses of Colin's battery were wounded during ammunition delivery to this advanced position that early morning. They had advanced over 5000 yards under fire.

'The German artillery in their 2nd line positions gave us a very uncomfortable time', says Colin, and caused two casualties during a bombardment on the 13th. Their task now was to cut the barbed wire of the 'second' German line in front of Bazentin Woods.

---

181 Lieutenant Pharazin, Captain Page also of the 106th battery, having been wounded earlier in the evening. Lieutenant Pharazin was himself wounded two days later.

An attack was planned for the 14th, and the 7th Division infantry were already back in the line after their short rest. They had a day to plan the assault and identify key points for destruction by the artillery, and this time, the planning was made much simpler by being within the structure of one division. Not only that, but the artillery were close enough to liaise effectively, and to observe properly.

The day before the attack, Colin scouted forward. *'I spent the day in our front line. By Jove, Mametz Wood is just about the biggest shell trap I have come across.'* He discovered that *'Staff have apparently been misinformed. The wire we have to cut does not exist, and there are still 1000 Germans in the Northern edge of the wood.'* This was markedly different from what he had been led to expect.[182]

Colin reported this back, but *'as the wire ought to be there, we were ordered to fire where it ought to be. It was suggested that it was hidden by long grass; and so it might have been, if there had been any long grass to hide it.'* The next morning, while it was still dark, the infantry crept across the open fields, stopping 100 yards short of the 'barbed wire'. At very first light, the artillery bombarded with precision. *'As the wire was not there, we demolished the trench instead.'* After the brief barrage, the infantry engaged with the enemy without any initial loss.

The artillery followed up with a timed rolling barrage. Seven brigades, including two brigades of heavy 60 pounders, (about 100 guns), shelled a front line 700 yards wide, uplifting 200 yards every half hour for three hours. *'We are side by side in action all in a row,'* Colin said of his divisional artillery. It was a well-planned attack.

---

182 The 'barbed wire' prominently marked on the original map below did not exist, and 36 hours before the attack, the German line was still through the top of Mametz Wood. *'The lack of information at Divisional Headquarters as to the situation was extraordinary'* said Colin.

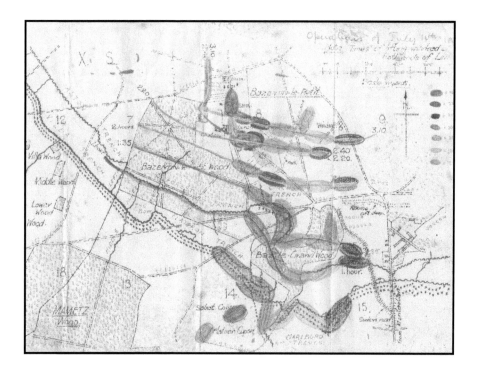

Operations of 14th July, showing the German lines in red, and the six lines of barrage (20 minutes each) for the seven brigades [183], which targeted Bazentin le Grand Wood and the fields to its left. Colin's 22nd brigade firing zone is in red, on the left of the line.

The infantry assault was at 3.30 am, and though the infantry closed with the enemy without loss, the subsequent fighting was savage and the casualties *'appalling'*. The rolling barrage did not prevent carnage. The 7th Division alone lost about 2800 casualties in the battle.

After the three-hour barrage, the observing officers moved further forward. Perhaps fortuitously, all unobserved fire was stopped at 9.55 am, because the cavalry had been ordered forward and nobody knew where they were. So, at 11.49 am, Lieutenant Baxter for Colin's 105th,

---

183 The seven artillery brigades supporting the 7th division were the 14th, 22nd, 35th, 80th, 81st, 120th and 122nd, keyed on the right. The poor quality of this map highlights the difficulties that both staff and regimental officers had in planning assaults intelligently. It shows only German positions, and covers only a small segment of the line. Often two such maps were required to cover one attack.

and Major Duff[184] of the 104th were not only in a position to report *'enemy counter attacking by the windmill,'* (see map above) but also able to do something about it. *'Heavy barrage supplied. Counter attack repulsed by artillery fire. Various barrages supplied during the day to assist the infantry in consolidating positions.'* This targeted support for the infantry repeated the tactics of the first day, yet again with great effectiveness, but again it happened by local initiative, not because it was planned.

Colin's next few letters home are cheerful. He knew he was doing well. *'Things have gone splendidly,'* though *'sleep has been a little scarce.'* And his mother was following instructions. *'I have received numerous parcels with soap, cigarettes, and chocolate.'* He had not lost his sweet tooth at times of danger.

Close enough now to be able to see what was going on and to maintain communications, Colin was enjoying himself. He would not have been anywhere else, nor with any other division. *'These are exciting times and I wouldn't have missed it for worlds.'*

But the work was hard, dangerous and unremitting. *'Every blessed night we are woken up, besides the telephone messages, by German gas shell and have been forced on three occasions to put on our helmets.'* *'A horrible dose of gas shells yesterday morning. They gave us a very rude awakening and we had to wear our helmets for some time.'* This was a dangerous lachrymatory (or tear) gas[185], designed to incapacitate in the first instance, rather than to kill.

---

184 Baxter lost a signaller sitting beside him, and *'poor Duff was wounded that day, not seriously though I am glad to say. I shall miss him very much. We were at Woolwich together and have been keeping each other company while shooting our batteries.'*

185 It was not the tear gas used for crowd control in modern times. This gas was phosgene, with an odour likened to that of 'musty hay'. It is colourless and highly toxic, since it reacts with proteins in the lungs causing fluid collection and death. Phosgene is a much more deadly gas than chlorine, though the symptoms take up to 48 hours to manifest. Its immediate effect is coughing, and irritation to the eyes. It is estimated that about 85% of the 91,000 deaths attributed to gas in World War 1 were as a result of phosgene or similar agents. www.compoundchem.com PerkinElmer copyright. The *'helmet'* used by Colin is described in note 245.

Colin does not admit to fearing it much, though he should have done. A few days later, *'the NCO of the guard came and asked me if he should get everyone out of the dugouts as gas was smelling pretty strong. I told him not to do this as it was not thick enough to worry about and there was a fairly decent breeze blowing. Just at that moment, another gas shell came whistling over and landed just downwind of us, covering the mess dugout with earth. I lay and wondered how long it would take my subalterns to get into the open air, as the gas gets very quickly down into the dugouts. Croft'* his senior subaltern, *'was quite undressed and mislaid his gas helmet, so he took one minute thirty seconds. He was thoroughly alarmed, not realising that it was one chance shell and would blow over at once. I forgot all about putting on my helmet, laughing at him. Luckily no more came over, as that one was much too close for comfort. The gas has a perfectly beastly smell, but so far no-one has had any ill effects, barring headache.'*

They stayed in the line firing continuously as the infantry of both sides suffered huge casualties in the battle for High Wood a mile beyond the Bazentin Woods. Again the range was lengthening and observation difficult.

And yet again, with the increasing range, coordination failed. On the 15th, *'at 5 pm, our artillery bombarded High Wood, and the infantry were supposed to attack after our fire lifted. However the orders to attack did not reach our infantry until about half an hour after the lift. The attack'* when it came *'had no earthly chance of success.'* A Colonel Owens in the Welsh division received the order, and rallied exhausted men from a mixture of units, most of whom had lost their junior officers, to perform the futile attack. Not only was part of the attack directed against a forward picket, but the German machine gun defences and a counterattack caused some of the men to break and run. *'It cannot be blamed on the men. Orders should never have been issued for those tired troops to attack.'* Major Walter of the 106th was observing there that evening and helped rally the survivors.

And on the 20th, *'an attack took place at 3.20 am this morning, plans altered at the last minute. I got the revised orders at 1 am at HQ, and had to prepare a scheme for bombardment to commence at 2 am. At least 3 hours warning is required by a battery for a barrage to be organised.'* He explains why all this time is needed. First he had to plot the coordinates, and calculate the range, for each lift. Then he had to work out which fuses would be needed and get them set up in order. Finally his battery director and gun captains had to be briefed. This series of tasks took 3 hours at the battery.

In addition, with each attack, the guns of his brigade were becoming less reliable. *'It is very difficult to get up to observe without getting hit in the back by our own guns,'* he says on the 18th. By the 20th, *'all our guns are absolutely worn out. Rounds are whistling, leaving the bore slowly.'* Later in the day, *'a shell exploded in a gun but luckily it did not burst. It only bulged.'*

That really was the last straw, and by that evening, he was firing only one gun; all the other guns had more than 50% of their rounds dropping short when they got hot. The infantry cannot have enjoyed it at all.

That evening, *'We are now back in rest[186], and just about time too.' 'We are very busy indeed getting things straight. We get a good sleep anyway, though it will take some time to make up the arrears.'*

The battery had been in continuous action for months[187] and in serious battle for the last four weeks. *'We are at last getting clean again, and it took some washing to manage it too. Had a simply glorious bath last night.'* He needed to get smart again as the division sorted itself out.

'My clothes are very disreputable, and I need more. I have written to Hawkes to make me another pair of breeches. Also could you let me have

---

186 They went into rest at Heilly, very close to Méricout-l'abbé Station on the river Ancre, not far back from the battle lines. It was very hot weather, but *'we are lucky because we are camped by the banks of the Ancre, a tiny little stream that runs through Albert, and we have plenty of cover from numerous trees. The main railway running to Valenciennes goes up the same valley, and is the one we went up by nearly two years ago now. It seems a long time ago now.'*

187 *'The first time since the 5th of February that the battery has been out of action.'*

another pair of puttees.[188] *I ruined two pairs on barbed wire during those operations. Please also send me out my new jacket.'*

They were scheduled for four weeks in rest and the infantry would need all of it after their heavy losses. *'I am afraid our division is now rather hors de combat.'*

Colin had been keeping a journal and he used the first few days of rest to bring it up to date and reflect on what had occurred. He wrote home. *'If the Germans really bring up many reserves they are bound to hold us on the Somme, and I'm not certain that this present pushing isn't rather a pity, the gains are very small and the cost just colossal.'* That is to say, why are we attacking the part of the German line that is now most heavily reinforced? He was of course aware of the wider war effort. *'Casualties have been dreadfully heavy, but if the success the Russians and Italians are having is helped by our pressure on this front, then it is worth it,'* he muses, but *'I'm afraid this year won't see us breaking the German lines here.'* He certainly did not share the general optimism that victory was close.

'Many of the places we have been fighting hard for this last fortnight were taken on the day of the attack[189]*, but had to be evacuated.'* That is to say, the further the infantry advanced in an attack, the further they were from their own covering artillery, and inevitably, the closer to enemy artillery. German counter attacks closely supported by their own artillery succeeded.

He considered the British artillery tactics. *'The advancing of the infantry within 100 yards of a curtain of fire has been a success, but it is not easy to make ones shell move in jumps of 50 yards a minute in front of advancing infantry.'* *'Some divisional artilleries give better support than others'* he says with typical understatement. But he was frustrated by the lack of precision, and appalled by the *'heavy casualties from our own*

---

188 These were strips of cloth wound spirally round the calf from below the knee to the ankle. The infantry wound them ankle to knee, but if a horseman did this, the knot that held them came undone.
189 At Mametz Wood, Bazentin and High Wood, amongst other examples.

artillery' which resulted from the unobserved 20 minute lifts used in other attacks.

On attacks in general, *'It is interesting how very easy it is, when one is on the spot, to tell if any particular attack is going to be a success. If someone on the spot could be trusted to push on, or hold back the attacks, according to the conditions actually seen, it would save great loss of life and morale. It was very obvious that the well prepared attack of the 14th would be a success.'* It was equally obvious that the futile attack in High Wood on the 15th July, would be a failure. Even colonels had no leeway on orders from behind.

Colin did not of course forget to complain a bit on his own behalf, having been in front line observation for a month. *'This sort of fighting, we have just about as strenuous a time as the infantry. 10 days in and 10 days out, same as the infantry, is just about enough.'*

But it seems that he was not given much opportunity to discuss these thoughts with the generals. *'The general[190] was round here this morning but was not particularly sociable. However, I'm told he means well.'* And *'we were interviewed in a bunch by the corps commander yesterday,'* (Lieutenant General Sir Henry Horne, unusually, himself from the artillery). *'He was very complimentary indeed about our division and spoke very highly about the work of the artillery, so I suppose our troubles and worries have been to some good.'* More an oration that an interview, one suspects.

And indeed, in view of the appalling casualties of the first day of the Somme battle, the surprise is not how bad the tactics on the day were, but how good. The battle was preceded by a bombardment which should have followed the example of the 7th Division Artillery in terms of planning and execution in every sector. For the first time in Colin's account, the British army had planned an assault of a siege-line with an appropriately targeted artillery bombardment based on detailed local reconnaissance and with enough time to do

---

190 Lieutenant-General Sir Herbert Edward Watts KCB KCMG of the 7th division, though he did take over the Welsh division for a few days on the 9th July.

the job. The infantry assault on the day was immediately preceded by a heavy bombardment of the front trenches to drive the defenders under cover, a well-tested and obvious step. At the moment of assault, the artillery moved to a pre-planned bombardment to hinder reinforcements and deter those defenders slightly further back, again obvious.

This phase was relatively short, and once the artillery forward observation officers were up, close liaison was established with the infantry, and the guns were used flexibly to provide support for the infantry. This was a recipe for success.

In the first few days of the battle, experienced junior commanders were to some extent allowed to use their initiative, even in stable defensive situations. Colonel Buckle on the 5th July, *'suggests a barrage to prevent counter attack at Mametz Wood'*, and gave co-ordinates. He was *'ordered to carry out his suggestion.'* He was of course, highly experienced. Inexperienced officers, even of higher rank, could not be expected to make these calls with any certainty.

But over the next week even the 7th Division did not follow the tactics of the first day. The guns were sited too far back to give the infantry the support they needed. This became a real problem on the 4th July by which time the infantry had advanced over 3000 yards into enemy territory. And they had advanced another 2000 yards before the guns moved on the night of the 10th July. It is very difficult to understand why they did not move before this.

The artillery forward observation officers had great difficulty moving forward so far each day, and then observing for their batteries, with their long communication wires being repeatedly cut. Liaison between infantry brigades and artillery brigades became more and more difficult. So unobserved timed barrages were substituted for intelligent targeted support, or the more difficult 'moving curtain' of fire.

The timed barrage was an attractive tactic. But it ossified attack plans, and as described, it often lost touch with reality on the ground.[191]

But when they defaulted to observed and targeted fire – *'German counterattacks were repulsed'* and *'barrages supplied to assist the infantry'* – suddenly the guns were altogether more helpful.

Of course, the officers, Colin included, of the 22nd Artillery Brigade and the 7th Division generally were regular army and very experienced. The difficulties of forward observation during a battle should not be underestimated. Even to get in to a position to see enough was difficult and very dangerous, and there was always the risk of directing your own battery while observing the fall of shells from another battery. But even at this stage of the battle, it was clear to Colin, and almost certainly to most officers in the front line, that close artillery support was crucial in dealing with the German counter attacks which were repeatedly nullifying the hard earned gains of the infantry. In short, without close artillery support, forward control on the battlefield was lost. When forward control on the battlefield was lost, the chances of significant success plummeted.

But they were back at rest now, out of the battle. 'Rest' however was a relative term. *'The mornings are pretty full with parade and one thing and another, and by the time that's done, one doesn't feel up to much else in the afternoon.'* Whatever his feelings, the men still had to be looked after. Morale suffered with inactivity, and the regular 7th division knew it better than most.

In the first week, Colin arranged *'a boxing competition in which our battery carried off 7 out of the 8 contests,'* and the next week, there was a sports day when *'the battery won all the men's jumping events outright, and were very unlucky to get beaten in the tug of war on horseback.'* Colin was a sportsman, and his men seem to have vied to emulate him.

But *'everybody is now having sports, and these all have to be attended.'* As, did cultural offerings, with even less enthusiasm. *'We had a sort*

---

191 Particularly if the officers controlling the rate of advance were killed.

of farewell concert last night, at least it rather developed into a farewell concert. It was got up by the brigade and the colonel's departure was learnt of on the same afternoon.' [192]

Sombre thoughts did intrude. *'It is exactly a year today that I got Fathers letter about Donald. It was hard then and it's hard now.'*

Perhaps as a consequence of this, he did manage to obtain 'Paris leave'. This was quite sought after, and allowed two nights away sampling the delights of the French capital. Colin met up with an old friend of the family. *'It is a splendid relief to get away from the khaki clad soldiers,'* he said. *'We made plans for today. A stroll to the taxi, the taxi round the Lake in the Bois, lunch at the Café de Paris, supposed to be the most chic place in Paris. Tonight we are going the Café Ciro to dinner and then on to some theatre.'* He clearly found Paris a strange and welcome contrast to the unremitting pressure of life in an army at war.

He was the only officer in the 7th division artillery to get leave of any sort in that month.

---

192 Colonel A.S. Buckle. He was promoted brigadier, but died of meningitis the next month. He was replaced by Colonel W.A. Short. Colin found both men difficult, and probably vice versa. But Colonel Buckle was a respected senior colonel, and Colin was settling under his leadership. He probably thought more of Colin than he let on, nominating him for a mention in dispatches, published not in January 1917, when Colin wryly said that *'recognition was hard to come by in the 7th Division'*, but as a surprise in the April. Colin had been commanded by the now promoted Major Short in 1913, and one gathers from a terse reference that their relationship then had not been entirely harmonious. Duke wrote in August that Colin *'doesn't like his new colonel.'*

CHAPTER TEN

1916 The 35th Division at the Somme

'A' Battery, 159th Brigade, 35th Division

'We have an idea we are moving today, but nothing definite so far.'

And what of Uncle Duke? The 35th Division had moved to behind Arras on the 3rd July. Here he was posted for a few days to the divisional artillery office. *'Did fool stunts with the brigadier; one-day battery staff, and later ammunition supply. No-one seemed to know quite what was happening.'* Enough said.

On the 5th July, they made another short move to behind Albert. *'This moving about is really quite fun. There is always anticipation with it and the wildest kind of rumours. Since we have got on the move, my bedroom has been a valise under a tree, and with luck a bundle of straw below, and the waterproof shirt for rain cover'* And then on down to the River Somme itself. *'We are now on the top of a hill and the view all around is simply beautiful; a large river runs below the hill.'*

On the 20th July, the same day that Colin and his battery moved into rest, Duke and his battery went to war. *'A couple of days ago we came up here, a short march, but very congested roads. We made a wagon line, and came up with the guns in the evening.'* [194] They had arrived at Maricourt, on the southern flank of the campaign, see map overleaf.

'We have been very busy ever since, digging ourselves into holes in the ground when we are not firing.' Their first task was wire cutting duties, but with *'observation posts unobtainable'*, according to the brigade diary,

---

194 The brigade diary says the colonel selected their position; Duke says that Captain Pinney did. The other two artillery brigades of the division were the 157th and 158th. The 159th brigade was designated 'B' group of the 35th division artillery and facing Guillemont. Their wagon lines were at Bray-sur-Somme.

it is not entirely clear how they did it. Imagine the derision in the 7th Division if that had been written by a brigade there.

'Everywhere bristles with our guns. The noise of battle is awful; cannot hear oneself speak. This warfare is quite different to anything we have had before. Last night we strafed the Hun, tonight he strafes us; such is life.'

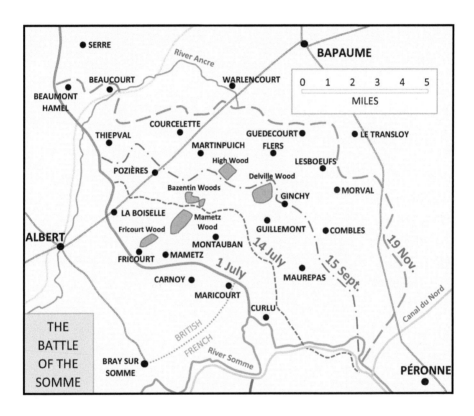

Duke's battery was at Maricourt, 3 miles east of Mametz.

'Although I wanted to sleep in my tent, the skipper absolutely objects to sleeping above ground, so that ever since we came in, we have spent all our time digging holes for ourselves to sleep and crawl into. Our guns are now fairly well protected from splinters and both officers and men have dugouts to hide in and sleep. The soil is clay above chalk, so we can go down to any depth without supporting the walls.'

The value of this exercise was soon demonstrated. *'A shell burst in our no. 4 gun pit, and the entire detachment were buried in the neighbouring dugout. Only one man was hurt, though he subsequently died of the wound. After this the detachment were very proud of their gun, which showed a lot of shell marks.'* Unbelievably they were the only battery to dig in.

'Our neighbours, a 60 pounder battery, have taken no precautions; indeed, their mess is a tent. This accounts for the very heavy casualties they are having.' 'We hear of casualties in the brigade and also the 157th. They too have not taken the precaution to dig as we have done.' In 1916 this was nothing short of criminal negligence.

A major attack was planned for the 30th on Guillemont. The colonel told off one junior officer to be the brigade observation officer. Again Captain Pinney impatiently took matters into his own hands. He sent Duke off to the left as far as Trones Wood, another subaltern forward to the front lines, while he himself scouted to the right for a suitable observation post. It was Captain Pinney who found an ideal spot about a mile east of Maricourt (in the French zone). The panoramic vista from this point was subsequently drawn by a war artist on the 7th August.

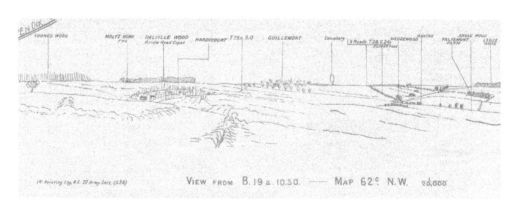

Trones and Delville Woods on the left, Guillemont in the centre. French zone of attack on the right. Map overleaf. Guillemont is 3000 yards away, too far for useful observation of battery fire.

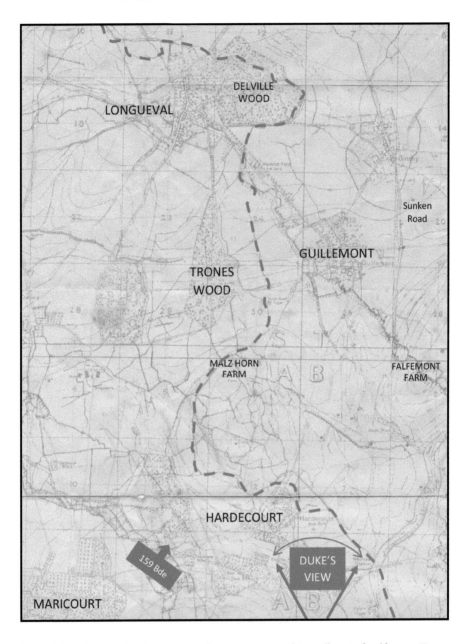

From his high point, Duke could see from Trones Wood to well east of Falfemont Farm. The Germans front line, in blue, is outlined approximately. Positions were very fluid.

Duke was the forward observer that day, though not forward, since he was due east of the battery. *'The Huns gave us a proper dose of gas overnight, and at 2.30 am the journey there was far from pleasant for we were in the beastly stuff all the way, and it catches you in the eyes and throat.*[195] *It was late when the mist rose, but I could see the whole battlefield, a thing they say only occurs once in a lifetime.'* *'The objectives on our left had been gained*[196]*, but what I (and the captain of a 30th Division Battery) saw was large numbers of Huns in full retreat across the open,'* in the French zone to the right.

'We immediately put the guns on, blazing away at them. Those who remained were rallied in the sunken road and even supported by others who came from a farm' see map, *'down a slope. We turned the batteries on this lot and simply gave them hell. Those who got this got into the sunken road, and with the others commenced a counter attack only to be met by our guns when they had to cross the open. Our two batteries simply stopped the attack.*

Sometime later again, they came down the hill further up – give them all credit – it was magnificent to see the way they were led and came forward in mass, only to be met by a hail of shells from our guns, pumping away like mad. This lot never reached anywhere except the shell zone. Some branched off towards the French zone and were no doubt taken care of by them.

It was a couple of hours before they attacked again, when they came on, in battalions. Unfortunately, there was a hitch with our wires and I could not get complete control of the battery, and the other battery was out of contact with

---

195 It was too much for the divisional trench mortar ammunition parties. They lost their way in the gas and fog, and the mortars were unable to fire in the preliminary bombardment. Brigadier not impressed.

196 Units of the leading 90th infantry brigade (30th division), attacking from Trones Wood, penetrated Guillemont, but the Germans reacted quickly and heavily shelled both behind the Wood, and the 700 yards of open fields between it and Guillemont, this all in thick fog. Communications broke down very early in the attack, and the second wave of troops of the 30th and 35th divisions failed to reinforce the lead battalions. Heavy German counterattacks later in the day overwhelmed the 2nd Royal Scots Fusiliers who were trapped in the village and almost annihilated. www.17thmanchesters.wordpress.com gives a good account.

broken wires, and I be hanged if they didn't get back in to Guillemont again.'

All well and good, and the divisional diary also records Duke's barrages, but *'the French officer put us off firing into a large formation on the right, thinking they were French troops, but I not knowing started in to fire on this lot. They broke and moved off to the right.'* One gets a sinking feeling. The French were attacking much of the line that Duke was observing. He was desperately inexperienced.

As for the 35ᵗʰ Division's artillery performance generally, the trench mortars failed to fire due to having no ammunition, and accounts of the battle make it clear that the pre-arranged barrages did little to support the infantry advance, or to break up the later German counter attacks. The one junior forward observer of the 159ᵗʰ Brigade was wounded, and observation of their early barrages was anyway obscured by the dense fog. The 'group liaison officer' with the leading infantry was a mere second lieutenant, and since infantry communications had broken down in the fog even before the attack started, his input to his colonel was largely based on rumour and wishful thinking.

As for the guns, secure positions had not been selected or constructed. *'Both our brigade and the divisional artillery have been very much knocked about. One brigade has lost all its commanding officers and many lost 50%.'* Duke had by this time learned to appreciate the competent leadership of his own battery, whose casualties had been light despite a heavy bombardment. *'Wonder if its lack of good management'* he mused, or *'if they have put in the amount of digging we have done.'*

Brigadier Staveley should at the very least have issued orders to his batteries to dig in. But he put too much faith in his colonels. He trusted them, as he himself had been trusted in command of Colin's brigade on the retreat in 1914, to divert *'batteries for fleeting opportunities, always returning to the main barrage,'* if the enemy were out in the open. But Duke was too far from Guillemont to observe for the much needed artillery support there, too inexperienced to authorise fire on units he observed in the French sector, and as Duke observed afterwards, *'none of the batteries saw what they were shooting at.'*

Immediately after the battle, Duke's colonel collapsed with trench fever (note 309), so Captain Pinney seized the opportunity to negotiate with the French and move his battery to the valley immediately behind the observation point used by Duke, *'an excellent position with just room between two French batteries'.* The advantages of better protection, and shorter wires to good observation were so self-evident that the *'brigade moved to join us a day or two later,'* though the brigade diary records that all the batteries moved together. Other units followed. *A heavy battery is being put in. They are truly reckless the way they send their wagons over the main road in broad daylight, for it's in observation'* from the German lines. More inexperience.

The generals discovered the observation post. It became *'a regular show-place and one day we had six up to view the country'.* A bit late, one would surmise.

As for Duke's battery, *'in the first four days in our new position, good work was done in digging for protection, but everyone got slack when reports of our going out of action began to be circulated'* on the 11th. *'When we did hand over, we were somewhat ashamed of the work we had done, given the length of time we were there.'*

Throughout his stint on the Somme battlefield, Duke was full of questions. Why were accurate direction finders not issued to forward observers? It seemed so simple and obvious. He designed one and sent a drawing back to Alec, his nephew at home, only to discover that the French already had such an instrument in use.

Why weren't engineers on hand to provide piped water? *'Some of our horses have to walk four miles three times a day just to get their water. There would be no difficulty in laying pipes and putting in pumps and concrete tanks.'*

Why wasn't the army more mechanised? *'Horses are being used for ammunition; all ought to be done by motor transport, much quicker and less risk of loss. Even the guns should be moved about by light tractors which would make roads as they go.'*

Why did the British Artillery fix so rigidly the timing of their Artillery uplifts? *'French methods are an eye opener to us. Their staff work is splendid, as is the communication between their advancing infantry and artillery. The lifting of their barrage is done by signal and not by time as we do. When a strong point is met, the advance is halted while the artillery concentrate, and not immediately rushed by the infantry, at terrible cost. They have a signal corps*[197] *which does all this work.'*

Colin too always praised the French Artillery staff work and asked why the British could not emulate it. Even Brigadier Staveley agreed with this, saying in his post-battle report that he favoured the French *'creeping barrage'* over the British *'jumping lifts'*, on the grounds that the *'final assault interval under rifle and machine gun fire is reduced to a minimum'* though he acknowledged that his division had neither the equipment, nor the skills, necessary for this approach.[198] He knew that his liaison with the infantry had not been good enough, and he asked for written reports from his liaison officers and feedback from the infantry after the battle.

But though incremental changes in resource allocation were occurring slowly, (both piped water and mechanised transport were not far in the future), step changes in operational tactics were another matter altogether. 'Jumping lift' barrages were the new British tactic, and it was not politic to question it. When Duke did so, he was told not to think, and to get on with his work.

---

197 The British did not. Each infantry Division had just one Royal Engineers Signals Company of about 160 men. It was organised into four Sections; one for Divisional HQ and one for each of the 3 infantry brigades, none allocated it seems to liaise with the artillery. They had their own signallers and telephonists.
198 National Archives' ref. WO 95/2471/2, p. 48. Brigadier Stavely had several complaints. He did not like the 'jumping lift' technique, since it meant firing without observation, and he complains at earlier being ordered to cut wire seen from the air, but out of view on the ground. In this respect, his report is conservative and would probably have been read with impatience, especially since his battle field control was based on erroneous reports, and from the evidence, it seems unlikely that his batteries managed to hit the targets he gave them.

Duke had a very low opinion of the intellectual calibre of his regular, more senior, officers. *'Few of them know how to use their authority,'* he said, and more forcefully, *'few have even the brains of chickens.'*

The 35th Division went out into rest on the 14th August; and did not return again to the Somme battlefield. They were sent to a quiet sector at Arras and stayed there for the next six months.

Duke was not surprised. *'I don't think they will trust our infantry to do anything again'*, he said, and *'I believe a major is responsible for our guns being away from it all'*. It was November, still at Arras, before Duke became more positive in his work. *'I've now got the battalion look-outs and snipers interested in spotting trench mortars and guns.'* It had taken all that time for his division to become an effective unit. Before then, he was not a happy man.

CHAPTER ELEVEN

1916 7ᵗʰ Division on the Somme

105ᵗʰ Battery, 22ⁿᵈ Brigade, 7ᵗʰ Division

'We are rather in the middle of it again here.'

On the 20ᵗʰ August, Colin was on the march back to the Somme. And for him it was more of the same. Very little progress had been made in the month they had been away. The British divisions were continuing their assaults, grinding forward a few yards at a time, with appalling losses. High Wood was still in German hands. Yet again Colin's battery was less than a 1000 yards from the front line, just back from Delville and Trones Wood, and only a few thousand yards north of his Uncle Duke's recently vacated positions.

And going into the battle, Colin disobeyed direct orders on the siting of his battery. *'Major Walter[199] is having a rotten time. He is across the valley to me, 400 yards away and has been subjected to very accurate shell fire, two gun pits have been hit by heavy shell. They wanted me to put my battery on his right, but I wasn't having it, no forward slope facing the enemy for me if I can help it. So in spite of a horse artillery colonel who first reconnoitred the position, I came across here and am very thankful I did so too.'* One would have thought that the lessons of terrain sensitive placement of batteries would have been learned by this time. But here, in 1916, is a colonel, trained for cavalry support, still thinking with pre-1914 military logic and choosing a site out in the open, without any thought of camouflage or protection.

Their first job was to dig in and dig in fast. *'We had a fairly rotten time of it the first two nights, as the Germans shell this ghastly valley pretty heavily at times.'*

199 Major Walter commanded the 106ᵗʰ battery in the brigade. Morrison was his senior subaltern, as Croft was Colin's. The four of them were the forward observation officers and they often worked together.

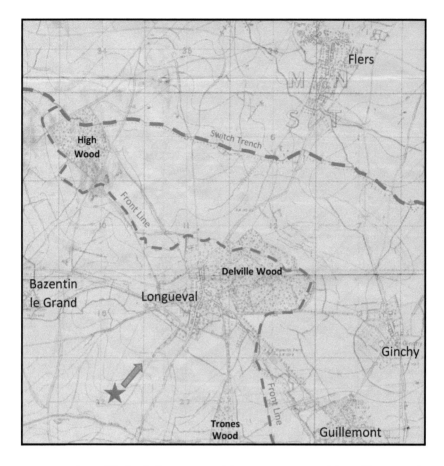

Somme trench map[200], dated 5th August. 105th battery position starred, line of fire arrowed. The German front trenches, and Switch Trench (east from High Wood), are marked in blue.

---

200 This map shows the system that had been developed by the British army to map the front lines. The scale is 1:20,000, though other scales were available. A letter was used first, in this map, S and T. The square so identified was divided into 30 numbered areas each 1000 yards square. Guillemont, for example, is in T19. Each enumerated square is divided into four, labelled a, b, c and d. The edges of each of these sub-squares were marked off 1 to 9, so that an exact map reference can be calculated. Thus Colin's first battery position was written as S.22.b.42. The first numeral 4 was west (0) to east (9), the second numeral 2 south (0) to north (9). For ranging purposes, the final figure was expressed to two decimal places, from 00 to 99, indicating an area five yards square.

The brigade diary that day enlarges, 'a howitzer shell landed on a party of men of the 105th working on a gun pit, killing one and wounding four.'

Both German ground observers and German planes were looking to register new targets. *'There have been any number of aeroplanes about here, the German ones are getting very bold and have been annoying us considerably. We have to duck to cover while the blighters are up. One can't even walk about in comfort near the battery position.'*

And it was not long before they were registered. Unlike at Ypres the year before, they elected to dig in and stay put. *'For some unknown reason a 10.5cm German Howitzer battery has fixed upon us for its nightly attention. For two nights he has put roughly 400 rounds per night into us. The night before last he put a gas shell through my dugout and has stunk me out of house and home. Four of our six gun pits were hit, one pit was hit six times, two shells going clean through the shield of the gun and a third blew a wheel to smithereens. The whole detachment were in the pit when the gun was first struck, and only one fellow was hurt. How the other four got off, I really don't know.'* But Colin moved his men quickly into cover for this and subsequent bombardments and the battery lost only two men killed and seven wounded that week.

Colin himself spent most of his time up at the front as forward observer in Delville Wood, with a couple of signallers, connected by their line of wire to the battery. Just rolling the wire out there was bad enough. *'We had a bad time going through the Wood.[201] German snipers were busy and dangerous.'* And the German artillery counter fire was such that the wire was always being cut by random shells. Every such cut meant a dangerous and lengthy search for the problem.

---

201 The battle for Longueval, and Delville Wood which dominates the village had been going on since the 14th July, with British attacks meeting with German counter-attacks in a war of attrition. Colin arrived on the 20th August, when most of the wood was in British hands, but it was another two weeks before it was taken. Duke has already described a failed British attempt to advance to Guillemont from Trones Wood.

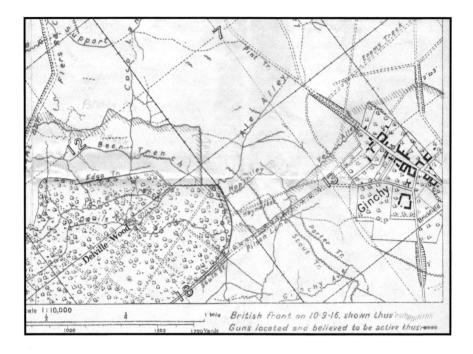

Trench map (10th Sep.) Delville Wood showing Inner Trench and Edge Trench.
The shaded trenches are in British hands that day.

'Delville Wood was not a healthy place to be in, for all sorts of reasons. '*Our observation post there*' (in Inner Trench) '*is in a most disgusting place and is continually under shell fire. There is only one trench to it and it is just one long grave. The stench is perfectly appalling, and a great many of the dead of both sides still remain unburied. I saw a German peeping through a loophole in their front line at a place where our trenches are only 40 yards apart. The blighters have built loopholes already, whereas I was using a periscope behind a parapet that would not have kept out a shotgun, leave alone a rifle bullet.' 'An awfully nice fellow in the Rifle Brigade was shot through the parapet while I was there, looking over it without a periscope I'm afraid.'*

'*Talking about that same spot, I was there and a German heavy shell landed just about 50 yards from us right into one of their own strongholds. At once they fired off a whole bouquet of rockets as a signal to their artillery to stop shelling them. We in the trench simply danced for joy as just about five minutes later another very ugly brute landed right in the same spot.'*

Colin seems to carry his luck with him! It could just as easily have landed on him.

But luck can be manufactured. *'In Paris, I had a very interesting talk with a French artillery captain and I have adapted a suggestion of his for dugouts in the battery. They sink a shaft like a well until they have about 12 feet of cover, which in this chalk will keep out most things. Then they tunnel under and make dugouts. Below the floor of the tunnel they dig down another 6 feet, so that even if a shell does burst on top of the shaft, the debris falls into this 6 foot excavated below the floor, and the dugouts are not blocked. Four dugouts can be constructed from one shaft.'*

He immediately took up the idea. *'We are living the life of rabbits just now, one ear wide open for the whistle of a German shell which sends us all below ground into the deep dugouts.'* *'If we had not started on our dugouts right away, we should have had terrible casualties. They have not left a square yard in the position untouched by direct hits and our number six gun is a very war-worn spectacle with two holes through its shield. They really are splendid things, but as you say take a terrible lot of digging.'*

And in a subsequent letter, *'my shallow dugout has had it again, this time a great armour piercing 8-inch shell. My rubber boots have disappeared into space, and my suitcase of valuables was buried by 5 foot of earth. The suitcase is completely done for this time, but the contents are practically intact. It has had an adventurous career, what with being hit by a train, then by a gas shell and now by an 8 inch.'* *'We were all down our deep dugout at the time. A shell fell only two yards from it and just part of the side of the shaft fell in. We are getting the shaft sunk to below floor level to receive any future landslides of that sort. Had awful visions of being buried for a second.'*

'You would have laughed to see Croft and I contemplating that colossal shell hole exactly where we thought our kit ought to be. I think that if one didn't laugh, the end would be an asylum. One jokes and laughs practically all day long. But we swore that if anybody laughed at us digging in that shell hole, we'd throw a shovel at them.'

Humour keeps creeping into the letters. *'By the way my nice little aluminium saucepan also tried conclusion with the 8 inch shell the other day and got the worst of it. I wonder if you could send me out another.'* *'The beggars landed a shell in our kitchen which has rather altered the shapes of the plates and saucers. It is nothing now to see a saucer waltzing across the table in a most ludicrous manner.'*

So he did his own manual labour, he got his deep dugouts constructed in days, and above all he led with a smile. *'The men are just perfectly wonderful, the conditions up in front here are terrible,'* he says in the same letter, and then goes on to acknowledge receipt of cigarettes for the men and supplies for the officers' mess. He worked hard to look after those under his command.

'The swine got a direct hit on one of the gun pits setting about 100 rounds of ammunition on fire. We had rather an exciting time putting the fire out. It would have been all right if one of the NCOs hadn't sat in the gun pit through the shelling, poor devil had his leg broken in two places I'm afraid. Croft did splendid work bandaging him up. They put another shell just about 10 yards in front during this operation and it did not explode. This is 'some life' as the Canadians would say.' [202]

His courageous, perhaps slightly colonial, ethos percolated the whole unit. *'We had a drawing room tea (no table) in the open air, enjoying a really nice evening, though there's the devil of a racket going on. We can't go into the mess because two hours ago, they landed a gas shell within five yards of it, and there are two fires burning in there to clear the gas out. The crater is still emitting gas and my eyes are running horribly. I will probably have to put on my goggles. This is really not conducive to good letter writing so you must excuse me.'*

Less than a mile behind the front line, the batteries were able to provide close support for the infantry in front of them. On the 27th August, Colin's 105th battery was ordered to support an attack in Delville Wood, by the 10th Durham Light Infantry. They were in

---

202 This on the 5th September. Lieutenant, later Captain Croft, was his senior subaltern.

Inner Trench (see map page 168) and at 5 am the battalion stormed the German held Edge Trench, on the north-east corner of the wood, before bombing up Ale Alley to the line of Beer Trench. They captured 50 prisoners with the loss of 6 officers (out of 20). 32 other ranks were killed, 159 wounded and 8 evacuated, 'shell-shocked'.

Colin was in Delville Wood that day, *'in a dreadful state, soaked through and covered with mud from head to foot'*, observing and directing his guns. The infantry brigade diary reports rapid planning of the operation, close liaison between Colin and Colonel Morant, who commanded; and then a 12-hour delay to ensure preparations were complete. There were quick responses during the day to hold-ups and counter attacks during the battle. And despite a general heavy bombardment from enemy artillery throughout, the new line outside the wood was held, a gain of several hundred yards towards the village of Ginchy. Close liaison between battalion and battery had led to local success.

An infantry officer and his slightly junior artillery counterpart were given a job to do together – as equal partners. Colin was solely responsible for the artillery support. He and the colonel planned the attack together and saw their plans through. Obviously the colonel was in overall command, but the ethos of this successful attack is clear; responsibility squarely on the front line regimental officers with no top down direction beyond a stated achievable objective. There were lessons to be learned. The little battle is not even mentioned in the divisional artillery war diary.

Colin had slightly mixed feelings about this conquest of Delville Wood. *'I'm not sure that it's a great benefit, as now that the Germans know we have the whole wood and that none of their own fellows are there, they can shell it as much as they like.'*

They did not have the whole wood for long. The map on page 168 which shows the gains involved is dated the 10th September and this attack was on the 27th August. The Germans always mounted large counter attacks to recover any lost ground, and they did so a few days later, recovering the lost ground, just as they had when an attack on the 24th had made the same gains. A British assault by the 7th Division a few days after that again recaptured Edge Trench, and briefly the village of Ginchy, but that was retaken by the Germans in another counter attack. Ginchy was not safely in British hands until the 9th September.

The losses on both sides were huge, and the artillery played their part in this war of attrition. But in contrast to the operational freedom Colin had enjoyed on the 27th, the divisional artillery staff generally gave strict orders each day to their artillery brigades on zones and map references to be bombarded with exact timings. The inflexibility of this approach continued to cause problems.

Examples have already been given of the disadvantage of the jumping, or rolling, barrage in this context. But even on quieter days, the orders, based on maps and reports, were sometimes just plain wrong. So if the batteries did not observe properly, or elected to blindly obey orders, they might well find themselves bombarding their own troops.

Colin had written the previous year, that *'a true gunner never fires a round without sending one of his own officers to report.'* He regarded friendly casualties as unforgivably unprofessional. Earlier in the battle, the colonel[203] had *'accused my battery of shooting into our own infantry and wouldn't listen to anything I said. It didn't seem to make any difference that I wasn't firing at the time. I asked to be relieved of my command.'* Permission denied, and Colin was not alone in making this request at this accusation in this regular army division. *'Three of us asked to be relieved of our command and I was the first.'* But there was not necessarily the same ethos in other divisions.

---

203 Colonel Short, though his enquiry probably pertained to the Welsh attack on Mametz Wood, when Colonel Buckle was in command. Colin presumably kept the papers relating to this attack for reference purposes. The letter quoted is dated the 9th September. Colin was pleased Colonel Short was away with dysentery!

So on the 13ᵗʰ September, Colin writes in forward observation that he '*had to take care throughout the day. One of our 4.5 Howitzer batteries was putting round after round just behind us. Our telephone wire was cut several times but very soon mended by linesmen.*' The next day, the same thing happened. '*We had to vacate the observation post and wait the pleasure of our own heavies who were doing some close shooting.*' They would have told their own batteries what was happening, but they had no authority to redirect the fire of any other battery, and no means of doing so. [204]

In other words, the senior staff often had insufficient up-to-date information from the front line. This was most obvious in battle, but it is clear that there were problems even on mildly fluid quiet days during the campaign.

But to return to the battle, with Delville Wood and Ginchy now firmly in British hands, thus eliminating the salient[205], there was an opportunity for another major assault by the Fourth Army on the German Switch trench between High Wood and Delville Wood, pushing north. Colin received orders on the 11ᵗʰ September '*to dig this forward position and take three guns up the same night.*' His battery was moved to the top end of Trones Wood, now firing due north. (See map page 166.)

On the 14ᵗʰ September, Colin went back up to observe for his battery's wire cutting, in preparation for the Battle of Flers which would open the next day. '*We started at 8 am and the absolute lack of trenches in Delville Wood, and the abundance of unburied decaying flesh made any movement in the wood very unpleasant. The heavy German*

---

204 The battery would inform brigade headquarters, and through them, divisional artillery who would check the fire zones of their own units. When, as likely, they found that it wasn't one of theirs, they would inform corps artillery headquarters. They in turn would check the zones of bombardment of each of their other four divisions, and issue revised orders, which then had to be implemented. This process took all day.

205 A salient was a bulge of line into the enemy line, which could be attacked from three sides. 458 battery had been in the salient at Ypres.

shelling caused us to lose direction, so we hit the wrong communication trench, and could not find the telephone wire which should have been there. We had to go back into the wood again and look for it. German snipers were busy and dangerous. We found the wire, cut to pieces, in a trench which was being heavily shelled, and was completely obliterated in parts. German machine guns were sniping anyone who showed themselves over the obliterated portions and we decided it was now no place for an observation post.' They found another spot from which to continue. But it was not the best and *'proceedings for the day were abruptly closed about 5.30pm by a German Howitzer of heavy calibre blowing in the trench 3 yards from us. We decided it was time we went back and had tea.'*

The 15th September was the day of the offensive, the Battle of Flers. The plan, as usual in a major assault, was for a long infantry advance with a breakthrough as the objective. This was the first time that tanks were used on the Western Front, and there were hopes that they might turn the battle in the allies' favour. *'Several armoured caterpillars moved up during the night. These contrivances are armoured with 2 Hotchkiss 7 pounders and several machine guns. They are reported to be absolutely indifferent to all obstacles, whether shell craters, trenches, barbed wire entanglements or even small houses.'* Colin was unimpressed. *'We shall see what we shall see.'*

After lunch, I met Major Walter to go up to Croft and Morrison who reported they were in Switch Trench[206]. We made our way across country along their telephone wires. The German were shelling pretty heavily just over Switch Trench, so we had to bolt through the barrage and found it occupied very thickly by our troops.[207]

The signallers were established in a deep German dugout, but as it was

206 Switch Trench, the strong German front line trench running along the crest of a low ridge, had been captured that morning. See map page 166. The map on page 157 shows the villages of Flers and Guedecourt which were further objectives in the battle.

207 *'KR., RBs, Guards, West York's, all mixed up in 100 yds of trench.'* It seems likely that these were units of the 14th Division. The Kings Royal Rifles and the Rifle Brigade both had battalions in this division.

just our side of the crest and we had been ordered to bring observed fire to bear on a German trench line just short of Guedecourt, it was necessary to bolt out 100 yards beyond and observe from a shell hole. We made our way out there and had a splendid view, five officers and five telephonists sitting in one shell hole. Our troops could be seen beyond Flers on our left and it was pretty clear we had been held up on the right. One caterpillar could be seen N.E of Flers stranded away in front of our front line. We had passed three of them on our way up to the Switch line. [208]

The guns were got on to the required target, and presently Germans were seen advancing towards Guedecourt. [209] *These were engaged, but the long range (6200 yards) at which we were firing made it impossible to get much result.*

The Germans just 1500 yards in front of us suddenly ran some field guns into the open, and commenced shelling some of our troops advancing on the right using direct laying. As our telephone wires were now all cut up, we decided to make a bolt the 100 yards to the Switch Trench. The barrage was between us and Switch Trench, and we decided to all start together. We all arrived safely at Switch Trench.

As soon as the wire was repaired, we decided to try and knock out the German field battery firing direct. Major Walter's wire was got going first so he made his way out to the shell hole again. I followed him soon afterwards with our wire and a signaller. By this time the light was starting to go, but unfortunately the Germans spotted us and opened rapid fire with one gun right onto the shell crater. The fourth round hit us. Major Walter was hit over the left eye and at the time I believed he was killed outright. The piece which passed through my cheek caused so much blood to flow that I could not see for a bit. We pulled Major Walter down in to the shell hole and bolted for the

---

208 While the new caterpillar 'tanks' worked they had some success, but few of them got very far.

209 The village of Guedecourt was to their front, about a mile beyond Flers. Yet again the plan for the battle, which was intended to force a break-through, had involved an infantry advance beyond the range of the artillery. Yet again, a German counterattack would negate much of the initial gains.

trench again. We made our way back to Croft and Morrison who went out at once and got the major in, the shelling having ceased somewhat.

It was dusk and everybody gave a hand to bring the major in on a stretcher. It took 2 ½ hours to get back to the battery, luckily no casualties being sustained on the way. I found a captain already due to take over the battery, walked on back to the dressing station, and was taken by ambulance to Corbie No 5 casualty clearing station[210], going in the same ambulance as poor Major Walter.[211] He was still unconscious.'

At the clearing station, he took time to write to his mother. *'Have a lot of letters to answer, but you must wait a bit as the Huns have cut my cheek open. Am rather afraid this won't reach you before the War Office telegram, but I hope it will.'* It did not, but the thought was there. The War Office telegram gave only minimal details and caused great anxiety. *'Will let you know where I land up.'*

He landed up at the Empress Eugenie's Hospital for Officers[212], in Farnborough on the 20th September. *'I was evacuated and taken by barge from Corbie to Abbeville – took 24 hours and a very comfortable journey it was. After 24 hours at the general hospital there, we came on by train to Havres and across to here last night. The piece of shell that hit me entered just below the cheekbone coming out two inches below, not touching any bones. The only trouble was the amount of blood I lost. The face has swollen up a bit. However they are putting fomentations on, and that will probably bring it down.'*

It was a nasty wound, badly damaging the salivary gland. But

---

210 There were about 60 casualty clearing station units on the Western Front and they moved as needed. No 5 was at Corbie, a small town on the Somme, about 30 kilometres back from the front line. www.1914-1918.net

211 *'A piece of shell had entered his brain and little hope is entertained that he will recover. He is a very great loss, and was much liked by everyone in the Brigade, besides being a very fine soldier indeed.'* Major Bertram Walter died, aged 34, the next day and is buried in Corbie communal cemetery extension.

212 The 'hospital' was really a private nursing home. Just eight officers were looked after, in the wing of the private house of the Empress Eugenie, the widow of Napoleon the Third of France.

luckily he avoided both an operation and infection, and the swelling gradually resolved. Yet again, he was not a very good patient! *'My face is going down quite quickly and ought to be normal in a day or two. The doctor is coming again on Tuesday'* (the 3ʳᵈ October). *'I will make a big agitation, but before then I don't see any way of getting away.'* His big agitation was a success and he got home on the 5th October.

Colin had been wounded on the 15ᵗʰ September. On a daily basis before that, he had been shelled at the battery and at his forward observation post. He had been gassed as he slept, and sniped at whenever he moved forward or about. And at least as dangerous as this targeted fire was the purely random fall of shells or bullets which came from all directions from either side. Colin lasted about 20 days, Captain Ferguson commanding a neighbouring battery lasted 5, wounded by 'friendly' fire in High Wood, and Major Walter of the 106ᵗʰ had been killed. A colonel and a captain were killed in their howitzer battery, and another officer wounded by shell fire. Four senior commanders in the brigade were incapacitated in less than three weeks. There was a steady trickle of casualties in the battery. His suitcase was 'killed' three times in as many weeks. Such was The Somme.

But as Colin recovered, he must have been happier about the handling of the artillery war than he was a year earlier, though perhaps that is not saying much. He would still have had three main complaints.

The first would have been the failure of the new divisions to achieve the results that the 7ᵗʰ Division achieved. Their artillery was simply not professional enough, their staffs not capable of the planning; and their regimental officers not capable of selecting good close positions and achieving the necessary accuracy to cut wire, and deal with strong points and observation posts.

Duke's account in full measure confirms the lack of professionalism in his 'dud' division. Lieutenant Colonel Staveley, commanding 35ᵗʰ Division Artillery, wrote in his divisional diary on embarkation that he *'had only 3 officers on the RA active list, of whom all had been promoted from the ranks'* in August 1915, and that *'training had been sadly impeded due to lack of equipment and instructors.'* Given the habitual understatement of the time, he was saying that his men were not fit for service. It is difficult to argue with this assessment.

His second would have been that the artillery was failing to provide close support to infantry attacks as they moved forward, largely due to increasing range. He notes this problem yet again on the day he was wounded. This complaint is all the more significant, because on the days they achieved this targeted support, notably on the first day and at the Battle of Bazentin, the infantry not only gained territory but more importantly held it. Always, if the infantry moved too far, and usually if the artillery stuck rigidly to predictable barrages, enemy counterattacks succeeded.

His third complaint would have pertained to forward control of the battlefield. Both he and the infantry they were supporting were shelled by their own side far too often for comfort. This occurred even on days where troops were not moving. There was no mechanism for a rapid general adjustment of artillery fire. And during a battle only seldom was the liaison good enough to enable the infantry to both request, and receive, an effective adjustment of the artillery barrage to help them achieve their objectives. The generals with the authority were too far back, or more accurately at the end of too long a command hierarchy.

The 7th Division Artillery generals[213] did to some extent tolerate individual initiative, and trusted the tactical acumen and liaison skills of their front line officers. They did allow the early breakdown of the pre-arranged rolling barrage to respond to hold-ups and counter attacks on the battlefield. And the fact that they did vastly increased the effectiveness of their guns. The less competent and newer divisions just did not have the ability to work in this way. The 35th Divisions

---

213 Brigadier General J.G. Rotton commanded the 7th Division artillery in July and Brigadier General H.S. Seligman in August 1916.

poorly sited batteries, with half their officers incapacitated, and with desperately inexperienced forward observation and liaison officers, were in no position to help the infantry. Even the best divisions must have realised that, as casualties and promotion took their best junior officers, so this informal process needed to be formalised, and their forward intelligence procedures strengthened.

A combination of poor intelligence and inflexible artillery planning was the worst of both worlds. The latter stages of unobserved rolling barrages were just that. They were by and large a disaster, causing hideous friendly casualties and relying on luck to help the infantry. This should have been obvious by the end of the first month on the Somme. Both Colin and Duke recognised the problem, and it is significant that Brigadier Staveley of the 35th Division did too, in his reports of the battle on the 30th July.

Like the 7th Division generals, he had encouraged some local autonomy, though probably with disastrous results, with his inexperienced colonels relying on long range and very junior observers. And he reported with admiration the way the French Signal Corps controlled the artillery lifts as their infantry progressed, doing away with the timed lifts which ossified the British attacks.

So changes in what had become conventional practice were urgently needed. The problems are fairly clear from Colin's and Duke's letters and from the associated war diaries. The crucial question was whether any of the very senior generals were seeing the problems as clearly as some of their front line officers, and pondering on possible solutions.

CHAPTER TWELVE

1917 A cold winter and Messines Ridge

'A' Battery, 113th Brigade, 25th Division.

'We are finding it jolly cold and this mess has no gramophone.'

In September 1916, the medical board had decided that Colin's facial injury was 'slight and non-permanent and that it was probable that he would be unfit for military duty for two months.' On the 29 November 1916, they found that he was fit for general service and he was posted to an officer's billet for reappointment.

'The whole duty of officers here consists of censoring letters. I have left it to the younger officers as I think I have done my share of that.' Colin was in no mood for menial duties. *'This place is dreadfully dull and is 6 miles from the town, which offers no inducements whatsoever.'* The town shall remain nameless.

'I hope to get back to Col. Lambarde. I have not had any word from him yet, and only hope he has had my letter and has applied for me to go to him.' With a facial wound, Colin wanted a commander he knew. He had. Orders came through.

Colonel Lambarde was delighted to get Colin back and welcomed him back to France[214] on the 1st January 1917. He appointed him an Acting Major, (*'the colonel has told me to put up the crown and tape'*) even before he had been gazetted captain.[215]

Colonel Lambarde needed every good officer he could get.

---

214 The 113th brigade was at St Yves in the quiet Ploegsteert Sector, where Colin had been in 1915.

215 Colin was made captain in December, gazetted on the 16th January 1917. He should have been gazetted Captain back in mid-1916, on taking command of a six gun battery, but the 7th division lost the paperwork.

Really professional officers were few and far between, and both were happy to be back with the other. He is *'doing too much as usual. He was walking all round the wagon lines today and arrived here at about 2.30 pm, having been soaked through during the course of the day. He's too old for that sort of thing you know.'* Colin could probably have chosen to go anywhere, but he chose Colonel Lambarde and so found himself in charge of the leading 'A' Battery of the 113th Brigade, which was still in the 25th Division.

But he arrived at a desperately difficult time. A big organisational change was occurring (over a few months) in that all batteries in the army were being standardised to six guns. Colonel Lambarde's 113th Brigade had had four batteries of four guns, but by mid-1916, he was down to two batteries of six guns. He now received twelve guns from other brigades which had been broken up, to increase his strength to four batteries of six guns. Every brigade, and indeed every battery, had its own ethos and this meant that there were a lot of confused officers and men trying to adjust to their new circumstances. New relationships had to be forged, new loyalties developed and minor differences in practice reconciled. [216]

'The battery is not doing so badly at present, but there is plenty of room for improvement,' said Colin a few weeks later.

The first three months of 1917 were exceptionally cold and Colin saw quickly that the men were suffering. *'I wonder if you know*

---

216 In May 1916, his two 6-gun howitzer batteries were replaced with three 4-gun field batteries. In late 1916, 'C' Battery was broken up and its two-gun sections went to 'A' and 'B' Batteries; and 507 (Howitzer) Battery, which came from the 7th Division, became the four-gun D (Howitzer) Battery. On the 22nd February 1917, 'B' Battery (field guns) of 172 Brigade of 36th (Ulster) Division became the new 'C' Battery and two guns from 'C' (Howitzer) Battery of 172 Brigade were used to bring 'D' (Howitzer) Battery up to six howitzers. www.1914-1918.ner/rfa Thus 'A', 'B' and 'C' were 6-gun field batteries, and 'D' was a 6-gun howitzer battery. In addition, there was a slimmed down brigade ammunition column. Most of the duties of the brigade ammunition columns (see note 57) had been transferred to the divisional ammunition column in March 1916.

of any sock knitting society who would like to send out some socks for the men. We are rather in want of a few.' Within three weeks, 150 pairs, *'three huge parcels of socks'* had arrived, and the men were *'very thankful'* for them.

And there were no officers in the battery buying supplies from home, so the mess was bleak. In literally his first letter home on the 2ⁿᵈ January, he wrote *'now for the wants, first two white tablecloths.'* Standards had to be maintained.

'The bread was frozen at lunch the day before yesterday; that will give you some idea of the cold. Lea and Perrin sauce is the only thing that has survived, vinegar and all the other sauces are blocks of frozen whatever they are.' But the nights were the worst. *'The frost has been the devil, nearly had my head frozen off last night. I am sleeping in a canvas hut which might just as well be the open air as far as cold is concerned. The hot water bottle has sprung a leak and it's just as bad tonight.'*

With his scarred face and receding hairline, his confidence was low. *'I had an awful shock yesterday. I met an officer and I suppose because of my major's badges, he took me to be older than himself. He must have taken me for 34. I'm really rather frightened over this.'* He was only just 24.

'I have not done all I should have done in a month but it has been difficult and I have had to go very slow.' *'We are more or less in the middle of changes, and there is rather a spirit of unrest everywhere which I hope will settle down soon,'* There were discipline problems. *'I am not in good writing form today. I have been sitting on a very boring court martial most of the morning.'* And at the end of January, *'the colonel is on leave and I now have to act in his place commanding the brigade until one of the more senior majors come back off a course.'*

So his responsibilities were high. He got very few letters and his to his mother were mostly demands for extra kit. *'You are sending me out my new service jacket, aren't you? I really need it rather badly to confront people with. It is essential to be respectably dressed just for a bit.'* And as he had the year before, he tried to get some better communication equipment for the battery. *'The D111 is not what I want, and is the one that is issued to us. The Ericson's which I asked for is a very much neater instrument.'* His mother (and father) sent everything without complaint, but his replies get positively ungracious. *'Your letter was most uninteresting, nothing in it at all.'*

Small wonder that that the quality of her letters – it was a hard winter in England too – dropped off. But she must have said something. His letter writing improves abruptly at the end of the month. He started thanking his mother again, especially when the gramophone and records arrived. He was pleased with the tablecloths too. The officer's mess was becoming a more cheerful place and he was finding his feet. And by that time, he had also looked up the Antoine girls[217], who still lived nearby.

Luckily his senior captain in the battery was Schooling[218], who had been in 458 Battery with him in 1915. He was a friendly face; he was reliable; and he thought the world of Colin. And *'I have Blackburn, an old hand, a ranker with 17 years' service in. He is invaluable, and a very tough nut to crack on all the tricks of the old soldier. Besides the experience, he has read a lot and is a very nice quiet fellow.'* Never once did Colin denigrate officers who had been promoted from the ranks through ability. In the artillery, competence counted, at least in 1917.

It took no longer than six or eight weeks for the battery and brigade to adjust to its enlargement. But this was not the only reorganisation taking place in January 1917.

The Royal Field Artillery as a whole was being redeployed. Half of all artillery brigades, including Colonel Lambarde's 113th Brigade, were taken away from their divisions and put under direct army

---

217 This was the French family who had looked after Donald's kit in 1915.

218 *'Schooling is with me, but I shall not have him for long as he is to command the Brigade Ammunition Column. However I am getting Pownall as my captain who is thoroughly to be trusted.'* F.H. Pownall was with him thereafter, as was Blackburn. *'Then there is Jones, a Welshman who was a schoolmaster and won a bard's seat at a Welsh university before the war. He speaks Welsh better than English, and is a very capable fellow. Swinford is a very nice youngster, who was some time in the yeomanry at the beginning of the war.'*

command, there being four British armies in France at the time. Prior to this, all artillery brigades had been permanently attached to divisions, now only half of them were. The army (in their case the Second Army) then immediately allocated the brigades back to an infantry division, but only on a temporary basis.

The advantage of this to the army was that artillery brigades could be concentrated by them in both attack and defence. It seemed a logical step.

But there were significant disadvantages. In late 1915, the generals had implied that their main problem was too few guns, rather than the way they used their existing ones. Now they were implying that their main problem was a failure to concentrate their guns, rather than their front line tactics. And the changes made liaison much more difficult for the artillery. The New Army brigades, constantly on the move, had no permanent hierarchy of command, answering to the divisional general of the moment. Friends in the divisions were hard to make, trust hard to build up. The junior officers, outside a divisional structure, were completely dependent on their colonels.

'113th brigade schedule, held by Army Headquarters.'

These were problems which took time to become obvious. As the above schedule shows, the 113th Brigade was initially left with the 25th Division and then had three weeks with the 36th division, before going into rest.

On the 12th March, Colin's battery was sent forward by the staff of the 36th Division. The roads were almost impassable and *'I had to take my guns into action in the middle of a bog. The men were all in mud up to their thighs and we had a horse in right over its back. It was raining hard part of the day, and not a scrap of cover. We were pretty wet by the time we were finished. It was only for one days shooting though.'* Both he and the brigade diary report this episode fairly positively as a team building exercise, but it was the type of poorly reconnoitred plan that became increasingly common and irritating, as they lost the warning gossip and mutual planning from contacts at divisional headquarters. *'One does not know from one day to the other what is going to happen next. We last went into action from a position well behind the lines at four hours' notice,'* he complains later in the year.

But for now, at rest, Colin amused himself in the cold weather by obtaining a couple of horses that none of his fellow officers felt were safe to ride and set about schooling them. *'I again rode over to the remount section having heard that they had got a fresh lot of horses in. I chose another chestnut. The remount sergeant singled the horse out for me. 'Ginger' is the finest looking horse in the division, but he is extremely trying at times, a bird or piece of paper flying across the road makes him shy like anything. A band was altogether too much for him and we both finished in a ditch. The other officers rather scoff at him and he wants a lot of schooling. He will be a splendid ride if I can cure him of his rearing.'*

His second horse wasn't much safer. *'I rode 'Peter' right up to the guns this morning, and jiggered if he didn't have me off, just as clean a toss as I've ever had. He's the first horse to put me off unwillingly since I left the shop. He did it jolly quick.'* Later in the year, *'my horse Peter has just come round. I'm just going to take him out for a little exercise. Incidentally he still gives me a lot of exercise!'*

Colin loved his horses, and refers to them individually throughout the war. Riding, and the care of horses was an integral part of his job. Every battery had about 200, including a personal one (or two) for every officer.

Later that year, he found Dolly, the horse he had ridden at the Somme. *'I found the 105th battery and had a long talk with my old Farrier Sergeant. I got Dolly back from them. McNaughton, commanding the 105th, is very Scotch and I gasped when he never asked for another horse in exchange. He could not resist saying at Dolly's expense that as he had no trap to put her in, I could have her. So I took her on the spot giving him no time to change his mind. Of course, she has a hard mouth and has been pretty touchy since she was shelled on the Somme, but she is looking very fit.'*

It was a considerable compliment to have been given a horse by his old unit, but now he had too many horses. *'The colonel has taken Dolly from me as he is short of a horse and he likes her. He will let me have her back at the end of the war.'* This did not stop him looking for more. *'There is a mobile veterinary section here and they have a little bay pony with a touch of Arab in her I would give a great deal to have. She is a little devil though and wouldn't be there if there wasn't something wrong with her.'*

But later in the year, *'I am very concerned about Ginger. We are having a tremendous lot of a disease which has all the symptoms of specific ophthalmia. Anyway the horses get successive attacks of running of the eyes, and eventually go totally blind. There is very little one can do to help them. They say it is not contagious, but there is a tremendous lot of cases. Ginger has now had two attacks of it with three weeks between.'*[219] Colin lost him a few months later.

It was not just the personal horses that got traded, this from a letter in 1918. *'I went down to the wagon lines yesterday, and exchanged 18 bay horses of mine for 18 blacks from 'C' battery. I wanted the blacks to make up my black section and 'C' battery wanted the bays to make them a complete*

---

219 The cause of Ophthalmia, an auto-immune uveitis, was then unknown. It is now known to be a late manifestation of some general bacterial infections. It can only be treated when it occurs, and not prevented.

bay battery. I'm very satisfied with the exchange and hope 'C' battery are likewise. These horse dealing transactions are the limit and this one was no exception, but I think things even out.'

But meanwhile in early spring, they had gone into rest.[220] *'We have a very nice billet here in quite a big farm. The horses are not so well off unfortunately. We had rain and snow last night, and they are standing in mud pretty well up to their knees. It's too early to have them out in the open after they have been under cover all winter. It will pull them down a good deal.'* And a week or so later, *'the mud is dreadful and the horses are standing deep in it. They are looking more tucked up than I have seen them for some time. The Blue Cross have sent me out the Epsom salts and iodine for them. Splendid isn't it? Means a subscription I'm afraid.'*

In April, *'the horses are in a terrible place again. Really we shall soon have no horses at all,'* and later in the month, *'Yes, this weather will do a great deal for our horses, but I'm afraid the poor beasts will take a great deal of pulling round. It was shocking how pulled down they were. We lost a good many of them from pure debility.'*[221]

He had other problems while they were in rest. *'The battery are having a concert tonight and I shall have to be there. I'd give a good deal to get out of it!'*

But worse than that. *'These men of mine are very trying sometimes. They robbed a neighbouring billet of some wood to make a fire and I'm jiggered if they didn't leave half of it lying about. This was found by the RAMC (the rightful owners) who didn't come and ask me to replace the wood in a gentlemanly manner, but at once reported it to division. If those fools had only come to me, the matter would have been squared right away. They got hold of the wrong number – the ammunition column – and Schooling was called*

---

220 They were at rest in Eecke just north east of Bailleul.

221 In this one month alone, 5% of the horses in Flanders were lost, due to a combination of a shortage of oats (which had to be imported) and the persistent wet and very cold weather. Just over 10% were lost in the whole of 1916, this according to Captain Sidney Galtrey's book, 'The Horse and the War' published in 1918.

upon to explain himself in writing to the GOC Corps. He showed me the correspondence, knowing full well it was my pigeon, and said it wasn't his unit, etc. etc. This correspondence went from them to division, from division to corps, from corps to division, from division to RAMC who were asked to give the matter their further consideration. They discovered their mistake, said it was me, back it goes to division, from division to brigade, and brigade to me. I write and say I'm sorry and it shan't happen again and send that back to brigade, who will forward it to division, who will forward it to corps, who will either let the matter drop, or devise something for our punishment. Each letter is on a separate sheet and there were 16 sheets when I got it and a shortage of paper too. And now the RAMC have waited some 16 days for their wood and are likely to wait another 16 days unless they fetch it themselves. By the time I hear again from corps I am hoping to be over the hills and far away.'

During this time at rest, Colonel Lambarde arranged a series of sports days and football matches to draw the brigade together as a unit, starting with a rugby match. The local champions were the South Wales Borderers and Colonel Lambarde issued a confident challenge without discussion, and then nominated Colin to captain the brigade team. *'The colonel landed us for it. I think he should turn out too,'* Colin said, but more pertinently he feared further damage to his facial scars, and had a quiet chat with the doctor. Only partially reassured, he played anyway.

'The South Wales Borderers produced a band which played before and after the match and there were about 1500 spectators. They had a very burly lot of forwards and we were outplayed in the scrums, but we had some very good players. One subaltern was a reserve for Ireland and another had played for Natal in South Africa and a very fine player he was too. We beat them by a goal and a try, to a goal. I took a kick almost in front of goal and missed it. I rather think they did not expect to be beaten and that we have spoilt an unbeaten record. It was a jolly good game and very much cleaner than a good many inter-regimental games I have played in.' The Colonel was so pleased at the victory he wrote to Colin's mother to tell her all about it!

And he acknowledged the leadership skills of his junior officers. *'I am getting very proud of my brigade. Your son is getting on splendidly with his battery and I am thankful I have got him. Schooling too is doing wonders with his ammunition column which was a terrible battle when he started with it.'*

Colin was very stiff after the rugby, but he loved all sport and appreciated the benefits.[222] My *'battery is playing 'C' Battery at football and I am very much afraid we are going to get a beating.'* But *'we won our game yesterday, much to the discomfiture of 'C' Battery who were too sure of themselves. What I liked about it was the way our team played together. It was not any particular piece of brilliance that won it, but sheer combination.'* Sport motivated him, and through him his men, making them a team, in battle as well as on the playing field. *'Always like to win,'* he says.

He was totally immersed in his army life. In March, his mother wrote for details of his personal finances. *'You ask me a terrible question in your letter. I really haven't the ghost of a notion what my income was, and really don't know how to find out.'* They kept a tally of his expenses from home, and he settled up irregularly. Sometimes he got into arrears, but he unhesitatingly signed all the financial papers his father sent out. Not surprisingly, he worried more about death than taxes.

The war intruded as the weather improved. Their brigade was with the 16th Irish Division, providing short-term relief for more settled divisional brigades, taking over their positions for two weeks, then moving on to the next emplacement, when their original owners returned from rest.

They took over *'a pleasant little emplacement'* in mid-April, but

---

222 The importance of sport and positive recreation to the units at rest is clear. Both Colin with the 118th brigade before Ypres, and Duke with his 159th brigade describe going into rest with no organised activities, and the subsequent adverse effect on fitness, morale and discipline. Officers could not truly rest in rest. Football was the staple sporting activity, but cricket, rugby, athletics and equestrian events also featured. Few episodes of rest occurred without Colin complaining he had to attend a concert.

found it was already being registered by the Germans. *'Here's a glorious day, but the Huns seem to have chosen to be particularly disagreeable to this poor battery. About two hours ago, they started deliberately ranging on us, first with a battery of fairly light calibre and now with heavier calibre.*[223] *I'm rather afraid they mean to give us a rotten dose like some of the other batteries have had round here. It's a horrid cold blooded procedure. They give one a couple of hours' rest and then open up.'*

Counter battery bombardment was a scientific art, as Colin knew from experience. *'Those shells came down while I was writing this letter and I only recovered this notebook out of the ruins of our mess the next day. The blighters got the battery all right. Their first salvo scored direct hits and smashed all our mess crockery to blazes. My kit was very lucky, not so the kit of Swinford and Blackburn. I am only sorry now that I did not have the guns pulled out during the ranging. It's a long job though, getting them out of these strongly prepared positions. They got four of the guns and destroyed the whole position, but they fired close on 2000 rounds*[224] *to do it.*

We are now sharing 'B' Battery's mess. Thank goodness the weather has been decent. It would have been rotten in the wet.'

'Shooting very good,' said the brigade diary with professional approval. *'At 1.30 pm, the men were moved off to a flank. At 3.45 pm the enemy suddenly opened fire. Five gun pits had at least five direct hits each.'*

Presumably Colin was with the signallers manning the telephones as he calmly wrote his letter. The experience did not seem to inconvenience them much. Only one of the damaged guns was salvageable, but the others were quickly replaced and the battery moved to a fresh position a week later, with a full complement of guns, but without any plates or cutlery.

'This is really a business letter to ask you for some things in the culinary

---

223 They were registered first by 10.5 cm (4.2 inch) Feldhaubitze 98/09 (a howitzer equivalent to the British 4.5 inch) and then by the heavier 15cm (5.9 inch) schwere Feldhaubitze 13.

224 They were bombarded twice, with an interval, but *'2000 rounds'* may have been an exaggeration. The brigade diary quotes 400 for the first bombardment.

department. The Germans have done ours in absolutely, confound them. Now saucepans, can you please get us a set of three that fit into each other for packing with handles separate. It would be an advantage if the handles were all the same size and interchangeable. Aluminium, they would have to be I suppose. The room they take up is a great consideration. Knives, could you get a set of six large and six small, horn or bone handled knives, good and strong. Forks, six large and six small, spoons table and tea ditto. Cups and saucers, I think will not be required but would you please send out 6 enamel ware soup or pudding plates, 6 cheese plates and six large plates for meat.'

Only the next day, he learned that his Uncle Duke had been dangerously wounded at his battery a few miles south.[225] A fragment of shell had shattered his spine. He was left paralysed and unable to walk. *'I dread to get your next letter. It's an awful war and much worse for the people at home. Things are so much easier for us out here. It's just what we have to expect. Cannot write any more just now. Tell Granny how sorry I am.'* Duke died of his wounds in 1919. From domestic anxieties to the horror of family tragedy, that was the nature of the war, and few families were spared.

But Colin had little time to reflect. On the 1st May, the brigade moved to the lines right in the middle of the Messines Ridge, south of Ypres. They were still with the 16th Division and still relieving divisional brigades to allow them a few weeks of rest.

'I never seem to have any time for writing these days, we are getting such a lot of moving about. No sooner do we get in to one position than we get moved to another. It's the absolute limit really. We are moving again tonight to another position which has to be built.' It is never stated explicitly but the implication was that their competent brigade was being used to get the divisional positions up to scratch.

---

225 He never left hospital. In May 1916, Duke Marshall had written, *'it will come to us all if this war lasts long enough.'* He was nothing if not a realist. His 35th division had been in the Arras sector till early February, but then moved south, to where the Germans were conducting a strategic withdrawal, forced by their difficult positions and a collapse in morale on the Somme. They fell back to their newly constructed Hindenburg Line. It was outside St Quentin, a stronghold on that line, that Duke was severely wounded on the 16th April.

Their brigade may have been a New Army one, but Colonel Lambarde set regular army standards of camouflage and protection. If the positions they took over were not good enough, they made them good. They dug the guns in, and they dug themselves in. Both Colin and the Colonel were lucky to be alive, but much of this luck was due to hard work and intelligent digging. They felt put upon, and with some reason. Colonel Lambarde expected Colin's 'A' battery to set the example for the rest. *'The men are jolly tired of doing other peoples' work,'* he said. And so was he.

In addition, the colonel and his battery commanders routinely made an assessment of their new positions; but Colin, at times, found this frustratingly pointless. They were ordered to move on before they could see the benefits. They were actually with the 16th division for eight weeks, and Colin later records how helpful the experienced Colonel Lambarde was to the 16th Divisional brigadier. But this involved moving his experienced batteries around the divisional front.

Back to the domestic, *'those saucepans, knives, spoons and forks and kettle have all arrived in splendid time and condition. Please tell Father I got the cigarettes two days ago. They are much appreciated by the men, especially up in the gun line where the men cannot buy anything at all.'*

Colin's demands from home were very often for the comfort and care of his men and officers as much as for himself. Family money helped of course, but it was family ethos as well. If pressed, Colin's parents would probably have agreed that buying cigarettes for the men and little luxuries for the officers' mess, would make the battery work better, thereby increasing Colin's chances of survival. But this would have been unfair. They did it because one did; because they could afford to; and because it supported the war effort.

And the war was at an important stage. The Germans had retreated on the Somme, and had lost Vimy Ridge at the Battle of Arras in April. The French had made progress at simultaneous offensives at

St Quentin and on the Aisne.[226] New British offensives were in the planning. General Plumer, in charge of the British Second Army was preparing an attack on Messines Ridge. And General Gough, commander of the British Fifth Army was planning a subsequent offensive further north.[227]

General Plumer planned his battle with care. He concentrated his artillery and after intensive reconnaissance systematically, and over some weeks, pounded the German Artillery and strongpoints to near destruction. With the contours favourable, he had ordered long mine passages to be dug under the German defences and packed them with explosives. Mines had been used before, but never on this scale. For the actual assault, he retained the barrage, but kept it fairly short.

So far this followed the intended tactics of the first day of the Somme, albeit with much more firepower. But the differences thereafter were striking.[228] He wanted his artillery to move forward almost with the first infantry assault. He wanted accurate targeted supporting fire for his infantry at a range close enough to be effective.

He abandoned the concept of planning for a breakthrough, and with it any attempt at a really long infantry advance on the first day. He knew that the enemy were expecting an attack and would have reinforcements in reserve. He scheduled delays into his infantry advance, so they could dig in and fight off the inevitable counter attacks, aided by close artillery support. He wanted to hold the ground he took.

---

226 It had been hoped that these French offensives would break through and win the war. German morale was damaged, but not yet sufficiently for total victory. In all the attacks most of the gains were made in the first few days. The French persisted, losing huge casualties, which precipitated unrest in their armies.

227 General Hubert Gough V.C. was from the cavalry, General Herbert Plumer had an infantry background. The differences in the ethos of their planning are striking.

228 He had analysed the failures on the Somme, and learnt further from the initial successes of the British attack at Arras, the Canadian attack at Vimy Ridge and the French advance on the Aisne, all in early 1917.

So he had addressed the problem of lack of artillery support for the infantry as they moved forward. He ensured air superiority to protect them. And he hoped to address the problem of forward direction of the battle by giving himself time during the scheduled delays for consolidation and reassessment. His instinct was for top down control, so he remained reliant on forward observation officers, both in the air and on the ground, to collect intelligence accurately and rapidly for processing up quite a long command chain. His own staff would then have to work fast to enable adjustments which might have a significant impact on the battlefield.

But though General Plumer controlled the actual battle, the planning for it was inclusive, at least on the 16th Divisional front. The opening day of the Battle of Messines Ridge was scheduled for the 7th June, and as early as the 13th May, Colonel Lambarde was *'ordered to pick positions for two brigades in advanced positions for the second phase of the attack on Wytschaete Ridge.'* Front line expertise was being used intelligently to increase the chances of success on the day.

Colonel Lambarde selected the dip in this field to shield the brigade for his position. The British infantry were on the forward ridge; the Germans were on Messines Ridge (now wooded), Wytschaete church spire is visible, centre left, dominating the area.

On the 15th, *'positions were'* agreed *'for the first phase of attack. The brigade will be the second brigade to move forward to occupy positions after the first phase of the attack on Wytschaete Ridge.'* Colonel Lambarde would not have been too happy at being given second place in the schedule, but the entry passes without further comment. And on the next day, the *'batteries started working on forward positions. Ammunition (300 rounds per gun) to be dumped there and camouflaged.'* More hard work, but now it was for themselves. *'We are at present putting Flanders into sandbags pretty hard and thriving at it,'* said Colin. He approved of the arrangements for the battle.

Colin though had doubts about the quality of the 16th Divisional Artillery as they moved from position to position. *'I'm disgusted with some of the things I've seen. There are damned few soldiers left nowadays.'* His battery had even been briefly seconded to a 16th Division brigade. *'We are at present under the command of one of the most inefficient soldiers I've met in this war, and that's saying a great deal.'* But he was back now with Colonel Lambarde who was determined to lead a 'fighting brigade'. He had no intention of allowing his brigade to sit at the back firing long range barrages. He was mentioned in dispatches[229] in the list that month.

'It was splendid the colonel getting a mention. He's doing jolly well and has done for some time. It's a damned shame they don't make him a brigadier general. He's about the only real soldier in our small area at present, and wants to be a jolly sight too close up. If I was his adjutant still, I should refuse point blank to take his box office up. I am afraid he gets things all his own way now.'

Colonel Lambarde would certainly have noted that his artillery brigade was not scheduled to be first up to the forward positions on the day. Neither Colin, leading the 'A' battery of his brigade, nor Colonel Lambarde himself liked to be second. Orders notwithstanding, we can be quite sure that some extra planning

---

229 As was Colin for his part in the Somme Battle. Every award in the hierarchy helped! As Colin said later in the war. *'I have fixed my MC on this coat to the Colonel's satisfaction. He complains that the Division we are now supporting has many such decorations, and it is time we showed them some of ours.'*

went into their arrangements for the advance. Second place was simply not acceptable.

Colin was involved to some extent in this planning and he would have spent time in Loker, where both the 16th Division and the 113th Brigade were headquartered. He made a friend there. That friend was Major Willie Redmond M.P.

There are sub-plots to every battle and this one was no exception. Major Redmond was a charismatic Irish Nationalist, known throughout the Empire for his belief that the Irish should be fighting the Germans to earn the right to Home Rule along the lines of Canada and Australia. He was 56, and despite his age, his political importance and his poor health, he was very keen to move from his staff post[230] at Loker back to the 6th Royal Irish Battalion from which he had been invalided home the previous year.

The day before the battle, Major Redmond, obtained permission to re-join his fighting unit, and made his way up to the Royal Irish Battalion. On the way, he dropped in on Colin in his battery. He *'was in our battery for nearly an hour and a half telling us all sorts of interesting things about parliament.'* Redmond that evening made a point of visiting every company of his battalion and apparently spoke to every man, so the fact that he spent so long with Colin at his battery on that day of all days is remarkable. They must have got on extraordinarily well.

On the morning of the 7th June 1917, the task of the 16th Irish Division and the 36th Ulster Division was to capture the village of Wytschaete, which was a mile from the British front line. At 3.10 am seventeen mine tunnels which had been drilled under the ridge

---

230 He had returned to France partly because his 16th Irish Division, from the mainly catholic South of Ireland, had been ordered as a political decision to fight side by side in the line with the protestant 36th Ulster Division. (There had been an Irish Rebellion at Easter in 1916, when a number of Dublin Irish had been executed after a failed insurgency.) There was some political distrust of the Irish Division and it was very important that the battle should go well.

were simultaneously exploded. *'From a high point of vantage, they were a most extraordinary sight and the ground rocked just like an earthquake.*[231] *It was more of a succession of explosions, and the most extraordinary part of them was the tongues of fire which came out of the ground.'* The detonations were heard in London and the effects totally demoralised the surviving German defenders.

The infantry assaulted and every preliminary objective on a seven-mile front had been taken by mid-morning.

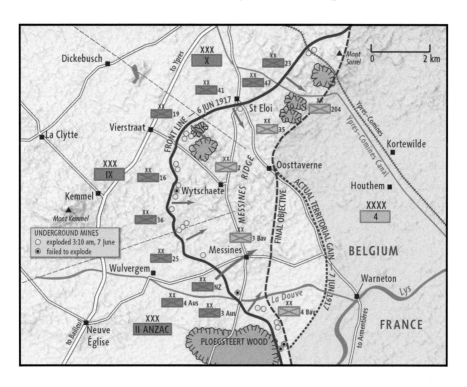

Messines Ridge, four miles south of Ypres, (map page 66).
113th Brigade positions were very close to 16th Division headquarters.

'At 8.55 am, upon the Infantry gaining the trench line just beyond Wytschaete, the batteries received orders to advance to forward positions.' The 113th Brigade, with its four batteries, instantly moved forward at the

---

231 In a letter from Colin, this sounds like a quote from a newspaper.

gallop. One hundred and forty-four horses, twenty-four limbers and guns, careered down the narrow country lanes to their forward position in the tiny valley of the Haringhebeek with mounted officers leading and alongside, and supporting wagons behind. They were in a hurry.

Colin as commanding officer of 'A' battery would have been at the front of the cavalcade. He and the colonel led the brigade forward with a random artillery barrage falling around them. They slowed as they reached their positions, in view of the old German lines, where they had stockpiled their ammunition in readiness. Colin had his battery *'walk into action',* the guns unhitched, set up, *'and the teams walked away.'* Still under fire, *'the colonel had a blind very close to him,'* they were ready for action by 10.05 am. The other brigade ordered forward at the same time was not in position for another hour. They were the first brigade forward.

'We did the advance in great style, really rather a fine performance!' Not often is Colin pleased enough to praise himself. And *'we fired hard to cover the fresh advance.'* Their job was to provide support to the middle phase of the infantry advance, and help to break up counter attacks for the next 24 hours.

It is probable that Colin moved forward as the observation officer, directing the fire of his battery. He describes the *'crater at Peckham near Wytschaete,'* as being *'big enough to take our house and whole garden,'* so presumably he went up there. The brigade diary records that the barrage in support of the further infantry advance at 3 pm was *'very good'*. All the divisional infantry objectives were achieved with unexpectedly few casualties.

Brigadier General Charlton of the 16th Divisional Artillery was delighted with them and the next evening wrote an almost illegible, but very complimentary, note to Colonel Lambarde on the conduct of the Brigade. *'I saw General Plumer and the army generals today and both asked me to convey their congratulations and thanks to all ranks. Everyone is full of praise for the artillery and I know how richly they are deserved. I hoped to come and thank you personally today, but spent too much time looking over the ridge. I am very sorry indeed that they are going to take your brigade away from us and I hope I shall again have the honour of including it in my command.'* So everything should have been good. The brigade had a lot to be proud of.

But Colin was not happy. Nor presumably was Colonel Lambarde, since he gave the note to Colin. Their forward battery positions had been leapfrogged later on the first day and they were not required to advance further forward and finish the battle. In fact, their Brigade was being removed from the battlefield within 24 hours, with almost indecent haste. The general wrote his note on the 8th, making it clear that it was not his wish or decision that they be moved on while the battle was still in progress and that they would be gone before he could get back to see them.

But their orders transferred them north, and within days the brigade found itself in a nasty little corner not far from Ypres. Colin gives no explanation for this sudden move, but presumably General Gough was demanding more artillery for his army.

Major Redmond was mortally wounded at Wytschaete at a very early stage in the advance of his battalion. Colin would have heard of his wounding that day up at the front line. It affected him profoundly. *'Major William Redmond is one of the greatest losses,'* he wrote. When, later in the week, the newspapers arrived, this was headline news. Colin would have hated the romanticised reports of his death, incorporating heart-warming accounts of his care from a wounded Ulsterman.

Probably this explains why his letter of the 15th June, a week after the battle, is so enigmatic and bitter. *'You ask about the battle,'* he says. *'The casualties to our attacking battalions were extraordinarily small, and there were very few dead of any kind to be seen. Most of the German guns got away, and the German infantry, barring those actually holding the front and support lines just were not there to bar any progress. In fact, it was a walk over. The Irish divisions distinguished themselves and the organisation was wonderful,'* followed by a big question mark. [232] *'I wish to goodness I'd got back to the 7ᵗʰ Division.'*

He has made it clear before this that he missed the competent leadership he was used to in the 7ᵗʰ Division, though he had watched and learned from Colonel Lambarde. He was anxious for his Uncle Duke; probably irritated by their sudden move to Ypres; and possibly still shaken by his narrow escape in the devastating bombardment of his battery the month before.

And if, as seems likely, he personally grieved for Redmond, he would not have wanted to spell this out in a letter. Colin was charmingly apolitical, but he would not have been the first young man to have fallen under the spell of a charismatic Irishman.

But the brigades dashing advance could be celebrated as a 19ᵗʰ century move in a 20ᵗʰ century war. Twenty-four guns were moved up under fire and into action in just over an hour. There was still a place for horsemanship and individual heroism. And better still, despite their *'hot time'*, they lost only one man killed on the day. [233]

As for the battle at Messines, the key had been the artillery preparation, which devastated the German positions, and then the massive mines terminally destabilised an already wobbly front line. At Wytschaete in the centre, the attack went to plan. In fact, a bit too much so, as the projected infantry casualties did not occur, and as a result there were too many troops and not enough shelter in the new intermediate front line, where the advance paused. As a consequence, the anticipated German barrage and counterattack, led to unnecessarily heavy casualties. And particularly on the right flank, the infantry overreached, making too much progress, and as

---

232 Again these words sound like a newspaper quote. Colin was very disparaging about the press coverage of the battle, and particularly about the literary efforts of William Beach Thomas, who wrote for the Daily Mail.

233 In their eight weeks with the 16ᵗʰ division at Messines Ridge, the brigade lost 1 officer and 4 other ranks killed, 3 officers and 19 other ranks wounded. Colin's battery lost not a man in their heavy bombardment.

a result the artillery several times fired heavily on their own troops, causing more unnecessary casualties.

So there were still lessons to be learned. The three-day attack had been successful, but it was clear that the coordination and control of the forward infantry, particularly in the later stages of the battle, had not been good enough. Most of the casualties had occurred well forward and too many had again been caused by friendly fire. Despite improving communications and the delays to dig in, it had still taken too long for the generals to react to events on the battlefield and to coordinate the artillery. But all the objectives were taken and the gains held, despite determined counter attacks.

This limited attack was the blueprint for success. Earlier in the year, Duke, mired in a sea of mud just south of the Somme, wondered *'if a front like this is worth holding at all, but the moral effect of retiring is too awful to think of.'* A few weeks later, the Germans decided that it was not worth holding and fell back,

'It's difficult to know what's going on with the Hun' said Duke, *'but the morale of his troops is certainly not as it used to be.'* And *'we are all pleased the Hun has retired. Retirement means the shaking of morale,'* though *'how far this counts in this war is impossible to say.'* He was right to be cautious. With such huge armies, poor morale at one point did not mean poor morale everywhere.

But not only had pressure on the Somme forced the German withdrawal in April, but at Vimy Ridge, at Arras and on the Aisne, the Germans had been attacked and lost ground. At each point their morale had suffered.

Colin before Messines Ridge also recognised the value of attacking morale. *'I can't think why we don't have a smack at them pretty well everywhere now, and upset their plans if possible.'*

Neither he nor Duke expected a breakthrough any time soon. *'It's impossible to move forward into country that has been made desolate, when the Hun, who even if driven out in a hurry, still has dugouts and houses to protect him,'* Duke wrote a few days before he was wounded.

Impossible is a strong word, and the Germans had systematically devastated the back areas as they retired at the Somme, burning and blowing up the villages, cratering every cross-road, and cutting down every orchard. Duke was depressed by the wanton destruction and he was very cold and very wet during the whole advance. But the inference is plain. A breakthrough is not to be expected.

There was a chance of another 'smack' further north. Perhaps the good work could be continued. General Gough and the Fifth Army were organising an attack from the Ypres sector. One of the targets was the village of Passchendaele. Colin's 113th Brigade was among the many army artillery brigades sent north to prepare for this new campaign.

CHAPTER THIRTEEN

1917 Passchendaele

'A' Battery, 113th Army Brigade

*'First Ypres in 1914 was bad, Second Ypres in 1915 worse
and I really haven't a name for this one.'*

On the 11th June, they were allocated to the 30th Division, which
was part of II Corps in General Gough's Fifth Army, centred on the
Ypres salient.

And the 30th Division, in the second half of June, was positioned
just east of Ypres. Colin knew the area well from 1915, but he *'could
hardly recognise a single landmark'*. Everything had been destroyed. *'I
have not been through Ypres since May 1915. There's not one house that has
two stories, most are just shapeless masses of bricks and shell craters. Standing
in the centre square, you can see all the country round.'*

He went for a walk to reconnoitre their forward position and
*'had as unpleasant a dusting yesterday as I've had for many a day. The
Germans are throwing about a lot of ammunition.'* Going for a walk in
any part of the Ypres Salient was not advisable. The Germans had
all the high ground. (See map page 66.)

They were moved to an even worse spot, a mile south-east of
Ypres, on the 19th June. *'We got hurried orders the day before yesterday
about coming in here. By special request we were asked for, being of course
the finest brigade in the British army. And though we, or rather I personally,
would much rather have been left out of the line and done without the
compliment, the colonel seemed quite pleased about it.*

*Everywhere else except this tiny little spot we are pounding the Bosch to
blazes. Just here, he has got it all his own way for the time being and he is
making the most of his opportunity.'* 'The Gun Line is very uncomfortable,'

as '*owing to the exposed ground, we couldn't come out of our burrows except between 3.30 and 4.30 am before the light got good.*'

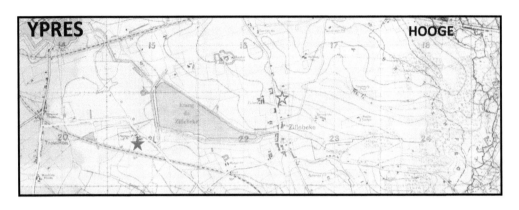

On June 19th, they were in position, just south-east of Ypres, starred in red.
On July 20th, they made the journey marked in yellow to a new position at Zillebeke.
The German lines were only 2000 yards away at that point, shown in red
running down from Hooge.

General Gough was concentrating his artillery for his offensive, which would start, after several postponements, on the 31st July. Unlike General Plumer he had a cavalry background, the same background as the colonel who had chosen battery positions at the Somme – on a downslope open to the enemy; the same background as the dragoons who had charged machine guns at High Wood. His plan was simplicity itself. Mass the artillery, kill everything within range, and then walk to victory.

The success at Messines Ridge had set the precedent. But Messines Ridge was a real hill; Passchendaele Ridge was a long low lifting plain. At Messines the German supply roads ran north south, and were easy to cut. At Ypres, the roads ran east-west and were not (see map, page 66). At Messines, the British artillery had cover, and high ground of their own. At Ypres, there was none, and worst of all, at Messines, the British were attacking a salient and thus able to bombard the German defences and access roads from the north, from the west and from the south. At Ypres, the British were in a salient with very exposed access roads being bombarded themselves from north round to the south-east.

Few saw any merit in the battlefield chosen, even leaving aside the waterlogged low lying terrain of the British front line, which made transport so difficult. It seems that General Haig had decided to lock horns with the German army at the worst possible spot.[234]

Colin and Colonel Lambarde both went on leave to England for a week in late June and Colin did not arrive back until the 7th July. He was glad to get away. On the 24th June, *'the area occupied by headquarters and the batteries was shelled incessantly from 9 am to 6.30 pm.'* Their brigade headquarters received eleven direct hits over the next few days.

Happily for Colin, the 30th Division then gave the brigade a short respite, though on their last day in the line, the 9th July, *'there was a heavy thunderstorm here this morning, and it has been raining on and off all day. We got thoroughly soaked through, right to the skin and had to change everything.'* The weather from now on was a crucial factor.

'We have been having glorious weather at rest back here[235] and the men have been thoroughly enjoying it.' 'The night before last I had dinner with Colonel Lambarde in Cassel. It is a beautiful place and you can see miles and miles of country from there. They say on a fine day one can see the sea quite clearly, and rumour has it, England.'

He went back there the next night with his colleagues. There were other attractions. *'There are two quite famous sisters who look after the Hotel Sauvage here. I cannot for the moment remember their names, but*

---

234 This is not to say that there was any lack of planning. The many conferences and relevant army memoranda make it clear that there was a great deal of it, and all these facts were known. What is clear, is that the army plan was imposed on the divisions. And that General Haig was the main architect of the scheme.

235 At Oudezeele, near Cassel.

there is an equally famous girl in a tiny little café in Bailleul called Tina[236]. *She had her portrait in the Tatler not so long ago, and another girl Agnes, of the Café Francais in Caestre. Perhaps the latter is not quite as famous as the other three. Caestre is rather out of the way.'*

They had only a few days in their wagon lines, able to relax, but even there, not far enough back to be entirely safe. *'We are enjoying the respite though the Bosch does not entirely leave us alone, even down here.' 'The records I bought are proving quite a success and they are making such a noise with Chu Chin Chow that it makes writing sensibly difficult.'*

'We march back to our old wagon lines tomorrow and go into action the next night. We have had glorious weather, but today it looks very threatening with thunder cloud and is raining a little.' Their battle was starting.

Even in 1915, before Second Ypres, they had had the opportunity to scout their battery position before they took it up. At the Somme in 1916 and at Messines Ridge earlier that year, they had not only scouted their positions, but prepared them as well. No such consideration under a cavalry general at Passchendaele. They were simply given a map reference and told to get on with it.

So on the 20th July, *'we are moving up into action tonight. We left the wagon line at 1.45 am and got safely almost to Shrapnel Corner,'* just south

---

236 'THE BRITISH ARMIES LITTLE SISTER – Tina, the teashop girl from Bailleul is one of those women with no official position, no medal, no title, who will nevertheless live in the memory of all this generation of fighting men. Tina keeps a teashop just behind the fighting line. In the street where it stands, shells have torn great holes in the walls. But in her teashop is English tea and sympathy for the young subalterns who gather there. Tina has even essayed making muffins and crumpets to make her 'boys' feel at home, but they were not quite a success. The men didn't tell her so for fear of hurting her feelings, bless them, but she knew. She is barely eighteen, this little teashop girl, and yet she has given comfort to a hundred hundred British lads. Her blue eyes would open wide with surprise if you told her this, and the little golden curls above her ear would go bobbing with laughter. 'I do but keep a bally teashop,' using the slang her guests have taught her. 'I do just be good pals to these boys.'' New Zealand Oamaru Mail, Volume XLVIII, Issue 13559, 16 September 1918.

of Ypres, '*but a motor lorry was burning hard in the middle of the road. This necessitated wheeling round to find another track. One was a mass of shell craters so we went round another and got back to Shrapnel Corner, crossing between rounds from a German gun that was shelling it. We had to trot most of the way in order to get in in the dark. We arrived at the battery position*' at Zillebeke, (map, page 204), '*about 5.15 am. Fortunately there was a mist, and the guns were set up without interruption.*'

Looking east from their battery position (now Zillebeke Cemetery), the Germans held the high ground visible on the horizon.

And they were spotted immediately. '*At about 5.45 two German aeroplanes flew low over our trenches. One shut off its engines, planed down over our positions and dropped two bombs onto us. I was hit on the nose by a very small splinter. I do not know whether it is still in or not.*' '*Absolute impertinence,*' he said in a later letter, '*but of about 30 of us there, I was the only one to be touched.*'

Despite the wound, he called in at headquarters to ask permission to leave the guns under guard, and to send the men back under cover to dugouts. '*I never dreamed that they could possibly make us shoot from such forward positions.'* Colin had not even been briefed and was horrified to learn *'that we had day and night tasks, and that we should have to fire that night.'* They had been given no opportunity to reconnoitre the position, and no time to dig the guns in or to make even elementary dugouts.

So leaving his men in danger, he made his way down to the dressing station to get treated. *'I had a rotten passage down, passing through one of the Australian batteries that had also just come in. They had been heavily shelled only half an hour previously losing 2 officers and 18 men killed with 16 wounded.'* His brigade had been lucky to get into position without a similar bombardment.

'I came down to the wagon line to get myself cleaned up a bit.[237] The piece hit my poor old nose and has lost itself in some air pockets; the nose apparently has air pockets somewhere. Anyway expert advice plied much iodine and said leave it there. I don't feel any the worse for it and am going up tomorrow morning with the colonel.'

When he returned the next morning, he noticed *'terrible blast marks'* caused by their night's firing. Out in the open and with a long black burn mark in front of each gun, they were quickly registered by *'Bosch balloons and aeroplanes, and it was impossible to leave the dugouts until evening.'* Colin has mentioned air power before, notably at the Somme, but it is clear that it is now a much more significant element in the battle.

On the 22nd, the brigade diary notes *'heavy shelling in front of batteries and on headquarters,[238] and during the night a gas shell bombardment –*

---

237 *'You'll probably see my name in due course in the wounded list. This is done so that if suppuration should set in, I get the privileges of a wounded soldier, and not those of one with a sore due to carelessness or something of that sort.'* The brigade medical officer dealt with all the minor injuries, sending the more serious casualties back to a Clearing Station. All British wounded, however trivial, were counted. The Germans did not record casualties who returned immediately into action. This means that British casualty figures were considerably higher than the Germans for the same battle loss (in all battles of the war), and are not comparable.

238 The brigade headquarters was actually in front of the battery positions.

mustard oil.' This was not pleasant. *'The Germans have got a new gas[239] now, which is all right as long as one gets the box respirator[240] on quick enough.' 'They gas us thoroughly at night every time it is calm enough.'*

'Mustard oil twice in the night. German planes come over the back areas very low each morning firing on to battery positions with machine guns,' says the brigade diary, a few days later. *'The Bosch are doing a tremendous lot of bomb dropping onto our battery positions and it is very unpleasant. They come pretty low over us and make quite fair shooting onto us.'*

This was a new intensity of warfare. Ypres and the Somme were nothing to this and within three days, *'just at present we are not keeping anybody at the gun line for more than two days at a stretch if we can help it. It's rather a rotten existence for the men up there. We are shooting a good deal.'*

Unsurprisingly by a week later, he is tired and irritable. *'We have not by any means been having a quiet time. Conditions lately (during the last six months) have changed very much, and present day war is very different and much harder than before.'*

---

239 This was the first large scale use of 'Mustard gas', a mixture of impure chlorinated organic sulphides. It is a yellow-brown colour and smells of garlic or horseradish. Delivered as a liquid, but rapidly becoming a gas, it causes chemical burns on contact with the skin, leading to very painful blisters. If inhaled, it causes life threatening blisters in the respiratory tract. Though dangerous and debilitating to its victims, its mortality rate was not high. But those who suffered severe chemical burns or breathing problems were put out of action for a considerable time. www.compoundchem.com

240 Box respirators had a mouthpiece connected via a hose to a box filter, which neutralized the gas, cleansing the air. Duke described the early version, the Large Box Respirator, in May 1916. *'I never saw such a thing. It weighs about a ton. It's a haversack arrangement, inside are a pair of large goggles which are put on over the eyes, then there is a tin box containing air attached to a thick piece of rubber hose to a mouth and nose piece which fits over the lower part of the face. I think if I put the thing on I should feel like climbing a tree.'* This was still in use, but it is more likely that Colin had, by this time, the more up to date "Small Box Respirator" (SBR), which had a close-fitting rubberized mask with eye-pieces. The box filter was worn around the neck. The SBR was upgraded as more effective filter technology was developed. www.worldwar1-history.com

'We're having a rotten time up at the gun line. The whole brigade is in line, in open positions of course. We're losing guns at the rate of about six every 24 hours. I have lost three these last two days. However, we're cheerful still, that's the main thing, isn't it? At least we're cheerful in the intervals, you know. It's been wet the last 24 hours.'

He does not sound cheerful at all. They were in *'open positions'*, because digging in created puddles and they had had no opportunity to build protection. Artillery had not routinely been placed in the open since 1914. And there was so much artillery.[241]

Their position was known to the yard. They were bombarded remorselessly and accurately. The men were out in the open, coated in mud, soaked to the skin, sleep deprived, respirators on through the night, and in constant action. The static nature of the battle field meant that the artillery of both sides had the time to pulverise each other.

Colin's Welsh subaltern, Jones, *'got a nasty piece of shell through his nose, which we thought had taken his left eye out, but apparently he can still see a little with it.'* In total, the brigade lost 82 men, nearly 10% of their strength, killed or wounded in the three weeks before the infantry battle even started. Three of their officers were killed and seven wounded, out of less than thirty.

And the brigade of 24 guns had 26 guns knocked out in their position in front of Zillebeke.[242] In contrast, they lost 27 men in eight weeks at Messines Ridge.

'The sickening point is that those behind have absolutely no conception of it. Nobody can have that has not been through it. What rankles is these people

---

241 Three thousand British artillery guns firing over four million shells in 10 days is the figure quoted by www.historylearningsite.co.uk which is 1040 rounds per eight gun battery per day. A higher figure is given by www.firstworldwar. com. On the 24th July, Colin's brigade was firing 600 rounds per battery per day, though the battery did fire 2600 rounds in a day later in the battle. With many guns out of action, ammunition losses from enemy action, and the heavier guns firing more slowly, all quoted figures should be treated with caution.
242 20th July to the 8th August. Brigade diary.

think they know and of course do the driving. I'd give anything to have some of them in our battery position for two nights. They wouldn't stand any more coming right into it. One kind of gets used to it gradually, and can just stand it with periodical rests.'

It is small wonder he was complaining. Colin always hated not being in control of his own destiny, and certainly he had no control over it now. They had to fire a schedule of barrages entirely at the behest of divisional and corps artillery staff.

Colin had been scathing about the deficiencies of the staff in 1915 and his complaints were not unreasonable. The staff in 1917 were certainly more experienced, but they were experienced in the warfare of 1916. Those who had been regimental officers had experienced everything that Colin's brigade were now encountering, but not all together, and not all together for days on end. *'They think they know,'* said Colin, and it is hard to blame them. Anybody who had been through the Somme had the right to think they knew what war was like. But this was indeed different, and indeed much harder. The frequent changes of command brought about by the army brigade system made things worse. (See schedule overleaf.) Nobody cared what happened to them. They were not treated as intelligent men, but as expendable pawns.

General Gough had postponed the assault because of the difficulties he was having with his artillery.[243] He drafted more in to replace his losses. But there is no evidence in Colin's letters that he did anything to try to improve the positions of those already there, not that that would have been easy. The ground they were on was flat and featureless, most woods and hedges long destroyed.

Colin had had some optimism before the opening of the Somme, and a sense of purpose before Messines Ridge. There is anger before the onset of this battle.

---

243 The French, on the left wing of the attack, also had difficulties with their artillery contributing to the delay.

	Division	Corps	Date From	To
	16th	IX	12.4.'17	9.6.'17
	30th	II	11.6.'17	9.7.'17
Rest	—	—	10.7.'17	15.7.'17
	30th	II	16.7.'17	3.8.'17
	18th	—"—	3.8.'17	10.8.'17
Rest	—	—	10.8.'17	22.8.'17
	25th	II	23.8.'17	25.8.'17
	47th	—"—	25.8.'17	4.9.'17
	25th	—"—	4.9.'17	5.9.'17
	25th	I Anz:	5.9.'17	10.9.'17
Wagon Lines	—	IX	11.9.'17	12.9.'17
	19th	—"—	13.9.'17	20.9.'17
Rest	—	—	21.9.'17	30.9.'17
	7th	X	1.10.'17	19.10.'17
	21st	—"—	19.10.'17	1.11.'17

113th Army Bde: R.F.A.

"A" "B" & "C" (18pdrs) "D" (4·5" How).

Every change meant new divisional staff and command to deal with; and with every change of corps, a new lieutenant general. In the twenty weeks of battle, the brigade had eleven such changes.

General Plumer had insisted on control of the skies before Messines and had gone a long way to winning the artillery battle there before the battle opened. The British did not have control in the air before Passchendaele; the German Artillery was far from defeated; and the sparsely manned concrete strong points on their deep front were largely intact. The situation could not have been more different.

With every other gun on that front, 113th Brigade fired practice barrages on the 26th July, and again on the 28th, rehearsing the assault plan, further churning the wet ground and adding to the destruction of the few remaining drainage ditches. General Gough had helpfully revealed his plan for a huge inflexible unobserved rolling barrage along the whole battle front.

The maps which follow show the plan for the six artillery brigades of the 30th Division. The divisional front is 1500 yards wide and the uplift from each line of barrage 100 yards, scheduled every four minutes with the guns firing at four rounds per gun per minute. Thus the 113th Brigade was firing 96 rounds per minute onto a line about 200 yards wide, with every exploding round throwing up smoke and water vapour, creating an dense smog.

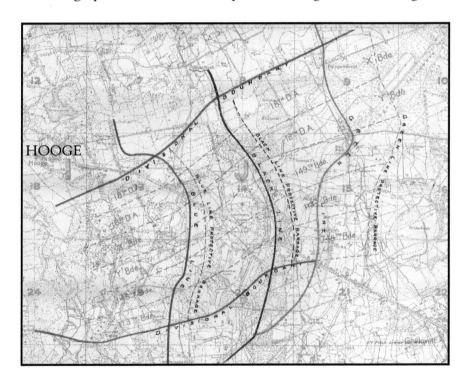

Artillery barrage map for the six brigades of the 30th Division on the 31st July. No allowance is made for strong points or terrain in the pace of the advance. There is one gun about every 12 yards of the divisional front. The green line is the final objective, about two miles from the front line. A short pause in the infantry advance was scheduled at the blue line, a longer one at the black line.

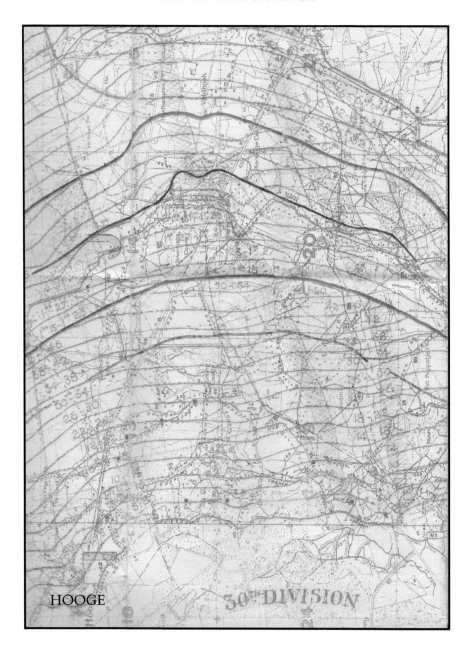

HOOGE

30TH DIVISION

This map shows the 30th Division sector, just the centre part of the corps artillery plan for its three divisions, the 8th, the 30th and the 4th. The 113th Brigade barrage is shaded and exact timings given for 8 hours and 40 minutes into the battle, with pauses at the blue and black lines

At 3.50 am on the 31st July 1917, the assault started. The infantry, laden with heavy kit, tried to advance at 25 yards a minute, keeping the bombardment to their front. It was raining hard. They were not crossing the pastured farmland, shown on the maps, but a glutinous swamp. After years of bombardment, the top soil was liquid mud, drainage ditches and root systems completely destroyed. Craters, full of water contaminated with mustard oil and explosive remnants, had to be circled. All this would have been dangerous enough, but they had an enemy to face as well.

Mud at Passchendaele

The 113th Brigade diary makes no attempt to gloss over the extent of the disaster on the day. *'Zero day. Attack launched at 3.50 am. Visibility very poor. 30th Division held up at first objective by machine gun fire and loss of direction. Ground so cut up that the infantry were unable to keep pace with the barrage, (lifts 100 yards every four minutes). Having lost the barrage, they lost direction and got stuck in the mud.'*

Colin had a friend in the division in front of them. *'We were supporting Lieutenant Colonel McDonald's battalion, the 19th Manchester's,'* (who were in the first wave of the attack). *'He spent the night of the 30th very close to where we were in action and I managed to get a note to him, but could not get over to see him myself'.*

The colonel replied a few days later. *'Well back for the moment. So sorry I missed you. If I had known you were there we might have sat and been gassed together all night.'* Colin does not mention till a month later that he lost his voice for a fortnight due to inhaling gas during the first days of the battle. *'I suppose you are still up there, poor devil! We had a hell of a battle, the worst I have ever been in. Everyone lost their way. I brought out 3 officers out of 20. I was too tired to look for you when I came out. I could barely walk, after being in cold water storage for three days. I will look you up if my battalion comes back into this fight – which God forbid! Best of luck to you!'*

The assault had been the predictable complete disaster. The conditions were truly appalling, and many men died of hypothermia or drowning.

At least, the division did instruct one battery in each brigade to *'respond to all zone calls in range'*, i.e. to liaise with the infantry, and target enemy strong points to assist with the advance. This was a nod to the lessons learned at the Somme. But the artillery observation officers could see nothing through the fog and smoke, and their wire communications were cut by German counter fire. Colin's orders to help the infantry by targeting any strong points they encountered were impossible to obey.

Most of the 30th Division troops did not even achieve the blue line on the first day and they got nowhere near the black line, let alone the green one. It is true that this was about the least successful sector, but few divisions did very much better.

There was no plan B. The infantry assaults continued. On the 3rd August, the brigade diary is not optimistic. *'The ground in front is already in a terrible condition. Weather still very bad. Hostile fire mostly on roads and known battery positions, at times very heavy. Ground so bad it is almost impossible to get up ammunition even by packs.'* And the artillery brigade adjutant even had time to pity the infantry; *'very great difficulty in getting the men back from the front line*[244] *owing to the mud.'*

The same day, Colin is equally pessimistic. *'This is the first letter I have been able to write to you since the 31*[st]*. We have been having a jolly hard time of it. This wet weather has of course put the lid on everything and goodness knows how the thing will end. From a combatant officer's point of view, it never looked good and why there was all that wretched optimism everywhere, I cannot make out. Things look black when the weathers bad. Let's hope things look a bit brighter when the weather clears.*

We are still in action and likely to remain so for some time, I'm afraid. It is just impossible to move anyone. The poor infantry are up to their necks almost in water, and only shell holes to live in.'

There was a lighter moment, if one could call it that. *'Major Osborne'* who commanded 'B' battery *'created a great diversion for us. Two German prisoners on their way down were given one of our wounded men on a stretcher to bring down. We were watching from a distance. A German shell burst near them, and the blighters dropped the stretcher and bolted down the track. Suddenly a wild figure dashed out of 'B' Battery's dugout with a pick handle and made for the two Bosches. When they saw him, they stopped in their flight and stood still, then turned round thinking better of it. However, this did not stop the major. He came after them with the pick handle and hitting them hard rushed them back to the stretcher they had dropped. The men were terrified but they faced the shell fire rather than Major Osborne who looked a terrible sight as he had not shaved for four days. Everybody who saw it enjoyed the show immensely.'* Major Osborne himself was not entirely proud of the incident. He told Colin that *'one of the fellows was crying all the time 'I go wounded man, I go wounded man'. He said he hit them pretty hard too.'* He knew he had lost control of himself.

---

244 The attacking division, the 30th, was relieved on day 3 by the 18th division. Colonel Lambarde had a new general to liaise with, not that liaison was a feature of the first month of this battle.

'We are still in action in the same place, and pigging it as a result of this rain. We are all very dirty and tired of this show. The battery is just about played out and I believe we are about the best off in the Brigade. The Colonel is pretty tired of this show also. He has been living in the cellar of a ruined house for 18 days now, and is lucky if he can get out for an hour during the day. One seldom gets a whole hour quiet enough.'

'By the way, will you please ask Father to double the output of cigarettes he is sending me for the men. We aren't getting enough.' Hardly surprising.

They were pulled out on the 10th August, having been in action for three weeks. 'We were all frightfully glad to get out for this rest.' 'Very good billets, very bad horse lines,' the brigade diary records.

The brigade was not in good shape. Colin himself had been both wounded and gassed. He had a painful ulcerated throat, his voice was hoarse, and the small open wound on his nose was giving him trouble. Ten officers and seventy-two other ranks had been incapacitated. And now, 'two of my subalterns have gone sick together with diarrhoea, Captain Pownall has gone sick, while on leave, and Blackburn, has taken over at the ammunition column. I have three subalterns, none of whom have been with me for three weeks.

This makes things difficult,' he says. But at least the surviving officers had the opportunity to let their hair down. 'We (the battery commanders[245]) gave the Colonel a dinner in St Omer yesterday and had quite a merry party. I think the Colonel enjoyed it, though he doesn't pretend to like these things. – Just been interrupted again, a wretched colonel come to tell us how to groom our horses I expect – and tonight I have arranged to go in again and hope to have another merry dinner.'

'And who do you think I have run into of all people? Gordon[246] now commanding the 81st Battery, RFA. He has been out in rest here after coming up from Vimy. And yesterday, after arranging for our respective batteries to

---

245 Colin, Major Willoughby Osborne and Major Bolitho. Major Glynn of 'D' battery had been wounded.

246 Major Roger Gordon MC was a Scottish international rugby player and contemporary of Colin at Woolwich.

play each other at football, we discovered that Tyler was still at the artillery school here. They have splendid quarters in a chateau, and the commandant, his colonel is a very nice man. Gordon and I rode over together to see him today and we are meeting for dinner.'[247]

Describing these dinners, he sounds a bit guilty. He is aware of the food shortages back in England. He advises his mother to discontinue the regular cake parcels, though she did not take much notice.

Too soon, they went back into action.[248] They had been out for twelve days, but of these four were spent marching the fifty kilometres to and from St Omer.

'Here we are in action again about 1800 yards north of where we were before and just a little forward of there. So far it has been very much better than our last position I am thankful to say, but this is still a rotten spot.' They were in the old British front line, a mile short of Hooge, just north of the Menin Road from Ypres to Hooge. (See map page 230.)

'Two of my subalterns arrived back the day before yesterday, so things are easier now. I have not got to be battery commander, captain, section commander and sergeant major all in one. Unfortunately, my new sergeant major is not strong enough to run this battery and I shall have to get rid of him.'

'This is our third night here and we are extraordinarily fortunate to have big dugouts to come down into, 30 feet underground here, a deserted infantry headquarters, cramped and very wet, but the sense of security is a wonderful blessing after the rotten time we had at Zillebeke. We can see our old position from here getting hammered.'

By the end of August, Colin is unable to contain his anger at the futile tactics of the first month of the battle and the way

---

247 *'We are just about the only three gunners left who were in the same set at 'the shop'.'* Of the 166 graduates of Woolwich from 1912 to 1914, 48 out of 166 are listed as killed in the war. (Firepower, Woolwich.)

248 No real rest for army brigades. They briefly joined the 25th division on 23rd August then moved to the 47th division on the 25th for the next ten days.

they were being treated. *'It is not like the good old days when war was interesting. The present method of running things destroys personal initiative. I suppose those who know find it best, but it's a terrible come-down from the old regular army ideas. I think the whole thing wants reorganising by energetic young blood.'* In the context of the French mutiny and Russian collapse,[249] these are strong words, not yet treasonous, but heading that way. The feelings in the infantry must have been incendiary.

He was not the only artilleryman severely discontented. The brigade diary, only the next day, records the frustration of Colonel Lambarde. *'Brigade did a standing barrage and smoke screen. No indication given to the artillery on this front what the infantry objectives were. Seems a mistake not to give the artillery some idea of what is going on.'* Criticism of a senior officer in the official brigade diary is almost unprecedented. But all the lessons of the importance of intelligent coordination between infantry and artillery had by now been completely forgotten.

Some relief was at hand. The day Colin wrote his complaint, the 25th August, General Haig, to his credit, sacked General Gough, the mastermind of the battle, to no-one's distress, and brought in General Plumer who had won the battle at Messines Ridge. Back in the early summer, plans had been submitted, based on his tactics at Messines, with shorter objectives. But these had been vetoed by General Haig. Now, back in command and assessing the strategic options, he wanted to call the offensive off. But it had to continue. British prestige with her allies was at stake, and there was a risk involved in allowing German troops to be released to attack the still wobbly French army further south. Besides General Haig still wanted a battle of attrition. So in the first half of September, there was a pause in the battle, while

---

249 French infantry had mutinied at the murderous losses they had incurred in the late spring of 1917, and the Russians were in the first throes of revolution. Colin is certainly aware of the latter, but he never mentions the French mutiny.

General Plumer took over and arranged his changes in planning and tactics. [250]

But the bombardments never stopped – on either side. *We do the same things more or less day after day. The Germans still seem to have a good deal of ammunition to spare, but they are always getting a little bit more than they give us. We have 1000 rounds of ammunition to cart up at 6 sharp tomorrow morning.'*

There was little more to say, but he tried to stay positive. *'Had a tremendous bit of luck today. I was walking along a track when the Germans suddenly took it into their heads to drop some high velocity shells very close by, and in the ensuing stampede, my old coat pocket split and everything fell out of it, including my revolver and two precious pencils. I did not discover the loss until I got back to the battery and after attending to a few orders, I set off back to the place to have a look for it and got there just in time to see an infantryman bring it along. The pencils however I could not find.'* The luck seems to have been finding his revolver, not avoiding the high velocity shells!

There were other hazards to avoid. *'Yes, that mustard gas is beastly stuff. I have been in some very strong concentrations of it. As a result, I lost my voice for about a fortnight. Its worst effect is on the lungs, a lot of men have died of pneumonia and bronchitis. Its effect on the skin is beastly. It is a terrible irritant and if you get any in your clothes, huge sores and blisters are formed. Of course any in the eyes would blind one. One learns just how much one can stand of it, and when the respirator has to be put on. It was the first surprise of it that cost us a good many casualties. I think our corps front was the first front they tried it on.'* [251]

---

250 Thus the Battle was in four phases. Phase one in August, phase two was a lull, lasting about three weeks, while General Plumer reorganised and reinforced his artillery, and planned achievable assaults. In phase three in September several successful assaults, blessed with better weather, gained ground with Plumer's revised tactics modelled on Messines. The artillery moved forward with each advance of the front line. But in October, the weather broke and the awful state of the ground meant the infantry again could not be supported by artillery advances, and the last small territorial gains were achieved at enormous cost.

251 It was. II corps in July 1917. Colin first records it on the 23rd, not mentioning it on the 20th.

General Plumer tried to arrange some protection for his artillery. *'We now have a machine gun section attached to the battery.'* So on the evening of the 7th September, Colin tried to get a little of his own back for his wounded nose. *'Those impertinent German airmen have been coming over very low, and turned a machine gun all round us while we were getting ammunition the other morning. Last night, I got the gunners to let me shoot the thing. I waited until two of them came jolly close and then emptied three drums at them as fast as I could. They swerved round at once and did not come back. I wish I'd bagged one. It was most exciting.'*

But the endless bombardments went on. *'They have been thumping us pretty well all night and all morning.'* And he was getting run down. *'It's trying, as one cannot spend all the time in a dugout.'* *'Living underground rather gets on one's nerves, but one does at least get a sleep. The great difficulty is keeping clean. My pyjamas have quite given way, and are absolutely in rags now. I wonder if I wrote asking for some more. I'm getting terribly absent minded these days, and do things without remembering whether I have done them or not.'* *'There is plenty of time to write, though it is very difficult to concentrate on it.'*

Letters from home did not necessarily cheer him up. *'Yes, that was quite true about General Peake being killed. Colonel Trench was killed with him who I also knew as captain at Bordon. If you get a chance, tell the Peake's how sorry I am about it.'* *'I had missed Baxter's name. He is not an only son, but his mother is very seedy. And Mr Jacob's brother. I'm awfully sorry.'*

In the second week of September, the brigade was briefly repositioned[252] to Hollebeke, right on the southern flank in readiness for a new limited offensive, the Battle of Menin Road which started on the 20th. There he had a pleasant surprise. We were *'hurried into action again in a semi-prepared position, and found my old battery, the 105th, preparing the position we were to come into. We actually*

---

252 Joining the 19th division in IX corps. Army brigades were transferred to where the action was. Yet another change of generals for Colonel Lambarde. Hollebeke is shown in the map on page 66.

took over the positions they had been in. I had dinner with Croft[253] and saw a lot of old friends. It was very nice seeing them all again.' 'But as usual it is getting pretty hot as a result of our coming here. One gets very tired of going out of the frying pan into the fire continuously. It's rather difficult to get touch with the world behind just now.'

But if the brigade had had precious little rest, Colonel Lambarde did manage to obtain a leave allocation for himself and his officers. 'These are very hard times just now and we all get exhausted to a certain extent.' This is the first time Colin has recorded that leave was allowed during a battle. He went first, accepting his allocation with relief. It was only ten weeks after his last leave. General Plumer must have been aware of the stress that his front line officers were under.

So Colin was away for the successful assault, before which the brigade fired practice barrages for four days, and then 2600 rounds per battery on the 20th September. Further successful, but limited, attacks occurred in the dry weather while he was away.

There is no mention of his leave in his letters. No thank you, no recollection of a happy event. It is as though it never happened. His letters just pick up where they left off. 'We could not cross over on the 4th October. It was terribly rough at Folkestone and I'm jolly glad they didn't send us over. It would have taken me weeks to recover. I was lucky getting here. A couple of Guards officers and I tackled the driver of a car who had just bought an officer to the boat. I had learned that we had moved[254], so I put up for the night at Cassel.' Finding one's unit could be quite a problem.

'I arrived back at the wagon line area I had left the batteries in, but these I found occupied by the 189th Brigade, which had replaced us on the 1st. Not knowing where the brigade was, I made my way to IX Corps headquarters to find out.'

---

253 Croft had been his captain in the 105th brigade at the Battle of the Somme.
254 There was a board in the port at Boulogne on which messages were posted for officers. There was an old message for Colonel Lambarde saying the brigade was moving, but not where; no message for Colin.

'I was kindly offered lunch there by the artillery intelligence officer.' The intelligence officer who offered him lunch was probably pleased to have the opportunity to learn something of a battery commander's views and to assess his morale. *'Apparently there are about 10 messes at a Corps headquarters, so a corps staff is pretty considerable, much larger than I ever dreamed of.*[255] *The usual optimism of such places prevailed there, but they were very good, and promised to take me on in a car that afternoon. Colonel Ellewes the Corps Horse-master and a gunner was very entertaining, besides which he has done a lot of regimental service through the war and understands. Of all staff appointments I think that of Corps Horse-master must require the most tact.*

One staff officer when it was suggested that this next winter would be the hardest of all, said in a very off hand manner 'Oh, they'll dig themselves in quick enough when the time comes.' Thank goodness not all staff officers are of that kind. Most pretend to know the hardships of this fighting, but not one in 100 has experienced it.'

So Colin probably acquitted himself well in the impromptu interview. But he had no time to think of this lunch, nor reason to do so. He now knew the brigade was with his old 7th Division, in a very exposed position just north of the Menin Road at Hooge. His mind was on returning to the fray. *'Just a line to let you know I have arrived back'* on the 7th October *'to find that the brigade has been in action for seven days or so. We are right in the middle of it again. I spent last night at the wagon line*[256] *and rode up into Ypres, and out again by the Menin Gate, down the Menin Road as far as Hell Fire Corner.'* (About a mile out of Ypres.) *'I left the horse there and went on foot through Hooge of which not one brick remains, and topped the rise to see shells falling fast in Chateau Wood which was our battery position.'*

---

255 It seems unbelievable, but this was his first ever visit to a corps headquarters. Yet another indication of the damaging segregation between the staff and the regimental officers.
256 Wagon lines were now miles behind the lines in relative safety. The lines of 113th brigade were five kilometres south west of Ypres at Dikkebus (or Dickebusch).

'Taking refuge in a pillbox by the side of the road, I waited for a lull, then made my way up, meeting Pownall who was on his way to see about an ambulance for Major Somerville Smith[257] and two of his subalterns who had just been wounded during the bombardment and one of whom died before they got him to the dressing station.

July 1917 1:10000 map showing Hooge, and a barrage within the arc of fire from Zillebeke at 3300 yards. On the 12th October, the battery advances from Chateau to Glencorse Woods (starred). The Menin Road runs from Ypres, through Hooge and on.

I found the battery very much shaken with the bombardment. There were no dugouts around the guns, so I decided to take all the men into some disused pillboxes on the side of the Menin Road about 250 yards from the battery, and to leave the battery absolutely on its own,' despite that *'making it impossible to man the battery under 3 minutes due to the state of the ground between the battery and the dugouts.'* He was thus disobeying an army directive. He had finally lost patience with obeying suicidal orders which were putting his men in danger.

'The Colonel is not back from leave yet. I hope to goodness he gets back

---

257 He was only slightly wounded. Captain Pownall from Colin's 'A' battery moved temporarily to command 'D' battery.

soon. *The Brigade wants a little looking after. Major Willoughby Osborne[258] has also lost a couple of subalterns wounded.'* To make matters worse, the weather broke. Between the 4th and 9th October, there was over an inch of rain.

'It rained nearly all yesterday and last night. We spent a couple of hours yesterday getting a wagon out of the main road just north of Hooge, bogged in the middle of the road, caused by shell craters of course. We have just about had our share in these parts. The trouble is we are such a damned good brigade, the people won't let us away from them. It is a nuisance being an army brigade.'[259]

They supported a 7th Division attack on the 9th October towards the village of Reutel. Infantry losses on both sides were hideous as attack was met with counter attack. That day, the remnants of three companies of infantry were reformed into two platoons[260] in front of them. The advance was over low ground into a salient, so they were being bombarded by German Artillery, from the east ahead of them, and from the south to their right. And the land they were fighting for was a swamp. The Germans who were contesting every inch of defensible land did not even bother to counterattack one small advance. They considered the land lost not worth the trouble of retaking.

For the first time in the war, Colin's account lacks any tactical coherence. He could see nothing to be gained by further attacks. *We ought to cease hostilities; one rather feels that the Bosche is having very much the best of these exchanges. We poor devils are living in a horrible waste of waterlogged shell holes, with not a vestige of anything, houses, foliage etc., to hide us. I really don't know how the poor wretched men stick this business.*

---

258 Major Willougby Osborne of 'B' battery was in command in the colonel's absence. Major Bolitho of 'C' battery had been wounded on the 9th. Colonel Lambarde got back from leave to find his brigade even more short-handed.

259 The divisional artillery brigadiers would press to be allocated the army brigades with the best reputation, and would not tell the army that a brigade needed a rest if it was doing its job. Colonel Lambarde was not going to tell the army that his brigade needed time out. Nobody looked after them.

260 The British Campaign in France and Flanders, Vol. IV : Arthur Conan Doyle

They get wet through and have nowhere to get a decent sleep even if the Bosche would give us quiet intervals. The weather has been absolutely vile and it's beginning to get cold too.'

His concern now was for his men and young officers. *'Cigarettes are very difficult to obtain now and your parcels are a great thing for the men.'* Many of them were new recruits and he worried about keeping the battery effective. *'We are hoping for a long rest. We need it for training our new gunners who have not had much instruction.' 'I think they'll have to take us out soon as some of our batteries have had a very trying time indeed.'* They stayed in.

He rotated his subalterns at the gun line. *'Poor Pilcher and Esson have been having rather a trying time of it. Dahl is back now and I have sent Esson down to the wagon line for a rest.'* And he forced himself to remain fairly upbeat.[261]

After the attack of the 9th, they were again ordered to move forward. And somebody, at last, felt that they deserved some protection. General Plumer knew the importance of conserving his forward guns. *'Working parties arrived to build beautiful sandbagged emplacements for the battery in Glencorse Wood'* (see map page 225) *'which we were moving forward to.'* But they were wasting their time. *'A German aeroplane flew over.'*

Colin refused to have anything to do with the new emplacements. *'We had learned that sandbags in the Ypres salient are an absolute curse even if exposed to the Bosche for only a very short while. So following our usual method, I had only a small party up, levelled 6 places for the guns and commenced salving a German pillbox which was flooded and filled with debris.'* This is the second time in a week that he has used his front

---

261 *'I expect people in England are pretty pleased with what is happening out here just now, though last Sunday's Observer is just a bit too optimistic, I think. Of course, the optimism just behind the Lines also is very wonderful; however it's not so difficult to be optimistic there. By the way, don't forget to get us a record of 'I'm on the Staff' as soon as it comes out. Goodness knows if they'll ever let us back to where we can enjoy the gramophone, but they might. There's no knowing. One thing is certain though that is there's mighty little rest for the guns these days.'* Haig ordered the battle to be continued. It was.

line instincts to disobey orders. (The brigade diary glosses over the subject.) Forget the sandbags, he wanted deep dugouts for his men. He put in a request for the necessary timber.

Three days later, *'those new positions built have been very heavily shelled and very little trace remains.'*[262] His guns though were still in place, still firing, though they were in *'bog positions'*. Their only shelter was the derelict German pill box, made of concrete, which was good; but with its entrance in line with German fire, which was bad. No sign as yet of the timber he had ordered.

They were now in Glencorse Wood behind Polygon Wood, though to call them woods was to stretch the definition of the word. Both were a mass of shell holes with no vegetation over three feet. Polygon Wood had in happier times been a pleasantly wooded army facility with a racecourse and shooting range. Now it was a gas polluted and crater ridden wasteland. There was an isolated hillock at the eastern end.

'I accompanied the colonel up to Polygon Mound and we searched the vicinity for an observation post with no success.' The brigade supplied a *'Forward Observation Officer, who in 12 days succeeded in getting no reports back whatever. The wire to forward observation (FO) was impossible to maintain.'* This forward observer was expected to have a position *'whence the ground beyond the final objective can be observed'*, difficult on the upslope of a low ridge. They cut their losses and decided to do away with forward observation. Several young officers had been wounded, and they had sent back no useful information at all.

The brigade was now required to supply both a *'liaison officer and an officer in rocket piquet, who could see well enough to give warning of all hostile concentrations or preliminary barrages. They were made responsible for*

---

262 This incident illustrates how the staff did not consult the front line troops, before conscientiously issuing orders to provide a service for it. Men would have been killed bringing up materials and preparing a position that was itself a death-trap. It was built by a working party of the 7th Division Trench Mortars.

observing, thus doing away with FO.' The 'rocket piquet' simply had to observe friendly lines to transmit requests for help (being a rocket sent up) in the event of a local attack. But liaison had at last been formalised. A junior liaison officer was now permanently attached to every infantry battalion, and he communicated with his senior liaison officer, a colonel, based at infantry brigade headquarters. At long last General Plumer had introduced a command structure to allow forward control of the artillery and cooperation with the infantry.

'There were three battalion headquarters in the Mound and every passage way was blocked by men trying to sleep standing up and in any other posture they could manage. The Germans of course kept up a continual fire, and were repeatedly blowing in the entrances. It is an open question now which is the worst for shell fire, our field batteries or the front trenches. Tracks also are being kept under continual fire.'

Every day for the next two weeks, (from the 13th October) the brigade diary simply records very heavy shelling of all batteries on a daily basis. *'The Bosche have been giving us a very bad time today. I don't quite know what they are up to, but he is not short of guns or munitions. And he still seems to have a plentiful supply of aeroplanes and competent pilots too.'*

'There seems to be a lot of optimism at home about the war ending by Christmas. I wish some of those wretched optimists could come out and take part in this, the Third Battle of Ypres.' It was generally believed that German morale would crack when the British finally achieved the summit of the ridge. Even if it had, the British would not have been able to capitalise. Further advance through the sea of mud would have taken days to organise.

'I shall really think of applying for a staff job if they keep us in much longer, or turn conscientious objector.' Colin had said earlier in the war that he would only consider joining the staff if he became too shell-shocked to run a battery. *'I'm depressed today so you must not take much notice of this.'*

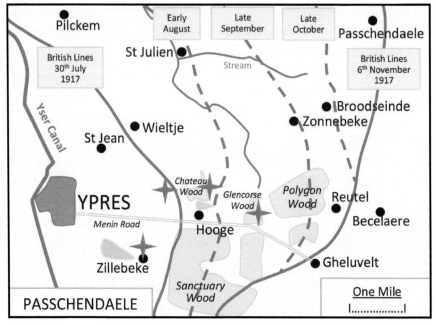

*The four brigade positions between July and October 1917 are starred,
left to right. In the forward position, they can be fired on from south to north-east.*

On the 18ᵗʰ October, he learns that their zone of fire has been changed. *'This means that all the positions in* Glencorse *Wood are useless. They have been sighted on a line 90 degrees left of the one now required.²⁶³ This will mean altering the gun pits. It is far simpler in these bog positions to select an entirely different area and start again. Supply however governs most things in these parts now and the track to Glencorse Wood was this morning impassable even to pack horses, the track at the positions having been literally blown to pieces.'* Despite the difficulties, they managed to get 2000 rounds of ammunition up as far as Chateau Wood the next morning.

---

263 *'Gheluvelt instead of Becelaere, is now reported to be the objective.'* The map above shows Gheluvelt. Becelaere is east of Reutel. The British advance at Reutel had created a salient, so that the troops at the point of the bulge were exposed both from in front, and from the side. General Plumer had organised a withdrawal in 1915 from just such a salient at Ypres. Both sides went to great lengths to avoid them. The British in this battle had gone to enormous lengths to create one. Nothing about this battle made sense.

The colonel was now in command of a 'group' of batteries[264] and had significant liaison responsibilities. Due to casualties, Colin was his senior major and he therefore had to take on some of the leadership of the brigade front line in Colonel Lambarde's absence. Colin had commanded the brigade briefly in the past, but this was a new and heavy responsibility. He was short-handed himself at the battery.

He started keeping a sort of personal brigade diary, writing on the 18th, *"B' Battery has had roughly 40 casualties in officers and men (2 officers wounded, including Major Bolitho) and about 40 horses. 105th Battery have had a very bad time losing 54 of their personnel in 10 days, including Major Beatson killed, their position being just 250 yards in front of ours. Our 'D' Battery has also up to the present lost 3 officers[265], 1 killed and about 40 men.'*

Colin was badly shaken by the bombardment that engulfed his old battery, the 105th. Major Beatson was an old friend from Woolwich. *'He has just been killed here sitting in a tank, the only cover they could find in a very much shelled locality. It was merely a matter of time before they hit the tank. That battery had 3 weeks' notice of going in there, which would have been ample time to have had a mine dugout built, if we are not capable of the concrete ones the Bosche strews all over the place.*

---

264 He was therefore the senior liaison officer based at infantry brigade headquarters, coordinating the reports of the junior liaison officers who were based at battalion headquarters. Groups were not a new concept and had been used extensively by divisions since 1915. A senior colonel commanded all the guns in a locality, ideally outlasting changes in divisional control to ensure tactical continuity, and to support less experienced brigade and battery commanders. But he was now formally required to liaise with the local infantry brigadier in the use of the guns. This moved control forward to minimise friendly casualties and maximise local support.

265 *'Somerville-Smith, commanding, had a miraculous escape having practically all his clothes torn to shreds, and getting off with several scratches and a terrible shaking. Several men were killed by the same shell.' 'Captain Deacon now commands 'C' Battery and Captain Pownall 'D' Battery.'* Promotion was rapid within the brigade. Captain Deacon was then wounded on the 21st.

Three weeks ago, I was ordered to take my battery up near his position. I at once applied for mine frames. Eight days later, a tunnelling officer[266] came round, recognised the use of making dugouts and started making them for the batteries four days after that. It had never occurred to them that the men doing the work need cover. The activity behind covering up HQ huts and things against bombs is colossal. By Jove, it makes me bitter to see these men being killed off like this, just because they don't grumble.' Colin was getting angry.

On the 22nd, *'we are having a tremendous struggle trying to get two guns that were knocked out the night before last, out of their 'pits'. We have managed after two and a half hours' work to get one gun 20 yards'* (one and a quarter tons dead weight) *'onto a piece of hard road. While we were pulling the first one out, the rope broke and Pilcher and the unlucky gunners had a mud bath.[267] We were getting on with the other when the Germans interrupted us to such purpose that we are leaving them for the present. We shall have to finish the job tomorrow morning.'*

'And talking about mud baths, Pownall had one with a vengeance going down to the wagon line the other day. He clambered on to the back board of a lorry going his way and was riding along happily enough when going over a shell hole in the road, the bump broke the chain holding the board up. He was deposited into the shell hole which was full of liquid mud. He arrived at the wagon line in an awful state.'

Colin was rotating his young officers and men as best he could. But he could do little to protect himself. *'I had 23 days at the gun line with only two breaks of one day apiece at the wagon line. I always had the feeling that casualties might occur during my absence that might have been avoided.'* He was only doing what Colonel Lambarde was doing. *'The colonel comes up to see us every morning and had to take refuge in here*

---

266 Tunnelling Units from the Royal Engineers were commanded at corps level and built the deep dugouts for the army. On the wide front that was constantly edging forward, they were in high demand, particularly for infantry brigade headquarters.

267 All had to be done manually. The horses were in wagon lines four miles away.

for some time this morning. We're getting very short of officers and it's rather a trying time for him.'

In the month of October alone, the brigade lost another 12 officers, though only one of them was killed, and the strain on those remaining was immense. Colin was the only original battery commander[268] left standing.

The 7th Division commanded them for 18 days[269], and then pulled back. Relief for the infantry, none it seems for the artillery. *'I shall be very pleased when we can get back for a rest, but they will probably keep us in until further fighting becomes impossible.' 'They keep us at it far too long. I laughed at responsibility 6 months ago, but I know what it is now, and can quite understand breakdowns.' 'I wish I could muster my former energy. The battery wants pulling together very badly, and it's deuced hard to do it under these conditions. It has come to the pass that I realise I must leave things to the junior officers if I want them to be done conscientiously, that's bad, isn't it?'* This was a scream for help in regular army parlance, as usual very understated. He is saying he is not fit for duty. But his mother was listening. She wrote to him almost every day for the next three months.

They participated in the bombardment for the assault on Passchendaele on the 26th October. The brigade diary sums up the result. *'Operation in support of corps north and south. Zero hour 5.40am. Operations south a failure due to the terrible state of the ground. Batteries very heavily shelled day and night.'* Or as Colin put it, *'the rain and wet made it absolutely impossible to push things through and the conditions in front were perfectly appalling.'*

They were still in action on the 30th. *'I don't know how we are going to keep up our reputation with the skeleton that is now left to the colonel.'* They were given replacements. *'I have had a perfectly terrible person sent to me as an officer. Goodness knows what he was before he got a commission.*

---

268 Major Willoughby Osborne of 'B' battery was wounded on 24th October. He lost his arm as a consequence.

269 On the 19th October, they moved to the 21st division, another new general.

The colonel has done it to get rid of him. He wants a report on him from me in a week's time. He said he expected I'd shoot either the officer or him when I saw him.' Both Colin and the Colonel were adept at moving on unsuitable junior officers, or negating the harm done by senior ones. It took Colonel Lambarde about six weeks to get rid of this one[270].

The battle went on till mid-November, with the British determined to capture the high ground and the Germans equally determined to deny it to them. *We are out here, wallowing in mud and waterlogged shell craters. The high ground we have captured is absolutely useless for observation because communication back through the mud and shell fire is impossible to maintain. The ground is getting worse and worse every day and the staff officers know less and less of the conditions of the regimental officers. We are getting the hell of a time, and it's all avoidable. Just a little organisation of tunnelling or dugout construction and hundreds of irreplaceable lives would not have been lost. By Jove, the wretched ignorance is astounding.*

Burn this letter when you've read it. Probably a concentrated gas bombardment right on top of us yesterday is responsible for it. The wretched stuff came through three blankets in enough quantity to make us put our box respirators on. Also they shelled us with 8 inch and 11 inch. There's a crater about 20 yards over this dugout which put 10 years onto my life when I saw it this morning, and I think of only three feet of concrete overhead.' Just one near miss like this would shake anybody's composure. It was just another day in his life.

Colin was getting more and more angry. *'By Jove, what a number of men and officers there are out here who literally know nothing about this war first-hand,'* in one letter. *'This newspaper optimism is just about the limit. They only see the front from a staff officer's point of view. We know what that is unfortunately,'* in another. *'What has really upset things is the damned optimism at HQ and home. The staff are very optimistic, HQ are very optimistic, and that damned ass Bottomley[271] has been writing the most*

---

270 The brigade diary records his coming and going. He shall remain nameless.
271 Horatio Bottomley was a serial swindler who used patriotic fervour, both in print and in lecture halls, to purloin money from a gullible public. He was a well-known, if not respectable, public figure.

absurd stuff and people are believing him,' in a third. All were reporting that German morale was about to collapse.

Colin could see no evidence to support this. He is accusing the generals behind the lines and the politicians at home of ignoring the reality on the front, and colluding in wishful thinking, persuaded by an ignorant and over-patriotic press. And he had not changed his mind about the battle a month later when he wrote again to his uncle. *'Things were certainly rather black when I wrote to you last, but there's still far too much truth in what I wrote for the general health of things out here.'*

By the last few days in the battle, Colin is frustrated at the pointlessness of their contribution. His guns are so far behind the infantry, they could barely support them. *'Our lines here are 6500 yards from Bosche. We barrage into a swamp, with only 500 yards available range for searching back. On average we fire two barrages a day, 300 rounds each time, 600 rounds in all. I'm sure it all looks all right on the map, and of course we are firing four shells to the enemy's one.'*

Yes, there was now good liaison between the infantry and artillery, and forward control of the battlefield was now a priority, but that was scant comfort to either party if the guns were too far back to accurately support the infantry units up in front. One cannot blame General Plumer. He was ordered to fight a war of attrition, on a hopelessly unsuitable battlefield in hopelessly unsuitable weather, and he did so. As ordered, he had created an almost useless salient in a sea of mud. He had not created a breakthrough of course, nor broken German morale, but that was no surprise.

Colin could see no solution. No longer were there continuous trench lines which, once breached, could be rolled up. Now the lines were held by a series of little forts, concrete pillboxes, each supported by artillery and each of which had to be outflanked and neutralised before the advance could continue.

'They can hold us in this country with a few pillboxes dotted about, and their guns are still there. They give us hell finishing off their ammunition

and then move back. The only way of making substantial advances is to go for their guns, making an advance of at least 5000 yards. They don't mind a damn losing 1000 yards on a five-mile front.' 'Our only chance is long range guns, masses of them, 18000 yards range for covering the long advances we want the infantry to make, before they can counter. Our 18 pounder has been obsolete for 6 months.'

But the British simply did not have any mobile guns of that range. [272] And even if they had, accurate fire relied on observation, requiring a massive expansion of aerial observation capability, and near total control of the air. Neither were practical aims in late 1917. *'Our whole method of warfare is wrong'* Colin concludes.

The battle officially finished on the 10th November, by which time the brigade was in rest. In the four months of battle, the British army had advanced four miles and lost something of the order of two hundred and fifty thousand men dead and wounded. The Germans probably lost more men than the British. So the British could be said to have won, in that they achieved their objectives, but one uses the word advisedly in describing such a ghastly and uninspired campaign. And the cost in morale was high. German morale at the end of 1917 was probably better than it had been six months before. That of the British and French was decidedly worse.

It was now clear to everybody from General Haig down that a single massive hammer blow was neither going to shatter the German lines, nor deal a terminal blow to their morale. So how to win the war?

---

272 The 6-inch 26 cwt howitzer introduced in 1915 weighed 3.6 tons, firing a 100 pound shell less than 10000 yards. It was moved by horses or 4wd lorry. The Ordnance BL 60-pounder, a 5 inch (127 mm) heavy field gun had a range of 10300 yards, later increased by redesigning the shell to 12300 yards. Weighing 4.4 tons, the gun required a team of 8 horses to tow it, with a maximum of 12 in difficult conditions. There were heavier railway guns of longer range, but with the obvious limitations on their movement. www.militaryfactory.com

CHAPTER FOURTEEN

1918 Prospects for Promotion to Staff

'We are getting our voices back again.'

'A' Battery, 113th Army Brigade

Colin had survived the battle. But he had hardly seen the Germans. For almost ninety days, he had faced unimaginable danger from an impersonal rain of bullets, bombs, gas and high explosive shells. The brigade had suffered well over 250[273] casualties, many of them his friends. He couldn't really blame the Germans for doing their job. But he could blame the men who put them there, held them there and did not seem to care. He could blame that impersonal entity, 'the staff'. So he did.

And at that time, in those circumstances, his hatred of the 'staff' became visceral. He could rub along with individuals, and he had forgotten the times when staff planning had been good. For three years the stereotypical image of the staff was that they were comfort loving, incompetent and aloof. And all his experience of Passchendaele went to confirm this. They lunched in comfort, they used scarce resources to protect their headquarters and they put his brigade in suicidal positions without consultation. Entirely unsurprisingly in the immediate aftermath of Passchendaele, he became obsessed with the injustice, the impersonality, and the sheer

---

273 From July to the end of October, 7 officers had been killed and 26 wounded, 37 other ranks killed and 191 wounded. Some of the wounded would have remained on duty, as Colin did, and the figures exclude September when the casualty numbers for the month are not recorded. More than 44 killed and 217 wounded to add to the 5 and 23 lost at Messines Ridge. Total strength would have been well under a 1000.

stupidity of a pointless battle for useless territory. He developed a fierce unforgiving anger. He blamed the 'staff' and at that moment he wanted nothing to do with them. They, more than the Germans, were the enemy.

With relief he accepted the offer of comfortable accommodation for the night of the 1ˢᵗ November as the brigade went in to rest for 18 days.[274] *'The night I spent at X Corps with Major Wynter who used to be brigade major at the 7ᵗʰ Division, but is now artillery brigade major at Corps.'*

He was probably glad to get away. Two of his best subaltern's were *'dreadfully upset. Pilcher's brother who was in the brigade has been killed. He got the news yesterday, and Esson's only brother who was in the infantry has also been killed. They both died of wounds in the same casualty clearing station.'*

And they had *'had rather a nasty dose of that wretched mustard gas the last two nights.'* Colin was not only *'suffering with loss of voice and sore throat,'* but also, *'my eyes are affected a little and unfortunately I got a little on the mouthpiece of my respirator. It has raised a blister in my mouth and on the right side of my tongue.'* These 'blisters', deep ulcers really, were very painful.

He had been hosted at lunch at IX Corps in early October, now he was having dinner by invitation at X Corps. He was being sounded out for promotion, and seems completely unaware of the fact. *'It was very nice being asked, as we had just come out of the line in the morning.'* Promotion meant a staff job. But with all his other worries, it was the last thing on his mind.

Even a week later, *'we are still not fit to go into action again. However, our voices are coming back. It is wretched stuff that gas.'* If he was complaining, it must have been bad. *'I have not been able to touch salt for the last few days owing to its making my mouth smart so.'* But at least they were in rest for a second week. *'We are not doing not much else than play football at present, getting up all sorts of league games and matches. Rugby we have not tackled yet!'*

The 'staff' had promised them a really good break and they

---

274 The brigade marched to a rest area 10 miles south west of Ypres that day.

needed it. After a month on the Somme, Colin's divisional artillery had had a month's rest. In the last six months of continuous battle in 1917, the brigade as a whole had had just three weeks of rests[275] and now they had another two weeks, in their wagon lines, still close to the front, but not in proper relaxed billets away from it all.

And, being so close, they were available at short notice if a problem arose. One did, and they barely had time to get over the gas before they were ordered back into the line. *'I am told by the colonel it will be for under 10 days as a stop gap only.'*

This was yet another promise made to be broken. *'They talk about sending us back for a decent rest. We've heard it before and these wonderful promises never come off. It's a rotten state of affairs, this continual bolstering up with false promises. I'd much rather be told the truth.'* The liars were the staff. They were still in action three months later without their promised rest.

So in the third week of November, back they went to Hooge, supposedly for just ten days. *'We are going in to action again tomorrow morning. They are taking us up in motor lorries, and then we do the rest on foot. I am going with them into action, then I am leaving Dahl[276] in charge, as I have to act as liaison officer between an infantry brigade headquarters and the artillery for three days. However, I shall be quite close to the battery, so shall be able to look after them too, I hope.'*

It is likely that his devotion to the battery was reciprocated. 'The men respected and trusted him absolutely.' So a friend wrote after the war. He had at least twice 'ignored' inconvenient orders to protect them. He was always at the point of danger. He got them cigarettes. He funded and supplied the officers' mess. He was a well-known sportsman, and above all he was lucky, a priceless asset in war.

---

275 Most of it in wagon lines close to the front, where they were 'on call', some of it on the march to their allocated billets. *'On the 10th August, they gave us a rest of 7 days, and 6 days marching,'* recorded at 12 days in the brigade schedule. They were in 'rest' from the moment they left the line. (See schedule page 212).
276 Lieutenant Dahl had only joined the battery in October 1917.

He was, by now, receiving almost no letters from home except from his mother. His young and very inexperienced officers were his family, and relied on him completely. He protected them by rotating them in and out of the line, staying in himself of course.

But just as in 1915, when Colin had been under prolonged heavy fire, but this time with the additional stress of being wounded once and heavily gassed at least twice, his mental state was distinctly wobbly. He describes no loss of nerve. Rather the reverse. But he does describe overwhelming tiredness, lack of concentration and irritability. He is resigned to the fact that his war will end soon. After all, everybody on both sides was trying to get him killed. As he said later, 'After Chateau Wood I was near worried out of my reason.'

Three days of infantry liaison turned into ten, but then the home leave that Colonel Lambarde had been trying to get him came through. He had seen Colin suffer in 1915 and knew the signs. He got him a whole month. He hoped it would be enough.

Colin's DSO came through on 1st January 1918 while he was still on leave. At some stage in the battle, he had been thought worthy of a Distinguished Service Order. The details of the citation are lost. At this stage of the war, medals were awarded within the army hierarchy, and not formally by the King. So it could have been any day during the battle, any spell of duty with any of the nine divisions they served under. They were all much the same. But if the specific reason he won this high honour is lost in mud, that somehow seems appropriate.

Colonel Lambarde meanwhile had been awarded the Legion of Honour by the French[277] and was still commanding an artillery group. Colin had half taken charge of the brigade when the colonel was concentrating on his group at Passchendaele; not an easy job, as

---

277 'The Colonel has just got a notice from Corps that he has to go and receive his Legion of Honour from some general or other commanding one of the French Armies. He doesn't seem to like the idea of the ceremony. However, I don't think he can get out of it, which is a good thing.' Letter 2nd December.

his fellow battery commanders were incapacitated one after another, and they lost subaltern after subaltern. Colin already had an M.C. which was official confirmation of his courage, and now his DSO indicated he was intelligent too. The combination was potent. He had been noticed, but he was still only 24.

The colonel was sounded out on Colin. He wrote to his mother just before Christmas. *'I have sent forward a very strong recommendation for him to be appointed a brigade major, so tell him to provide himself with plenty of coloured pencils and other office gear.'*[278]

The colonel's real reason for writing was a simple thank you. *'I have just received some mince pies and a plum pudding from you for which I am most awfully obliged.'*[279] But he added, *'Tell Colin I will write to him soon, but at present I am being rather harassed by an absolutely impossible territorial brigadier.'* Colin has complained of the poor leadership, to put it mildly, that most of their divisions supplied during 1917. Here is Colonel Lambarde irritated enough to indiscreetly make the same complaint.

Colin returned to France on the 6ᵗʰ January 1918 to take over the command of the brigade as the colonel went on leave. So now he had to deal with the problems generated by their inconsistent command structure, this time a change of corps.[280] *'Every general that comes round to see us suggests we should do different things. I have been dreadfully busy. There is a tremendous amount of work to get through and very few men to do it with. The poor gunners never get an atom of outside help.'* They were providing working parties to repair their own roads and tracks, and firing four *'bursts of fire'* every twenty-four hours on enemy *'roads, tracks, etc.'*

---

278 *'And tell him that his 'impossible' young subaltern has been ordered off to another brigade.'* Note 270.

279 *'Your plum pudding and mince pies made quite an impression on Brigade Headquarters. At any rate the subaltern signal officer keeps talking about them. The Battery got theirs all right, and had a great dinner, I'm told,'* said Colin later.

280 He actually took command of the whole group according to the brigade diary. They were currently under the 66ᵗʰ division, but on the 1ˢᵗ January, the 66ᵗʰ was transferred from II Anzac corps to XII corps. See page 245 for schedule.

But *'just now it is all we can do to keep the men from getting drowned. Poor old Blackburn[281] woke up two mornings ago at 10 am to find 2 feet of water in his dugout, all the lower bunks with a lot of his kit being absolutely under water. I think I'm lucky to be here.[282] It only drips here.'*

During the last week in January, he received news of the death in England of one of his best friends, Croft of the 105th battery, who had been all through the Somme with him, and Passchendaele too. He had fallen off a balcony of the Piccadilly Hotel during a dinner a few days before his wedding. The coroner said he was drunk and ruled it a death unrelated to the war. Colin had seen him have *'fainting attacks'* in France and was very indignant at the verdict. Yet another injustice, as he saw it, perpetrated by an ignorant civilian 'staff officer'.

He was kept very busy, with Colonel Lambarde on his month's leave, and Colin put the thought of the brigade major's course out of his mind. But the staff were closing in. On the 29th January, he *'had quite a big lunch party today, the staff captain corps, brigade major of a division and a flying liaison major,'* and he learned that his brigade major's course started on the 5th February. Colonel Lambarde returned.

Colin had been led to believe his course was to be based with the New Zealand Division, where he had lively friends. But at the last minute, he found himself with a West Riding Territorial Division, a much dourer proposition. *'Tomorrow I am going on the learner's course for brigade major. I now learn that it entails another fortnight at corps headquarters, after I have finished the month of division headquarters, six weeks in all – a jolly sight more than I anticipated. I'm really sick about it'*

As a career soldier, this promotion was exactly what he needed. To become a brigade major at just 25, possibly confirmed in the rank of major, would have pushed him right up the queue at the end of the war for higher rank.

---

281 Captain Blackburn M.C. was his 'ranker' captain, temporarily commanding Colin's 'A' battery.

282 The brigade was back at Railway dugouts, now a cemetery, just south east of Ypres. They had been there in the weeks before the onset of Passchendaele.

But Colin was filled with doubts as he went for his training. He was not with friends. And unlike 1915, no barrage of letters from supportive friends, no messages from Miss Ferguson, no quiet talks with the padre, no rowdy parties with fellow young officers, no paternal support from Colonel Lambarde. Even his mother's letters stopped for a week due to misdirection.

'This is a fine Chateau we are living in, but I'm not sure that I wasn't happier in the eternal darkness of a pillbox,' he says. He did not sleep well. He tells of his distress and feelings of guilt at being away from the battery. He records his poor concentration. *'Just a very short note today as I don't feel I can write any sense at all tonight.'* I have a *'war weary distorted brain'* he says. Traumatic stress we would call it today. He was not well.

The course itself was undemanding. *'The division is not going into the line for another two weeks, which means there is very little to do.'* He went for lonely walks, but the general did his best to get him involved. *'I hear the general coming in now. He's been away to a conference and he likes to talk. I must stop.'*

Things did improve. *'These last few days I have been working very hard on a defence scheme on the divisional front. Half past twelve to bed last night, then got up at 5.30 this morning and walked practically round the whole divisional area just behind the front line.'* He knew what he was seeing. His input was useful.

And *'yesterday I went over with a Colonel Stanley to see some of his batteries shooting on a range, and we had lunch with Tyler at the School. I enjoyed the outing immensely as we took the General's car, and today I went up with the General to have a look at the Artillery we are going to relieve in the Line.'*

But he was learning nothing new for himself. *'I was out for a long walk with the general yesterday. We walked from 9 till 4 without any lunch and then had an egg for tea. Just lately I have found myself with too little to do, and just waiting for every meal, eating far too much when it did come.*

While we are on that subject, don't you think you had better cut the cake supply down to one parcel a month if you do not cut it out altogether? We really get very well fed out here, and I expect you want things far more at home. It must be hard not being able to get any meat. We have plenty of bacon and beef out here. The men's ration is exceedingly good, though not too much for the energetic open air life they lead.' 'P.S. One of the beautiful battery tea pots has had its spout blown off. I wonder if you could find us another.' The battery was never far from his thoughts.

When the month finished, he was away. *'I was really very glad indeed to get back to the battery, felt quite like a release. Brigade Major's job will be very nice when I get so badly shell-shocked I cannot command a battery any longer.'*

He refused point blank to sign up for the remaining fortnight at Corps headquarters, which only 50% of applicants were offered. *'I've had a struggle to get out of the clutches of the staff. They were keen I should undergo some more instruction, but that I kicked at. I feel perfectly capable of doing a brigade major's job.'* He convinced himself that the second half of the course was unnecessary. *'I have been recommended for the job, so my name is on the list.'* It wasn't, of course. The corps brigade major tried to talk him into doing the course, but failed.

His mother told him off, *'You speak about my being foolish not to have finished the course,'* and the colonel was *'in an infernal bad temper over something. I don't know who had upset him.'* Sometimes Colin's lack of awareness is breath-taking. Colonel Lambarde had recommended him for promotion in glowing terms, had chosen the best new subalterns[283] for 'A' battery to help its new commander, and now Colin was back, having told the staff what they could do with themselves. He was not pleased!

And nor presumably was the rest of the army. It is relevant of course that he was sent for staff training to an infantry division where he had no ties; no friends to support him; nobody who knew personally what he had been through. The army brigade system had made such relationships so difficult to build up, and all but destroyed his divisional loyalty.

---

283 Captain Blackburn and Lieutenant Dahl had both commanded the battery for short periods. Lieutenants Esson and Pilcher had joined in August 1917. Lieutenants Wethered and Pilling were new to the battery.

113th Army Bde: R.F.A. (Continued).

	Division	Corps	Date From	To
	New Zea:	XXII	9.2.'18	11.2.'18.
	20th	–"–	11.2.'18	17.2.'18.
	37th	–"–	17.2.'18	13.3.'18.
Rest	—	—	14.3.'18	21.3.'18.
	49th	XXII	22.3.'18	12.4.'18.
	33rd	XV	12.4.'18	25.4.'18.
	25th	–"–	25.4.'18	30.4.'18.
	1st Aus:	–"–	30.4.'18	9.5.'18.
	30th	–"–	9.5.'18	27.5.'18.
	9th	–"–	27.5.'18	2.8.'18.
Rest	—		3.8.'18	15.8.'18.
	9th	XV	16.8.'18	23.8.'18.
Rest	—		24.8.'18	3.9.'18.
	35th	II	4.9.'18	6.9.'18.
	14th	–"–	6.9.'18	19.9.'18.
	9th	–"–	19.9.'18	20.9.'18.
	29th	–"–	20.9.'18	6.10.'18.
Rest	—		7.10.'18	12.10.'18.
	36th	II	13.10.'18	16.10.'18.
	29th	–"–	16.10.'18	23.10.'18.
	36th	–"–	23.10.'18	26.10.'18.
	34th	–"–	26.10.'18	1.11.'18.
Rest	—		2.11.'18	6.11.'18.
	40th	XV	7.11.'18	Onwards.

"C" Battery to Second Army Artillery School 20th August 1918 till ?

The 113th Army Brigade in 1918 – they were with the 66th division till 9th February.

In fact, the army brigade system had a lot to answer for. Half the artillery brigades were still with divisions, and their officers had hierarchical stability. It was different for the army brigades. Every time they moved, they had to prove themselves as a 'fighting brigade'. Colonel Lambarde did not want to sit and passively obey orders to fire mindless barrages. He wanted to be proactive and he wanted to enhance his brigade's reputation. But it is difficult to be noticed if your general changes every fortnight.

So Colonel Lambarde did not seek rest for his brigade if there was work to be done. He kept the men in their wagon lines and available for new tasks, seeing it as a weakness to ask for rest. Only he was really aware that his brigade had been tested almost to destruction, and Colin along with it.

And so far as the 'staff' were concerned, Colin could only make decisions on the basis of his own experience. He had been serving without a break for over three years in successful fighting units. His perceptions of the 'staff' had been negative at almost every level for all that time. He was unable, just after Passchendaele to see that in order to beat them, he had to join them. That for him was a step too far.

The corps brigade major (Major Wynter) knew him well from his time as divisional brigade major in the 7th Division. He was one of the very few staff officers that Colin liked and respected. If he could not get through, nobody could. But if Colin had been posted back to the 7th Division in early 1917, it is likely he would have accepted. His staff and front line experience would have been so very different.[284]

There were other factors of course. Colin at the time was commanding the brigade in Colonel Lambarde's absence, doing a colonel's job. Moving to the staff meant accepting a junior post in a stable hierarchy. He would have had to be polite and tactful, not necessarily his strong points. And he thrived on the adrenaline of

---

284 It is also likely that he would been killed before he had the chance. The 105th, Colin's old battery had had its commander killed and 50 men incapacitated in one week alone at Passchendaele.

constant danger. Addiction is a strong word, but one could say that he was addicted to the dangers and hardships he faced. He simply could not give it up.

But Colin's offered promotion reflects better on the health of the army as a whole. His promotion to that point had been opportunistic, growing into more senior roles as required by circumstances, sponsored by one or two senior officers. This was different. A promising young officer had been identified by staff at corps. He had been interviewed, references taken, and deemed suitable for assessment. A month's course was required (with a fifty per cent failure rate). Other similarly assessed officers would have gone on to improve the staff quality. But it seems likely that few would have had Colin's wide experience, working as he had with so many divisions in the last year. His enthusiasm on the one day he had been out planning the divisional defence scheme suggest that he might have been good at it.

But his first letters on his return to the battery in early March are lyrical in their contentment as he catches up with his young officers and settles back in. *'The battery is at present in action, but a long way back in reserve positions*[285]*,'* but *'yesterday morning, I was up at 5.30 am and Pilling and I went up to build a gun pit close up for a special purpose. We put in four good hours of work, and got back here about half past eleven as the clearing mist stopped us working.'*

He gave his mother a situation report. *'I'm up at the guns alone with Pilling at present. Pilcher is coming up tomorrow morning too, I hope, leaving Blackburn and Royle down at the wagon line. Wethered is away at a gas course for a week, but will be back shortly.*[286] The horses at the wagon

---

285 The brigade was still just south east of Ypres.

286 Captain Blackburn was now his second in command. Lieutenants Pilcher, Wethered and Pilling and Royle were his young subalterns. (Lieutenant Esson was on leave.) 2nd Lieutenant Royle was the son of a family friend, just out of school and Woolwich, whom Colin had met when on leave at Christmas. Colin had asked Colonel Lambarde to apply for him, and promised his family he would look after him.

line I thought were looking very well indeed, but we have a new institution at the brigade now, a horse master[287] has been posted to us. The colonel would have turned the fellow out if he hadn't been vouched for as being quite a good fellow. I rather fancy he doesn't like the way I'm doing things in the wagon line. However, he'll soon learn to leave 'A' Battery alone. I'll be polite as long as I can, but there's no sharing this battery with anybody else as long as I'm commanding it.'

Colonel Lambarde had already met 2nd Lieutenant Royle, Colin's protégé fresh from Woolwich. He kept him for a week as his 'orderly officer', and then passed him to Captain Blackburn for orientation at the wagon line. Colin took over and introduced him to life in the front line. *'Royle and I have been working very hard cleaning up our dugout which we found in a filthy state and under two inches of water.'*

Even in their reserve positions in early March, the line was not a safe place to be. *'The Bosche have been somewhat noisy all day,'* and *'two nights ago, it was a little warm.[288] I was up with Pilling who positively revelled in it.'* Almost the same day in another battery in the brigade, *'a couple of officers got hit by the same shell, neither of them badly hit. One was no loss, but the other was rather a useful subaltern.'*

His own new subalterns were not only useful, but very young. Pilling and Pilcher *'have been having a great afternoon, shooting at a bottle that they threw into the moat of a ruined farm. They have used up all their revolver ammunition and have been scheming all evening how they can get a further supply out of the Quarter Master Sergeant who is a great miser of it – which is a good thing as goodness knows what they wouldn't be doing if they had an unlimited supply. We want some bricks to build a fireplace down at the mess, and they are now thinking of building a raft to float the bricks*

---

287 Corps Horse-masters were introduced after the loss of horses in early 1917. Colin had enjoyed the company of Colonel Ellewes of IX corps the year before. (page 224) Even at the time, tact was deemed a most necessary attribute to those allocated to active units. Ref: The Horse and the War by Captain Sidney Galtrey. 288 *'Warm'* is no more than seriously dangerous. *'Hot'* and *'very hot'* are the next stages up!

across the moat to the road, instead of carrying them 30 yards over the bridge. Probably the raft will take a week to make, so I have stipulated for the bricks by tomorrow, by the bridge if necessary. They are like a couple of schoolboys home for the holidays.'

He checked up on the mess. *'The tea pot has arrived and will do splendidly. One will grow quite fond of its unnatural shape in time and it holds a lot of tea which is what is wanted at present.'* He had never had so many junior officers. *'Captain Blackburn and I have a little cubicle each off the mess, and the four youngsters live in a hut next door. Everyone has gone to bed now. We were up pretty early this morning.'*

He was home. *'Just had a wire from Pilcher up at the guns that all is well with him. I'm very relieved as there was a lot of shooting up his way this morning. I hate being so far away from them, especially now when rumours are going round of Bosche attacks. I am going to move up closer to the guns tomorrow, and am taking Royle up with me. They're such children though, it seems a shame to have them out here.'*

'My regular round of walking amounts to close on 15 miles a day in the salient, I should think.' He was back in his element, if not entirely happy. He was home.

And in truth, once he had got his battery organised, and settled to the mild boredom of defensive duties, he realised he was not happy. Everybody was on edge, with a major German offensive already starting in the south and another expected against the British; who knew where? And Colonel Lambarde was asserting firmer control on his brigade, not now distracted by battle command. On the 16th March, *'the colonel came to inspect the teams that came to fetch my guns this morning. He is never pleasant in the early morning, and I have rather developed a silent period for the early hours too, copied from him I suppose, so the inspection was fraught with tension all through. He has no right to come round and inspect teams that had to harness up and start out before daylight, with consequent lack of attention to details which are of course evident to a close inspection.'* He had every right.

So Colin, who had taken on so much brigade duty over the last months, now had less responsibility than he was used to. With good junior officers at his disposal he had less to do. He was a bit confused too. After all he was only a few years older than the boys who were his subalterns. Their youthful high spirits reminded him of what he had missed, of what he had lost. He found no pleasure in shooting at bottles. There was work to be done, Germans to kill. That was serious business, and to do it efficiently, he had to be terse in the mornings. That was rather a sad thought.

CHAPTER FIFTEEN

1918 The Spring Offensive

'A' Battery, 113th Army Brigade

'We can fight a defensive battle better than anybody in the world.'

By the early spring of 1918, the strategic situation had completely changed. The German armies released from the Russian Front started to arrive on the Western Front. For a brief window, before the Americans arrived, the Germans had massive numerical superiority. An offensive was inevitable.

Defensive tactics had changed. Artillery was now so dominant that any infantry in front line trenches quickly became casualties. So both sides had adopted a policy of defence in depth, with very lightly manned front trenches and linked strong points for several miles back, held by the majority of the available infantry. In defence, artillery batteries were split up and the guns placed individually. *'We are all manning single guns used for a special purpose,'* Colin says on the 17th March. But in many areas both infantry and artillery positions were incomplete or poorly sited.

So like all the army, they were kept busy, improving the defences for the inevitable hammer blow. *'I took 20 men to manhandle a gun 800 yards over bad shell hole country in the dark and pouring rain. Just as we got to the gun, the Bosche put a box barrage all round us, quite unintentionally as he couldn't have seen us. But it was damned uncomfortable for a bit, and no joke with 20 of my best men all together. We did it in one and a quarter hours. One or two Bosche machine guns and 77[289] batteries egged the men on most successfully, but all the same it was quite a feat, especially as at one place, the*

---

289 The 7.7 cm Feldkanone 16 (7.7 cm FK 16) was the main German field gun.

wretched thing slipped off a couple of planks and subsided into a trench with the muzzle holding it up on one side and the trail at the other.'

And a few days later, *'I had rather a long day of it yesterday, getting up at 5.30 am. Our lorry didn't turn up, so I got on a bicycle, and half an hour's strenuous exercise got me to the park. I found our lorry had looked for us in the wrong place, and the driver was having his breakfast. I had him out of that park breakfastless quicker than he was accustomed to be moved, and we started off from our wagon line two hours late. I made him drive to within two thousand yards of the Bosche line. The lorry driver won't forget it in a hurry. The Germans shelled the spot, only 60 seconds after he got turned round, and the last sight we caught of our conveyance was a great cloud of dust. It's a terrible rough road too. Our guns are spread over a big area, and we had a long tramp before I had posted all the detachments. It was a hot day too.*

I arrived back at the wagon line about 4 pm to find the colonel carrying out an inspection of the horses in an infernal bad temper. Probably my sergeant major had upset him. He is a jolly sight too talkative sometimes. We were a pair, as I was tired and out of sorts, never having recovered from the lorry being late. The colonel and I snapped for about an hour. The real grouse is he's dead against clipping horses, and six weeks ago while I was commanding the brigade, we had an epidemic of mange[290], and I clipped a whole section right out to stamp it out. The sight of those clipped out horses upset him. They are wonderfully fit considering they had to be clipped out at a bad time, and some Major General from the cavalry came round the day before yesterday and was

---

290 Mange (From 1914 field service pocket book). *'Symptoms are marked skin irritation. Horse rubs himself against any available object. Hair comes off in patches and skin becomes thickened. Prevent spread by obtaining veterinarian aid without delay. Very contagious. Isolate affected and suspicious cases with their equipment. Men may carry infection in their clothing. Disinfect all stables, utensils, harness. Treat by clipping, burn clippings, dress all over with a mixture of paraffin and soap in 1 gallon of water. Regular exercise and dress immediately on return every third day. Mange is contagious to man; suspect any rash.'*

Mange is caused by several different mites whose life-cycles are confined to the horse. By 1917, the use of sulphide dips to treat the horses was routine. There was debate on the best timing of routine clipping, which allowed early diagnosis of a winter disease, but exposed the animal to the cold if done too early in the year.

very pleased with them. Their coats are coming on well, aided by two rugs a horse, and one or two other method's not altogether sound from a condition point of view, but eminently satisfactory from the 'eyewash' point of view. One must take a few risks when there is a reputation at stake.' Presumably the colonel begged to differ. They had argued about this before.

But Colin was still the right hand man. A few days later, *'I am feeling rather sleepy as the colonel had me up at 6 am to walk down with him to a forward post one is not supposed to go to in day time.'* Such rules were made to be broken.

And there was another reason why he was more sleepy than usual. *'I had a bad night with the mice in this wretched dugout last night. They crawl and romp over my face at night and there seems absolutely no way of driving them away. I caught one this morning though. The wretch had made its bed in the lining of my steel helmet. When I put my helmet on, there was an unaccustomed bump, so I moved it round, and was rewarded by having my hair pulled quite violently. I took it off and the little brute's tail was sticking out under the lining. Gunner Nichol dealt with it for me.'*

But more serious warfare was now afoot. As they had all been expecting, the main German Spring Offensive started. They struck in the south, on the 21st March, heading straight for Paris. Outnumbering the allies three or four to one, the German attacks resulted in unprecedented territorial gains as the British and French lines buckled alarmingly. They advanced 40 miles.

'Things have been happening pretty quickly down south and here we are' on the 28th, *'sitting on our thumbs doing peace warfare. However I expect we shall have our turn presently. Pretty serious business and hard to tell how it is going to end.*

According to today's report, the Bosche have taken 34000 prisoners[291] and 600 guns. It is a different class of British Army facing him now to what it was in 1914 and he has had any amount of recent training in manoeuvre and

---

291 21,000 at this stage according to military history online.

open warfare[292]*. Funnily enough, our staff still seem happy and optimistic. They say it is only cut up ground they have taken back, and that we are bound to hold them. But it looks pretty black for Paris to me.'*

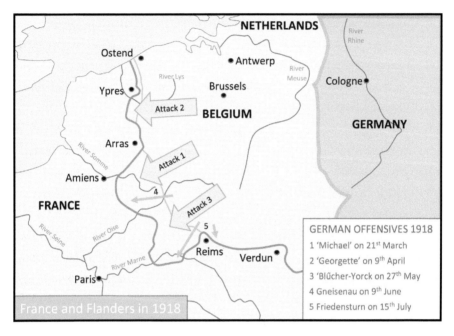

The German Spring Offensives of 1918

And the next day, *'Yes, the news from down south is certainly disquieting to put it very mildly. I think we shall do remarkably well if we can keep them out of Amiens, and that is a lot to hope for. The German staff work and organisation is amazing. They apparently at one place threw about 25 divisions at us, which got badly hammered; and two days after that threw sixty divisions in, which of course broke us.'*[293]

---

292 Nearly 50 divisions were available to the Germans following the end of the war on their eastern front with Russia. They used only a short, but very heavy artillery bombardment prior to the attack to achieve surprise and then storm troopers advanced through the defences to disrupt the artillery and headquarters, leaving the strong points in the British line to be mopped up behind them. It was an effective tactic.

293 The Germans attacked with 58 divisions from three armies against the 16 British divisions of the 5th army under General Gough (of Passchendaele fame).

The line did hold, but only just! It was a very scary time. *'There seems to be a pause down south, but I expect they are bringing up their reserves and will make several more colossal thrusts before we are done with them.'*

The 113th Brigade redoubled their efforts to strengthen their positions in the line east of Ypres. *'We have been dreadfully busy these last few days. This morning we were up for breakfast at half past six. We shifted two guns over to fresh positions until half past eleven, had lunch at 12, got the wires laid out at 1 pm, then I went up to the observation post to register at 2, and got back at half past five. I had a lot of orders to work through until dinner at 8 pm which should have been at 7.30 pm. It is now 9 pm and I'm going straight to bed when I've finished this.'*

But Colin was desperate for proper action and frustrated by the boring routine of defensive duties. He wanted to move to where the action was, down south. He wasn't really thinking straight. But the colonel knew his Colin!

'The colonel has been very trying lately, and I went prepared to have an appalling row with him, and to apply to be sent to a battery down south requiring a commander. But when I mildly made several requests about being excused liaison duties, that I didn't think he would grant, he agreed with everything and let me off them all. So I am not going south today.'

Nobody knew where the next assault would be and Colonel Lambarde wanted his best man with him, if and when it fell on them. Only two days later on the 1st April, he let Colin off going to what he regarded as a frivolous gymkhana. *'The colonel asked me to stay and look after the brigade while he was away at a horseshow.'*

A second German offensive was launched on the 9th April as the first ground to a halt. *'There are rumours tonight of doings fairly close to us, and there is a fair row on, but we cannot tell its extent, and have not yet been enlightened.'* The attack was just eight miles south of Ypres. Again surprise and massive numerical superiority lead to a near breakthrough. The first attack had targeted Paris, which might have won the war; the second targeted the Channel ports which again might be decisive.

The situation again became critical. On the 11th April, General Haig issued a general order, *'There is no course open to us but to* fight it out! Every position must be held to the last man; there must be no retirement. With our backs to the wall, believing in the justice of our cause, each one of us must fight on to the end'. Many infantry units did just that and whole battalions were virtually annihilated.

Reinforcements were urgently needed and Colin's 113th Brigade was briefed for a swift move south.[294] He did not expect to survive the experience. *'We have got to hold these wretched Bosche but it will probably take our last man.'* On the 12th, *'The colonel sent for me at 9 am and we went off in a car to reconnoitre positions in an area about 8 miles south of here. We knew that country well.'* They chose positions west of Bailleul, just outside Meteren, on the main road to Dunkirk and the Channel Ports, ten miles back from the original front line.

The next day *'at 7 am we reported as ordered, moved to our positions and set up for action,'* moving forward again at 10 pm that night, so that on the 14th *'we were in action in our new positions at dawn.'* See map overleaf.

The British army was in a desperate state that day, fighting to save Bailleul, but German patrols had leaked through the defence. *'When we came in, we landed up behind the most nondescript infantry[295] you can imagine. Army clerks, cooks, servants, army school personnel and labour battalions with rifles hurriedly thrust on them. They were not much use and a Bosche patrol made them run. There wasn't a gun behind them and they couldn't get in touch with anybody, right or left. They nearly wept on the neck of the first gunner officer that went up to see where they were. We are about the only artillery here.'* Every possible man had been mobilised.

---

294 The attack fell first on General Horne's First Army. On his left, General Plumer's Second Army held Ypres and his right flank came under attack the next day. On the 12th, General Horne's left flank, held by XV corps, with the 33rd division in reserve, was transferred to General Plumer. The 113th brigade was moved to support the 33rd division but arrived in position before it had advanced to the new front line. The situation was fluid and confused, and many units up to divisional level were fighting on their own initiative.

295 Probably units of the French 133rd division, who had mobilised every man to face the German patrols who had penetrated the British lines around Bailleul.

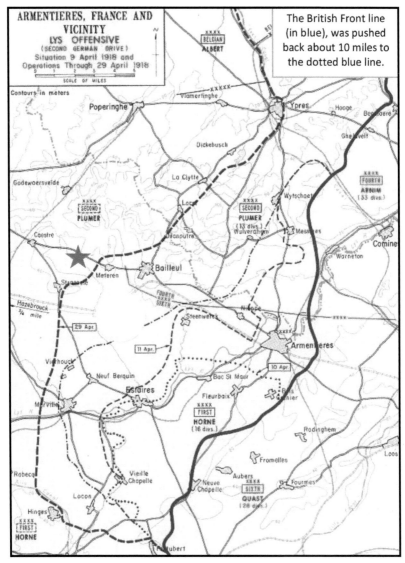

The 113th brigade (starred) straddled the main road from Bailleul to Coestre

'The Bosche were taking liberties that first day and paid for them. We let about 150 come over 500 yards of open country and collect behind a rise. We let them have it, and then they had to cross 500 yards back again. Our shrapnel is wonderful stuff when you get the blighters in the open. It was very pleasant shooting at the Bosche before his guns came up.'

Looking west from the first low ridge out of Meteren. Observation was very good from the far ridge. Flêtre (the hamlet on the right) is at the top of the hill out of Meteren heading towards Coestre.

The next evening, the 15th, *'we are now in very nice country, almost open warfare. The terribly sad part of it is the devastating of such nice country which is bound to result from the Bosch advance. We have a farmhouse to live in at present, but I don't suppose it will last very long when things get going again.'* And that same evening, the brigade came firmly under the orders of the 33rd Division whose infantry slotted in in front of them during the course of the night. The next day was decisive, as the British struggled to form a defensible line.

'We had a fairly good day today, saw Bosche all right. We've been scrapping all day with them and I hope accounted for a few. I think we did to tell you the truth. It's fine to see the blighters at the end of our guns.' Colin *'had found a convenient farm house for an observation post, saw Bosche and shot at them,'* spending *'most of the day watching them collecting into parties in lanes where they thought they could not be seen, and then dropping a perfect hail of about 100 shells onto them in a minutes burst of fire. I had eight such targets during the day. The guns shot splendidly too, and never once let me down over being slow.'*

A neighbouring farmhouse on the same ridge was briefly captured by the Germans[296] as they pressed home their assault, and the infantry brigade in front of them was under considerable

---

296 'The British Campaign in France and Flanders' Vol 5. Sir Arthur Conan Doyle.

pressure. *'Our infantry brigadier, as jumpy as blazes, came to find a refuge in our farm, having been shelled out of his.'*

'But we made the Bosche, who I think were under the impression that they were going to advance, dig themselves in like fury, and once they get dug in, tired infantry are very hard to move forward again. So we have arrested their advance, anyway over the tract of country we can see from the post. I think that with the troops that have now come up, we ought to hold them.[297]

---

297 General Ludendorff in his Spring Offensive for the Germans got the tactics right. He used storm troopers, who were ordered to keep moving forward, ignoring strong points which were mopped up by those behind, all the more easily (though they lost heavily in so doing) because the leading troops disrupted both command posts and the supporting artillery further back behind the British lines. But he got the strategy wrong.

He was looking for a breakthrough. He failed to heed the lessons of previous campaigns. With defence so dominant over offence, it was virtually impossible. A successful breakthrough had first to neutralise defence in depth on a wide enough front to avoid creating a salient. The advancing infantry had to be supplied, and the artillery moved forward, at the same time as a rotation of fresh infantry was being brought up for the third day to take up the ongoing offensive, and of course the wounded moved back. This was all much easier said than done, over devastated ground with no surviving roads and no cover of any sort. With every delay in this re-supply and reinforcement process, the chances of success diminished. With only horse-drawn transport feasible over damaged supply routes, delays were inevitable. The enemy were given time to move reinforcements on undamaged roads from further up the line to restore the status quo. The only way such a battle could be won was if the enemy sustained a terminal collapse in morale.

So as Ludendorff discovered, and despite the impressive territorial gains he made, his hammer blow assaults carried within themselves the seeds of their own failure. The best German infantry suffered the greatest casualties, their supply lines lengthened over war ravaged ground, the artillery did not keep up with the infantry, and when the German forward troops, who could not be re-supplied, captured the British supply dumps they stopped to gorge themselves. They advanced tens of miles and gave the allied armies a very nasty shock. But their will to fight was sustained and that was enough. Given that morale did not collapse, the situation seemed worse than it actually was. The lines were held and it was German morale, weakened by heavy losses, increasing shortages and unrest at home that was the more fragile.

You were right. Bailleul has gone, and I expect him to try hard for Mount Kemmel[298], which would give him a most extensive observation. However we hope we may defend that. Four days ago, we were about the only artillery here, and things were quite like the old days, but things have stiffened up somewhat now.' The German infantry were up in force, but now facing massed artillery. Yet again defence proved easier than offence.

By the 18th, *'the Bosche here are at a temporary standstill, I suppose until they can bring up their heavier guns.'* And the temporary standstill became a more permanent one. *'Your letter of the 14th and a paper of the 15th are the first news of the outer world that we have had for four days. We learn that we have been fighting desperately in our quarter of the globe, and that a glorious resistance is being offered to the Bosche. It is all most interesting.'*

Like at Second Ypres in 1915, the good positions they took up ensured defensive success. The brigade got to the right place just in time. Probably fortuitously, there was no opportunity for the staff to choose exact positions, or to otherwise interfere. Colonel Lambarde of the artillery had been ordered to select the battleground for the infantry falling back, and for the infantry coming up. He chose a defensible ridge with good forward observation and good fields of fire. He put Colin and his battery astride the main road at the point of maximum danger, and told him to liaise with any infantry officers he could find, or who could find him. And he left him to it with total confidence. All Colin had to do was fire at any enemy units he saw threatening the slowly stiffening line in front of him.

---

298 Mount Kemmel was an area of high ground about five miles north east of their position, close to Loker where the brigade had been posted during the battle of Messines Ridge. It was of considerable local tactical importance since it dominated the land between Meteren and Ypres. See maps page 66 and 257.

18-pounder battery in action near Meteren on April 13, 1918

The key to success was forward control of the battlefield, well sited guns firing opportunistically at what they could see of the enemy and his intentions. Artillery and infantry worked together. The brigadier sought out his artillery support, and rallied his men round it. 'Jumpy' or not, he had done the job.

But for now congratulations were in order. The 33rd Division were in no doubt how much they owed to the artillery in choosing their battlefield and supporting their infantry line.

Colin explained. The infantry brigadier *'was apparently so overcome,'* on the 16th, *'at finding the Bosche being shot at, (sort of implying that batteries are quite remarkable when they shoot on targets which they can see), that he passed some remark to the divisional artillery which called forth an enquiring telegram.'*

The enquiring telegram came the next day to Colonel Lambarde from General Mayne of the 19th Infantry Brigade who was *'very congratulatory of the artillery work of the brigade and especially of an officer who was observing from the same observation post as himself. The officer was a battery commander.'*

Colonel Lambarde immediately scribbled a note to Colin, '*I have just received the enclosed message. I have let them know it was you.*' So he had won his second Military Cross, 'for conspicuous gallantry and devotion to duty. Under heavy fire he established close liaison with the infantry whom he was supporting and by continually engaging targets that were harassing them, he materially assisted them to resist all attempts of the enemy to advance.' He never mentioned he had been '*getting it hot*'!

Colonel Lambarde told Colin's mother a month or two later, '*I am very pleased about it. I forwarded the recommendation when we had the scrap at Meteren, on which day Colin did some wonderful good work, in his usual quiet way.*' Even Major General Pinney of the 33rd Division sent him a personal note of thanks and congratulations.

Four other officers of the brigade got honours that day. And when the general in charge of the divisional artillery was away at the end of April, it was Colonel Lambarde who stood in for him, leaving Colin to command the brigade for a week or two.

But at the time it seemed merely a lull in the storm. '*We (Pilcher and I) have been up in the observation post all day chivvying about detached parties of the enemy who were silly enough to come within view or range. It was quite amusing, but not up to the excitement of a few days ago.*' Colin had time to assess the tactical situation. '*I sincerely hope we are going to hold the Bosche here, so as to be able to fairly hammer him out of the salient[299] he has made for himself as soon as our turn comes.*'

And the battery was able to relax slightly. '*I've just sent Blackburn away to look for lines for our horses a bit further back than this. They have been right up close to the guns till now[300], in case of trouble, and I'm rather frightened of getting*

---

299 For once, it was the Germans, who found themselves in a salient created by an advance, with the British on the high ground at Meteren and Kemmel.
300 As had the horses for all batteries. They had half expected a further withdrawal.

a lot of them knocked out.' And they had a roof over their heads. *'We are pretty comfortable here, but our farm house unfortunately is very ramshackle with a thatch roof which will burn like blazes. It cannot last long.'* It didn't.

On the 25th April, the Germans did, as expected, attack Kemmel. *'I started a letter to you yesterday but it never got finished. The notebook got in the way of a 15cm German shell, so that is the end of that letter.'* *'Unfortunately 200 cigarettes 'went west' as the soldiers say, along with the afore-mentioned notebook and letter. Those cigars too, now I come to think of it, have gone. Situation gets worse and worse!'*

They were on the edge of the bombardment which preceded the German assault on Kemmel, just north of them. *'We are all rather anxious to know what has happened up Kemmel way. One cannot help feeling that it must be his last effort. There is, and has been, the deuce of a battle raging these last two days.'[301]*

A bit more chat and he finishes the letter. *'Incidentally our beautiful farm house mess went at the same time as the notebook and now we are destitute of civilised dwellings again.'* The German shell had taken out their whole billet. *'In a way it is a relief to have had the business settled. It served us right for sticking to the farm for so long.'*

It was now an artillery battle, though more infantry attacks were expected. *'The battle is a pretty ding dong one at present. We were busy yesterday as they put a very unfair concentration of artillery onto our battery position[302], and I decided to make things a bit stronger. We were up working*

---

301 Mount Kemmel was indeed lost in this battle, but the German losses were very heavy. And the psychology had changed. *'There has been a lull these last few days since the loss of Kemmel, so wonderfully turned into a victory by all the accounts in the papers I see. It's an extraordinary thing, but it seems to have put up the morale of our troops no end.'* Another possible breakthrough had been averted. The capture of another few yards of front line was not regarded as significant, despite the local tactical importance of the high ground lost. *'The loss of Kemmel seemed to buck everyone up in the most extraordinary fashion. Personally I should have called it rather a disaster.'*
302 *'I hope to goodness that we shall not have to move, as it would mean the Bosche getting the high ground which we should have great difficulty in retaking.'* By taking the high ground at Kemmel, the Germans had flattened the salient.

until midnight and at the same time doing a fair amount of shooting. I'm feeling sleepy now, but I will probably go up to the observation post this evening to see if we cannot get a little of our own back.' 'Royle was at liaison with the infantry and Pilcher at the observation post when they dosed us yesterday and I haven't liked to leave the position in case they repeat the performance.'

A few days later, *'there was great excitement this morning. A Bosche aeroplane landed close to the battery, the pilot had been hit in the thigh by one of our airmen. Royle and Pilcher and a lot of the men had a tremendous race across to get to him before he could burn his machine, but he couldn't get out because of his injury and they got everything intact.'*[303]

'I had two journeys up to the guns yesterday, as the colonel called us up in the afternoon to see about a little show last night for which we had to do a good deal of shooting, and then I went up with a lot of ammunition after dark.'

Colin had not expected to survive their move to the eye of the storm. But even he began to believe the Germans had shot their bolt. The British casualties in the ongoing battle had been enormous with whole battalions and artillery brigades being virtually annihilated.[304] But the British line was now bolstered with French reinforcements. *'The optimism of our French allies is extraordinary in these parts, they seem perfectly confident the Bosche is beat, and that it is only a question of time before he is a ready prey for us all. I hope I see the last stage of it.'* This was written on the 29th April 1918. He had never dared write such a sentiment before, in nearly a thousand letters.

'We still hang on to our same spot and I suppose we shall stay here until

---

303 Air power was now a significant factor in war. The brigade had suffered 3 killed and 9 wounded when two 320 pound bombs were dropped on their wagon lines in February. From the 20th to 27th April, the brigade diary reports *'German planes very active, all over the front, flying very low over back areas.'* A month later on the 31st May, *'bombing all night is still kept up',* but by the 23rd June, *'We seem to have a very large number of planes about and it is now unusual to see an enemy plane except at dawn or late in the evening.'*

304 Casualty estimates for the battle vary wildly depending on how they are calculated, but both sides lost at least 80,000 men just in this second phase of the German Spring Offensive, the battle of Lys.

the Bosche turns us out. The colonel as well as commanding his own brigade, now commands a group consisting of three brigades including ours. He is highly pleased with life in consequence. My battery position is very close to his headquarters[305], and he thinks my firing draws retaliation of which he has been receiving a portion. He thinks I ought to move my battery.'

Colin argued his case. The men and the guns were dug in, and 'it is the best position here, as I can cover all the ground in front of me without having to move my guns. I have worked the men terribly hard to build good dugouts and to get them secure. To keep our position hidden, we have uprooted the whole of a growing wheat field. I had to keep the men hard at it to get it finished in one sitting. It would never have done to have left the job half done for the Bosch to photograph from the air.' The men probably complained at the work, because he added, 'I'm all for keeping them at it if it is going to keep them alive.'

He was given a reprieve from moving. But as second in command of the brigade, and by far the senior battery commander[306], he had a lot of responsibility. Among other things, his fluent French meant he had to do most of the liaison work with them. 'The area round here is simply packed with troops, French and ours, and there does not look as though there is going to be any repose.[307] We are unfortunately in the French

---

305 Colonel Lambarde had briefly commanded 33rd divisional artillery, but on the 3rd May he 'came back to Headquarters to command his group of three Brigades from there, so I had no further need to stay there, for which I was very thankful.' Colin did not like dealing with the staff. 'The divisional staff for the most part are good, but not allowed to do anything on their own.'

306 The brigade had lost four more officers, including Major Deacon of 'C' battery, wounded yet again, this time with a broken leg. He had been wounded at Passchendaele twice. 'I have to tackle the Colonel on my own over everything. I get absolutely no support from the other battery commanders,' says Colin.

307 They were never under the command of the French, but from April 25th, when the 33rd division left, they were under four different divisions in a month, as XV corps, of Plumer's Second Army sorted itself out. Colin would probably not have minded being under the French. 'We have seen a lot of the French lately and it always makes me dissatisfied when one compares the staff work of the two.'

area and may be ordered out of our wagon lines any minute;' this on the 3rd May. Reinforcements flooded in and the brigade cooperated. *'The French on our left advanced their line; the group put down a barrage to cover the flank.'*

But sometimes the battle was not with the enemy. Access to fresh milk in a billeting area was highly prized. *'I was sitting in our billet down at the wagon line, when a French non-commissioned officer came up to the farm and I heard him explaining to the owner how he had been nearly murdered by about 25 British soldiers. The captain of 'B' battery told me what had happened. The Frenchmen had without asking just walked in and bagged our cows. They had been spotted by a gunner just as they were getting away with them. The battery gunners at once gave chase after the Frenchmen whom they outnumbered 10 to 1 and rescued the cows. The Frenchmen when they heard 'B' battery's howling mob of gunners descending on them apparently thought their last hour had come. Their non-commissioned officer came to me, as nobody in 'B' battery could speak French. He asked me to allow him to fetch the cows that we have been keeping, as he had orders to take all livestock back to a safe area. I told him I would like to keep one for each battery which we would return to him directly we moved. I don't think the Frenchmen will again attempt to take things without asking first. They were pretty well frightened out of their lives.'*

Colin's fluent French had sorted what could have become a nasty diplomatic incident, but relations were generally good. *'Some more French soldiers have come back to this billet now, infantry this time, I think. However they turned up long before I was up this morning and seem to be pretty well settled in already. They don't take long making themselves comfortable.'* A few weeks later, *'the French officer who has been sharing the field with us as a billet came in to say goodbye, and we sat discussing our respective method of shooting guns until I don't know what hour.'*

But the same day that he had expressed the thought he might survive the war, *'I think I must have eaten something which has very much disagreed with me. I have horrible diarrhoea and have been pretty sick on and off for the last 24 hours. I ate a bit of toast this evening, first bite since lunch yesterday.'* He was quite unwell during the first week of May. *'The colonel calls it gastric influenza, though the doctor has yet to give it a name'.* He had *'leakage from both ends'*, a high fever, a bad cough and was in bed for several days. He still felt *'weak as a child'* a week later. [308]

It was a highly infectious illness. *'I now have two subalterns down with this flu, and also a good many of the men, which makes it very hard for the only two subalterns, who are left up at the gun line.' 'It is pretty virulent while it lasts and fairly knocks one up, the chief trouble being the lack of interest one has in food. Most of us who have had it did not touch food for 36 hours, but once the fever subsides one gets well very quickly. Several of the men had temperatures as high as 105.' 'Thank goodness we do not seem to get it twice over, in which way it is different from trench fever[309]'.*

He still felt queasy into the second week of May. *'I'm still down at the wagon line though I have been up to see them at the guns every other day. The battery is not exactly tired, but they have got terribly stale and it is rather disquieting. Blackburn has been just a little hard with them down here. They are like a lot of petulant children and want a good deal of tactful handling.' 'I sent Blackburn up to the guns.'*

And one of his subalterns was also causing trouble. *'I bought Royle down here to the wagon line for a couple of days. I'm afraid he must be rather spoilt by his people. I have to find fault and check his over keenness a good deal. It is a pity. He is an extraordinary nice lad, but confoundedly conceited and self-opinionated, and has not gained sufficient experience to*

---

308 This was the flu that caused the lethal outbreak in 1919 which killed millions in the aftermath of the War. Nobody knows why it was a fairly mild illness in 1918 and such a killer on its return the following year. But for those who had it in 1918, it was their flu jab. They were safe in 1919.

309 Trench fever was, and is, an infectious disease characterized by sudden onset, fever, headache, aching joints and skin sores. It is transmitted from one person to another by body lice infected with a bacterium, *Rochalimaea* (formerly *Rickettsia*) *quintana*. The fever may be relapsing at intervals of four to five days. Most people recover, but about one person in 20 becomes a carrier and can infect a new louse if bitten. It was a major medical problem during World War I. The control of body lice is the chief means of prevention.

keep his mouth shut. It is rather hard being told how things can be done by a lad just out from school. I don't usually bother with them, life being too short, I just get rid of them. But I'm afraid I shall have to play the father over him, and see if I cannot keep him quiet. I don't mind how much he talks as long as he does what I ask quickly. He is rather apt to upset the others (though I think they like him) which is the last thing I can have.'

It seems that his bumptious young officer did listen to Colin because a few weeks later, *'Royle is down with the flu pretty badly now and it will probably leave him a bit weak. I don't think it is anything for Mrs Royle to worry about. He is really an extraordinarily nice fellow, below his conceit, and very willing indeed, always offering to do things and I would be sorry to lose him in spite of what I wrote the other day.'*[310]

It was not quiet in their sector. There was 'heavy gas shelling of back areas at night,' and 'the usual harassing fire night and day,' according to the brigade diary on the 12th May. Colin himself was not feeling his best. *'Things are looking up since that wretched flu has subsided. But the battery is tired with continual work, and the worst culprit of the lot is myself. The number of things I leave undone that should be done sickens me these days. I suppose in a way it is staleness but there is really no excuse for it.*[311]*'*

He was not alone in feeling tired. *"I hear the flu is getting to London now. The disease is common throughout the whole district here and I don't think the Germans are free from it. If reports are true, they have got it pretty badly. It is, I think, delaying their attack which ought to have taken place three days ago. They are all ready for one.'*

---

310 Royle was an intelligent boy, and got the message very quickly. He represented Britain in the 1924 Olympics, had a successful business career and chaired the NAAFI through the second war. He finished life as Sir Lancelot Royle. He and Colin remained lifelong friends.

311 There was every excuse for his *'staleness'*. Nowadays post-viral syndrome is well recognised – six weeks of muscle weakness and tiredness after a viral infection, particularly likely to be severe in combination with post-traumatic stress. It would not have been at all surprising if Colin had collapsed under the strain at this stage. Many would have done.

The significance of the flu should not be underestimated. It was not till mid-June that Colin was able to write *'I think we are getting gradually over our bouts of flu. Somerville Smith and Pownall are both down with it, but Wethered is almost recovered and Pilling totally recovered.* [312] *Some of the men are down, but not many of them now.'*

For the whole of May, a major German offensive was expected.[313] *'We are still in the same place, and waiting for the next Bosche offensive to come off as all the papers (and common sense really also) say it will.'* But they were relatively comfortable. *'This wrecked farmhouse we are living in leaks a bit, and the cellar collected water in a downpour last night. However it might have been very much worse and there is really little cause to grumble. This morning is a glorious morning, made especially nice and fresh by last night's rain.'*

A few days later on the 18ᵗʰ May, *'I started off up to the observation post early this morning and did quite a long shoot with the guns, and then went down to the wagon lines for the day and had a very busy time down there, teaming horses and allocating remounts to different sections etc. It's been a glorious boiling hot day too. It's now 11.15 pm The moon is very bright there is a continual humming in the air just now and for the last two hours, with great aerial bombings. They are laying their eggs pretty indiscriminately all over the place.'*

His mother mentions a big air raid on London, but he can cap the story. *'One of their wretched big aeroplanes[314] was over here the other night and made two huge craters with one ton bombs, happily doing no damage, except shattering most of the little remaining glass at the wagon*

---

312 The former were battery commanders. Wethered, Pilling and Royle were all subalterns. Captain Blackburn is the only officer who seems to avoid it.

313 Ludendorff blamed the disease for the failure of Germany's major spring offensives. It was a grievous business, he said, having to listen every morning to the chiefs of staff's recital of the number of influenza cases, and their complaints about the weakness of their troops. www.historynet.com

314 Probably a Gotha G IV or Gotha G V. These big German bombers were capable of bombing London and did so. According to www.militaryfactory.com, standard pay-load was a 660 lb bomb and 4 x 220 lb bombs.

line farm.' And if the Germans weren't dropping bombs, they were making their presence felt in other ways. On the 20th, *'I walked back from the wagon line in the evening after dinner. It was a beautiful evening, but rather spoilt by the Bosche, who shelled our back areas pretty heavily.'* And he disliked the hot still days – *'there's a good wind blowing today, which is a blessing these days of gas shelling. One wants plenty of wind to clear it away. The Germans are making a tremendous use of gas shells and it is beastly stuff too.'* *'Esson',* one of his subalterns, *'is down at the wagon line recovering from a slight dose of gas.'*

They were all on tenterhooks. *'We are still in the same place and waiting for the Bosche to make a move. Cigarettes are a great difficulty out here and have been received very regularly, but the supply by no means meets the demand.'*[315]

He was still in touch with Tyler, who *'came across one of our old 458 battery men and managed to send him up to my battery. I would like a few more of our old men here.'* But most of his other friends were dead or alienated. His mother was almost his sole correspondent.

He was tired, irritated by some of his daily tasks. *'The battery commanders have to send in useless intelligence reports on gun flashes. We are bothered to death about them by headquarters, and we know from the inaccuracy of our means of taking them that they are of absolutely no use to the survey companies who their own ops have established.'* He was still using only a telescope, compass and stop watch to try to pinpoint enemy batteries.[316]

And finally, on the 27th May, the German's long awaited offensive came. But it was well away from them on the Aisne, where he had

---

315 *'Would you please ask them to double the supply. The trouble is the turnover of money. I will have to pay you by cheque from battery funds, instead of using the cash to cash cheques for my officers as I have been doing up to date.'* Father's note in margin of letter – 'ordered 8000 Players 29/5/18.'

316 Survey companies had used aerial photography, flash and smoke puff triangulation, and sophisticated microphone sound analysis to pinpoint enemy formations since late 1916. Front line observations were much less accurate.

been in 1914.[317] And as soon as the offensive on the Aisne started, Colin started to relax. The brigade had been continuously in the line since the 9th December, with the exception of seven days in March, and his 'A' battery had been in action even then. But there was still no sign of the brigade moving from its position at Meteren. Colonel Lambarde was in no mood to ask the army for their promised rest while there was any possibility of a further German offensive in their sector.[318] And it was still half expected by the British high command.

So Colin's letters become mildly bolshie. He and Pownall, who commanded 'B' battery went off for a day on the 2nd June to Dunkirk where we *'seemed to be about the only two English people in the town. We made straight for the sea after doing a little shopping, and just lazed on the sands until it was time for a splendid lunch, and then out to the beach again, to enjoy the sea breeze, and waited until it was time to get a cup of tea and catch the train back. All together it was a delightful day.'*[319]

Colonel Lambarde kept a baleful eye on them both to stop them repeating the performance. *'If possible we'll sneak off to Dunkirk again,*

---

317 The Third Battle of the Aisne followed precisely the same path as the two previous assaults. A promising early breakthrough, considerable territorial gains, heavy casualties on both sides, and then supply problems for the Germans as the attack got bogged down on the third and fourth days. And it failed to force the British to redeploy further south and thus weaken their northern sectors, where Ludendorff wanted to attack again. The Americans were by now providing the extra men needed to reinforce the lines.

318 *'The Colonel is dead against our having any rest, and always finds an excuse for not letting us out. '* Colonel Lambarde was in command of three brigades. His other two brigades came from the division currently covering their area. Thus on the 7th May, the 1st Australian division left and their artillery brigades were relieved by those of the 9th division. On the 27th May, the 9th divisional artillery relieved the 30th divisional artillery. The 113th brigade however remained and was still in place at the end of June. An Army Brigade colonel could not be seen to admit weakness and kept his brigade in, whereas a divisional brigadier would very likely have recognised the problem and ordered rest.

319 It sounds a pretty boring day, but this was a letter to his mother.

except the colonel won't like us gadding about,' and their plans were foiled when *'the colonel seems bent on having us up back at our guns at the slightest sign of anything happening. I don't mean on the part of the Bosche – I mean on our own part.'*

But he managed to slip away alone on the 9th June to see the Antoine girls, who were fairly local. He does not record what the colonel thought of that.

His travails at the brigade constantly reminded him that he was alone of his generation. *'At present I have to tackle the colonel on my own over everything. I get absolutely no support from the others, whereas when Major Osborne and Major Bolitho were here we were a pretty tough combine.'*

Colin may have been edgy, and worried about his men and about the state of his battery, *'we are terribly stale,'* but that June was warm and sunny. *'Well here's the 1st of July and a real scorcher it is too. Poor Daisy (our favourite cow) is terribly worried by the flies. She gives beautiful milk and the porridge and cream we have been living on for the last 9 weeks has been splendid.'*

The horses too were enjoying life. *'They are an absolute picture. This warm sun has made their coats shine like anything and they are getting a great deal of extra grass and clover and stuff that we cut from the forward areas. We are having glorious weather all this time.'*

But it was all a bit of an anti-climax. *'Things remain the same here. I cannot quite make out what the Bosch are playing at. He is certainly giving the Americans plenty of time to get over here. We have all sorts of wild rumours to account for his quietness, but he cannot possibly do other than strike here again I should think.*

If he doesn't strike soon, I expect we shall be doing something to him. They must see that America is going to be right in this business now, and the yanks are a splendid lot, the trouble is to get behind their talk though. I think they are very surprised (and full of admiration) at the type of British officer and soldier they are meeting, in this division anyway; it is a Scotch Division,' the 9th Scottish.

CHAPTER SIXTEEN

1918 The Hundred Day Offensive

'A' Battery, 113th Army Brigade

'The battery is in fine fettle, though we all hate this country.'

The failed German offensives were over by the end of July 1918 and at the last of them they actually lost ground when the French counterattacked on the Marne in early August. It was obvious now to the senior generals of both sides that Germany could not win the war. But could the allies? If the Germans could cause huge casualties resisting a new allied offensive, she might be able to negotiate a peace on reasonable terms. Another Somme or another Passchendaele would do it. And they had built a very strong back line, the Hindenburg Line, which they resolved to defend to the last man.

The allies had nothing to lose by waiting to gather their strength. The Americans were arriving in huge numbers and British troops were returning from other theatres of war. From their relatively strong position on the ridge above Meteren, the 113th Brigade was used purely defensively through May, and into the first half of June.

But as June progressed, local raids were being planned and on the 25th June, the British felt confident enough to give a little push. *'Infantry brigade (9th Division) and Australian Division on their right advanced their line about 300 yards. All objectives taken. 30 prisoners and 10 machine guns taken. About 50 enemy killed. Brigade fired on various targets including a short creeping barrage for 60 minutes,'* reports the brigade diary.[320] Another attack three days later yielded another 300

---

320 Short barrage, limited objectives, observed fire to support the infantry consolidating and holding their gains. Primarily a morale sapping exercise. This was just what should have been occurring in 1917.

prisoners. And the battery advanced too. *'We are pretty busy working on new positions. I have to superintend the work. I dare not leave it to any of the subalterns yet,'* Colin says the next day.[321]

But he was still very on edge. The lack of rest for his men had built up in his mind into a real issue. *'The colonel has got it into his head that we do not need a rest whereas we need one very badly indeed. It is leading to rather a lot of quarrelling and trouble. You may hear I'm up for a court martial soon. I have no objection to working hard and fighting hard endlessly if it is necessary, but see no reason why we should be the only brigade to go without rest.'* (See note 318) *'It is getting beyond a joke, and I see no other way out of the difficulty than to tell the colonel I don't feel I can conscientiously do all he wants done, and apply for an exchange to another brigade.'*

Colonel Lambarde, though still commanding his group, was taking back some of the work he had delegated to Colin when the fighting had been intense. He again started to reassert his control. Colin, predictably, did not like being told what to do when he had been managing perfectly well on his own for so long. And as he was wont to do, he let his resentment build up a good head of steam. The catalyst for an explosion soon came. He *'issued a very silly order last night giving the subaltern officers who are already pretty hard worked a lot of extra observation post duty which is quite unnecessary and an invention of his own. None of the other brigades are doing anything like the duties we are.'*

So on the 2nd July, *'Well, I've been and gone and done it. Have just had a real bust-up with Colonel Lambarde. The truth of it is we are both war weary, and damnably pig-headed. The colonel has lately been really making rather a fool of himself, and of course strongly objected to my airing these opinions to him. However I was forced to speak out too openly, which was really quite unwarranted. But to my way of thinking the job had to be done and I've done it. It's a tremendous relief to have got it off my chest. But leaving the battery will hit me pretty hard. I've got such a splendid lot of men, horses and officers and we usually get on pretty happily.'*

---

321 Colin's junior subalterns would never be allowed to choose and build positions.

Yet again, Colonel Lambarde knew his man. The next day, '*he came over and said we had soldiered much too long together to quarrel, which of course meant I had to apologise for what I had said, and the incident closes I hope.*' And four days later, '*Whether it is a hit back on the colonel's part I really do not know, but he has decided I need leave, and I won't contradict him.*'

The colonel worked fast. Colin was home within a week, so he missed two more local assaults when more ground was retaken towards Meteren and another 360 prisoners captured.

He did not get back to France for over two weeks, but when he did in late July, nothing much had changed. '*We were inspected by a general and had rather bad luck over the horses. It was fairly warm in the morning, and at the time the general should have turned up the horses were looking splendid. But a cold wind and a little rain came on and took all the shine out of them and that together with one or two little faux pas where things just went wrong instead of right gave the general rather a poor impression of the battery, which is a little sickening. However I ought to have looked more carefully into things myself.*'

As for Colonel Lambarde, he 'has *been rather seedy during my absence, having had an abscess in his face, which was very painful until it burst.*' So Colonel Lambarde measured up the situation, and, for both their sakes and with almost indecent haste, he shunted Colin off on a soft job on the 13th August.

'*I was shot off today to help equip Americans away behind the lines,*' he says in a postcard, enlarging later. '*I got a chit from the colonel telling me I was to meet a car at 10.30 am, and go off with my kit and servant. That car took me to 7th Corps headquarters, and my job is to find billets for, and kit out the artillery of an American Division, in a most delightful area near St Omer. I have been hard on the go these last four days and it is cut and dried now as far as my work is concerned. I am now waiting for the Americans to whom I have to give 3000 odd horses, and then help them fit their harness on, etc. A territorial colonel, who comes from Aberdeen, is running the arrangements for rations etc., but the organisation of the whole thing is left to me and I have rather enjoyed it. They have put a car at my disposal.*'

By the way, there are any amount of fine trout in a stream practically at our door. Bombs and soldiers' poaching has killed most of them, but I saw several fish rising yesterday.[322] I wonder if you could send out my old line and reel, and also that box of dry flies.' A week later, and his fishing rod had arrived. He thoroughly enjoyed his placement, waiting for the Americans. He fished *'practically every evening.'* And to make things even better, the brigade had at last moved into rest, and close by.

The Americans never did arrive, and he re-joined the brigade as it went back to war on the 6th September. And surprise, surprise, they were back at Ypres, not that there was anything left of the town itself. More specifically they were astride the Menin Road, looking down towards Hooge, not there was anything left of that either. Colin was not happy about it. *'Things are quiet here at present. We are absolutely sick of this northern part of the world. I wish we could get down to where there is something happening.'*

General Ferdinand Foch, a Frenchman, the Supreme Commander on the Western Front, was the man making things happen. Both he and General Haig had at last learned from the repeated failures of all previous allied (and German) offensives.[323] Foch's first success was his counter attack on the German offensive on the Marne in early August. Since then, he and General Haig had been overseeing a series of large local offensives which were rolling from south to north, few lasting more than three or four days, biting off manageable chunks of German territory with each one. The German lines were being 'smacked', just as they had been in early 1917, but not now to set up for a massive major attack, but

---

322 *'The little stream here (a tributary of the River Aa) must have been beautifully stocked before the War. It runs up our valley, and is quite a fast little gravel stream suitable for either wet or dry fly.'*

323 The attacks were made after only short, but very heavy bombardments so as to achieve surprise. They were not allowed to over-reach. Artillery support going forward was the priority. Supplies and reinforcements were brought up quickly to consolidate the gains and resist counter attacks. At last the recipe for sustained, if limited, success had been found. The cavalry were almost forgotten!

as an end in itself, using numerical superiority intelligently to push the German's back sector by sector.

The first attacks by the French army had started in the south in August and they continued every few days for the next three months.[324] *'Yesterday's papers have just reached us with news of another attack down south which seems to have been fairly successful though to no great depth. General Foch is certainly doing extraordinarily well,'* Colin writes. The allies got closer and closer to the Hindenburg Line and by mid-September, it was being breached. The German generals had known for some time that they had no chance of winning the war. It was now becoming obvious to the men. German morale plummeted.

Colin, with General Plumer's Second Army in the north, got increasingly impatient as he listened to the news of success.

And then a bombshell. On September 12th, *'the colonel was promoted brigadier general yesterday. He got the news at 12.30 pm and was taken off in a car at 2.30 the same afternoon. He had to pack his kit up and go. Bad luck too as he was suffering from an abscess on the same tooth as six weeks ago and it was just on the point of bursting. He wanted to stay here until it burst but they would not let him. He is rather cut up about it, says he is too old for it now and would rather be left to command his brigade. The 30th Division Artillery, to which he is going, sent him a telegram to say they*

---

324 Haig launched the successful Battle of Amiens on the 8th August. He very sensibly refused to accept Foch's advice to continue past the three days as the assaults stalled. But instead attacked at Albert, and then when that faltered, at Arras and then at Bapaume, further north. The Germans started to retreat, and once they started, the contagion spread to the whole line. Another six, major but limited, assaults drove the Germans back to the Hindenburg Line, from which they had launched their attacks in the spring. Like a boxer, the Allies were standing back and aiming their punches to weaken their opponent and to force him back. The Germans fought hard, and casualties in these battles were not light. More men died on the Western Front in 1918 than in any other year. But the Allies were not now expecting a breakthrough and knock-out blow. Superiority had to be established in all sectors, not just one, before that could be attempted.

were delighted with the news. We know the 30th quite well, so he can feel he is going to friends. I am very glad indeed he has got the thing at last, even though in a battle he is very good indeed, and we shall not get anyone as good in his place.'

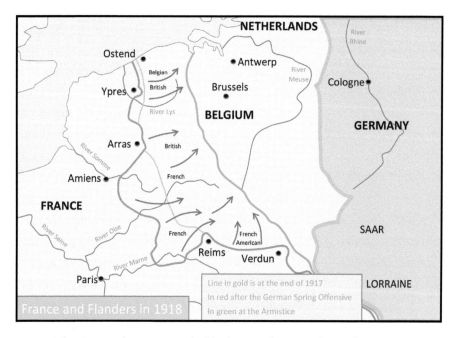

France and Flanders in 1918

Line in gold is at the end of 1917
In red after the German Spring Offensive
In green at the Armistice

The German lines were pushed back, sector by sector, the northern sector being the last to be involved, between August and October.

Colin briefly commanded the brigade, until their new colonel arrived. Colin had been in charge many times in Colonel Lambarde's absence, and knew it inside out. The poor man[325] does not feature much in Colin's letters!

On the 28th September, under the nominal leadership of the King of Belgium, the northern sector got its turn. General Plumer had been allowed to plan the British assault at Ypres, and using

---

325 Colin was mildly disparaging about him, probably unjustly and there is little to be gained by naming him. He *'has been training recruits and waiting to get a Brigade for a long time. He is rather inexperienced as far as recent fighting is concerned,'* and *'I have to do a certain amount of discussing things with him.'*

the new template, which he himself had pioneered, he kept the objectives simple and flexible. There was no special bombardment in the days before. He attacked with four divisions behind a heavy rolling barrage, keeping two divisions in reserve. The French and Belgians north and east of his sector attacked at the same time. The German lines were weak due to the needs of their armies further south, and crucially surprise was achieved. Colin had been in the first four Battles of Ypres, now he was in the Fifth, fought over the same ground.

When the battle started, his battery was with the 29th Division, whose brief was to attack following the line of the Menin Road, precisely the same route that his battery had followed the year before. The brigade, as the battle started, was in Ypres itself[326] and true to form, it was raining.

Colin, as by far the most experienced forward observing officer in the brigade, went forward with the 29th Division infantry, leaving Captain Blackburn to supervise the battery in its rolling barrage.[327] *'We had to supply the forward observing officers, so I left the battery to do the barrage and started off early with Lieutenant Pilling to get into the front line trench, the starting point of our telephone wire that we had to run forward. The attack started at 5.30 am and we started off about 25 minutes after the infantry in pouring rain with a tremendous lot of wire to run out.[328]*

I went a couple of miles with Pilling and then came back to reconnoitre ways for our guns to advance across the captured German lines. Having got

---

326 'A' battery was sited on the southern ramparts of Ypres for the barrage.

327 25% smoke to hinder the enemy response. General Plumer of course knew the terrain well. Tanks were not used.

328 If the infantry had been held up, targeted support would quickly have been available. But by nightfall the attack had penetrated nearly four miles to take Gheluvelt, well out of range, and beyond the furthest limit of the ground gained at Passchendaele the year before. The two divisions (the 9th and 29th) of Jacobs II corps took 2100 prisoners, more than 100 guns, and lost 1100 men. The Belgians on their left and IX corps on their right had equal success. The British Campaign in France and Flanders, Vol. IV, Sir Arthur Conan Doyle.

all the information I needed as to roads, I thought I'd let the brigade know how the attack was going, so I made my way back to the original front line. 40 German prisoners, coming back on their own, attached themselves to me. I kept sending them away, four here and four there, to carry wounded back, but I couldn't shake them off.' Outnumbered, demoralised and hungry, many of the Germans were keen to surrender.

'The telephone wire was cut to pieces at the front line, the only place the Germans were shelling. So we mended that and got word back to the colonel. Then we trudged back to the battery position to find them perfectly happy and the barrage shoot all over.' 'The colonel was just starting off on a reconnoitre on a bicycle. So we (battery commanders) all started off on bikes together and had the dickens of a ride forward in the pouring rain and slush.'

'We found the infantry had advanced much further than expected, so that our previously selected positions were quite useless. We would have to push our guns forward at least 4 miles. The colonel gave me permission to go and find Pilling, so I followed his line away up over very familiar country and then into country we had not held since 1914. The infantry were well in front of where his wire had reached and I found him at a loose end. I took him forward and we found some serviceable German guns on the crest of a ridge looking down on the German lines.[329] With the help of a few infantry, we succeeded in turning a gun round. But unfortunately while we were doing it, the divisional artillery general spotted us, called me over to him and ordered me to go back and see that our guns got up to support the infantry at once'.

Nothing better illustrates the importance now given to flexibility and forward control of the battlefield better than the fact that the divisional artillery general[330] was with the infantry brigadiers that morning, forward and out of range of his own guns, and that the

---

329 He had followed the Menin road from Ypres, through Hooge to just beyond Gheluvelt. See map page 66.

330 This was Brigadier R.M. Johnson of the 29th division. It was for this sort of energy and awareness, that Colonel Lambarde had been promoted. *'I'm sure he will be very popular with the infantry generals, but fancy the gunners will find him rather a trying taskmaster,'* wrote Colin.

brigade colonel had already reconnoitred forward. Both had seen for themselves that the artillery support needed to advance quicker and further than planned.

'I knew it was a four hours job to put the tracks right before we could think of advancing.' The British Labour Battalions had moved forward immediately to make good the one main road across the shell-torn mud. *'I told him that we were coming on as fast as we could, but there was no getting out of it and I had to go back. I was rather sore about being done out of the fun with the Bosche guns. We could see splendid targets, German batteries still firing and all sorts of things. But I left Pilling with the gun, and he had great fun shooting at the Bosche over open sights all day. I managed to pinch a horse to take me half way down'* (one hopes it was not the general's horse!) *'and so got back to the battery by about 1 pm'*

'We started the guns off at about 3 o'clock in the afternoon and managed to get our last gun into action at about 9 pm, pitch black and raining hard, the roads being blocked continually by vehicles in ditches where they stuck for hours at a time. You never saw such a mess. The men really worked wonders.'[331]

This was the same country, the same road, the same weather as Passchendaele. But this time the Germans were worn down by attrition, had minimal reserves, and were taken by surprise. The British infantry advance was quick enough for German forward guns[332] to be captured and for crucial high ground to be occupied. However the ongoing assault could not and would not proceed without artillery support. Despite the rain, the deep mud and the narrow congested tracks, Colin's brigade was nearly four miles forward only fifteen hours after the first infantry advance started.

---

331 The brigade diary reports that the infantry were out of range by 9 am, that the brigade moved forward at 11.15 am, and that the road from Ypres to past Hooge was 'very bad'. Colin's 'A' battery moved from Ypres down the Menin Road to just south of Glencorse Wood, one of his worst positions at Passchendaele, J14 on the map on page 230, past Hooge towards Gheluvelt.

332 Wikipedia says 300 guns captured, but it is not clear where that figure comes from.

The weather continued diabolical, and the difficulties of a rapid advance obvious. On the 29th, the second day *'they tried to get the cavalry through, which blocked all traffic, and stopped us getting anything up. The next day the same thing happened, the roads being blocked continually by vehicles in ditches and there they just stayed on the road where they stuck for hours at a time. You never saw such a mess.'*

But the guns needed to be still further forward. On the 30th, *'we got orders to move forward again. We succeeded in getting our horses up to the guns at 6 o'clock in the evening along the blocked roads, but no vehicles at all got up that day. The wagons started from Ypres at 10 am and took 23 hours to travel the 4 miles up to our first forward positions in pouring rain. In the meantime, our six teams of horses moved our six guns forward to the new position. It took us two and a half hours to get the last three guns out of the first position. The torches we had ran down and it was hailing and raining all night. We got the last gun in at 3 o'clock in the morning. The next day was fine, and some hot tea and rum soon had the men all quite happy again in spite of the fact the rations hadn't got up, and we didn't get breakfast proper until 12 noon.'*

It was another 24 hours before the wagons caught up. *'It was a tremendous pity we could not have advanced quicker as we'd have been miles further on into beautiful country if the guns could have followed the infantry on the first day. We have moved about four miles further east*[333], *and had to come by vile roads. Our new position is only about 1500 yards from the enemy and we had to come into view to get there and unfortunately got it pretty hot with our last lot of wagons. The Bosche gunners were terribly full of themselves as there was none of our heavy artillery to keep them quiet. To make matters worse, it was raining most of the day.'*

---

333 On the 30th, the 113th brigade moved another 4 miles up the Menin Road to Polderhoek to support the new infantry front line. On the 29th, the 29th division had advanced about two miles beyond Gheluvelt. The division on their right took Zandvoorde (map page 66) and the divisions further south joined the battle and captured Messines. The final line extended north east from Zandvoorde to Dadizele which is about a mile off the map. Here the offensive paused to address the supply problems. They had advanced about 10 miles.

'*Our supply wagon with our waterproof sheets etc. was badly stuck about a mile away, behind about ten other vehicles belonging to some other unit. It was impossible to get at it. So after eating some bread and bacon for dinner, I slept under an old bit of corrugated iron which had been riddled by shrapnel, and the others found corners of shell holes for the night.*'

But unlike the previous year, the offensive stopped to give time for consolidation. Along with the infantry of the 29th Division, they were given a few days break.[334] '*There is an awful babel going on in the mess. These young subalterns of mine are as rowdy a crowd as I've ever come across. We are out for a rest for a day or so, and there's no holding them. I cannot write sense tonight.*' Morale was high.

He was pleased with them all. '*I've got a splendid lot of officers and young Royle is the pick of them now, so quick to understand things. Pilcher is a great stand by, especially when we are getting things hot. They all beg to be allowed to stay up at the guns.*'

Blackburn had done wonders '*hauling guns and wagons etc. out of ditches all night*' to clear a path for his wagon lines to get up to the guns, and had also been given a bar to his M.C. that week. Colin immediately wrote home. '*Could you send out one of those clipping ones for him. I'd give him one of mine only I cannot get it off.*' He knew the importance of medals for morale.

And on the 14th October they were involved in another general advance on the German lines, the Battle of Courtrai.[335] '*We had a grand show that day, but the brigade had not much fun as we were not*

---

334 Pausing at Polderhoek, they left their guns under guard as they rested in their wagon lines from the 6th to the 13th. German reinforcements were arriving, but the British Fourth Army attacked at St Quentin on the 29th. The French and Americans had opened a new battle front at Verdun in the Meuse-Argonne Offensive on the 26th, with further attacks through to the 3rd October. German reserves were spread very thin.

335 They advanced to Dadizele after the barrage on the 14th, then on to Moorsele, now a north western suburb of Kortrijk (or Courtrai as it is in French), encircling the town from the north, heading for Cappelle-St-Catherine (now known as Sint Katerina), a village a mile north of the present day Kortrijk ring road.

allowed to advance until the next morning. However we started early on the 15th, marched about 6 miles forward and shot another barrage at 10 am the same day which took the infantry on another 4 or 5 miles. On the night of the 15th we marched forward again, and fired a barrage at dawn on the 16th. Had a good sleep on the night of the 16th, and now we march in the early hours of tomorrow morning to positions we have been reconnoitring forward all day today.'

This fighting was not particularly testing. *'We are in civilised country now, and the Bosch runs every time we bring our guns up.'* But they were constantly in action, much of the time close behind the infantry. So they suffered a steady trickle of casualties. The brigade lost seven killed and forty wounded in the month. And most significantly, their new colonel was lightly wounded on the 19th. This left Colin again in temporary command of the brigade.

They had reached a village, just north of Courtrai and were rapidly advancing round this strategically important town, standing as it does on the eastern bank of the River Lys which curved north across the line of the army's advance. Courtrai was a significant fortress town and railway junction and to maintain the momentum of the advance, it needed to be captured quickly. The plan was to encircle it from the north, which meant crossing the river, a task easier said than done.

They were back with the 29th Division whom they had supported on the first day of the battle on the 28th September. The infantry were leading the way. *'Patrols could not get across the river last night owing to machine gun fire making it impossible for the Royal Engineers to get pontoons in the water.' 'I stayed with General Freyberg V.C.[336] who commanded the infantry brigade we were covering.'* And *'just before noon we received orders*

---

336 General Freyberg got his V.C. on the Dardanelles, and was one of the youngest and most heavily decorated generals in the Army. The 113th artillery brigade had supported his 88th infantry brigade on the first day of the advance at Ypres the month before. Colin probably met him with the artillery brigadier on that first day when he was trying to get the captured German guns into action.

from 29ᵗʰ Division that the passage of the Lys must be forced tonight. Our artillery brigade was to be the one to go over the river and be the first to support the infantry on the other side. I must say it looked rather a sticky proposition at first.' [337]

River Lys between Harelbeke and Kortrijk (Courtrai)

The supporting artillery barrage[338] started at 6 am but could only protect the infantry for the first mile. By 8.30, the Leinsters were that far over the river. *'We got our batteries over the pontoon bridge. They stopped shelling just as our horses arrived which was extremely lucky for us. That day we did two advances, and were able to support the infantry over a*

---

337 *'The plan of attack will be as follows: – the 2ⁿᵈ Hampshire Regiment will be ferried across to make good the Harelbeke to Courtrai road and as soon as bridges are constructed by the Royal Engineers, the 2ⁿᵈ Leinsters will cross and will advance over the railway to a line beyond, which they will hold as the artillery brigade bridging is completed.'* Infantry brigade diary.

338 This was provided by the guns attached to the 29ᵗʰ division. It was not a divisional artillery brigade that went over the river with the 88ᵗʰ infantry brigade. The divisional war diary on the 19ᵗʰ October is explicit. *'113ᵗʰ Army Brigade will be the first to cross the river. Batteries to move under orders of brigade commander as the situation develops.'* Colin was ordered to liaise with General Freyberg, but was given freedom to move his guns as he saw fit.

very sticky piece of ridge which proved of great importance. Consequently they were pretty pleased with us.'

And pleased with themselves. *'I think the brigade has done pretty well the last show. We advanced twice including a river crossing three days ago, then the day before yesterday we advanced to within 800 yards of the Bosche, having to reconnoitre and occupy positions during darkness, owing to the orders being hurried, and then the next day we pushed 'B' battery forward to within 600 yards of the infantry, who however had to retire a bit at night so we pulled it back again to where we now are.'*

At Courtrai, Colin was the artillery 'general'. His orders from the brigadier gave him total freedom to move his batteries 'as the situation develops'. He simply had to liaise with General Freyberg, to provide the maximum of support to his infantry in a fluid ongoing battle. This was unprecedented freedom. The contrast with 1917 is stark. Then they were bogged down in mud, and in stifling control from above. Now his brigadier had the confidence to delegate total control to his front line commander.

The army brigade system had had disadvantages. But Colonel Lambarde had used it to maintain his autonomy, and to train up a fighting brigade which showed 1914 initiative. Colin had learned from him, and had feared the loss of this quality when he left. *'They have all had the surprise of their lives when we have proved ourselves without Colonel Lambarde,'* he wrote. The brigade, under their new colonel (whom Colin had disparaged), had done everything that was asked of it by the 29th Division at Ypres, but now with him wounded, Colin reaped the benefit, revelling in the new freedom the brigade had earned. It is possible though, that his close advance of 'B' battery was a bit over-enthusiastic.[339]

Nevertheless the attack at Courtrai was completely successful. General Freyberg's infantry brigade was personally congratulated by Marshal Foch. And it is clear that both he and the 29th Division

---

339 Acting Captain Dahl, in command, was wounded and one of his subalterns killed in a particularly violent bombardment of their close-up position.

wanted its supporting artillery to be included when the plaudits went round. Somebody in the division must have pressed quite hard to get a second DSO lined up for Colin. Pilling and Pilcher, his subalterns, both got M.C.'s.

And Major General Cayley, commanding the division, wrote Colin a personal note. *'This is unusual, as it is generally only the brigadier that writes.'*[340] (He had already had an effusive note[341] from him.) *'Dear Hutchison, Will you please convey to your battery commanders and to all ranks of your brigade the appreciation of this division for the splendid way in which your brigade has supported us in the late successful operations. Their cooperation has been invaluable and has helped most materially to our success. I hope it may be our good fortune to find ourselves covered by you again before long.'* The 29th Divisional war diary released them to 'go into rest'.

But there was no rest for army brigades. *'The same night as we drew out, I got orders to report to another division'* (the 36th) *'to support them with another attack'* (the action at Ooteghem). *'We had a lot of rounds to get up to the position too and most of our ammunition wagons empty. We had a terrible rush to manage it as we had to march about 8 or 9 miles to our new positions. How the men managed it in time I don't know, but everything worked without a hitch and it was done.'*

---

340 This new punctiliousness was significant. General Pinney of the 33rd Division on the Lys in April, and General Cayley now, both knew that they would not have won their battles without proactive artillery in support. The brigade had had a note from Brigadier Charlton of the 16th Divisional Artillery at Messines in early 1917, but the artillery were not even mentioned in the 7th divisional battle summary of the first five days of the Somme. This progression illustrates the change in their status from servants of the infantry to partners with them.

341 From Brigadier R.M. Johnson, who commanded 29th Division Artillery; *'I am writing to thank you and all ranks of your brigade for the excellent work you have done during the short periods during which you have been attached to us. It has been a real pleasure to me to have such a splendid brigade under my orders and I am really sorry that we are parting company – I hope for the time being only. You have given us full to overflowing measure of everything we have asked of you. Best of luck to you all, and may we soon have the pleasure of fighting alongside you again.'* He was thanking them for their support both at Courtrai and 5th Ypres, three weeks earlier.

Colin gives little detail of his personal involvement in these battles in his letters though he was obviously pleased with himself. The citation for his DSO says much more. 'For conspicuous gallantry in command of a brigade RFA near Courtrai. On 20th October 1918, he established an observation post right forward and directed the fire of his brigade on to a strong locality, thereby assisting the infantry to capture it. And on the 22nd October he carried out forward reconnaissance under very heavy fire, and brought part of his brigade close behind the infantry to support their further advance. His fine behaviour inspired all ranks under his command.'

It was clear now, even to Colin, that the war was won. But he was expecting a more drawn out conclusion, and he pressed the corps staff hard to give him 'a good fighting colonel' to take over the brigade.

As late as the 23rd October, he wrote *'It is rather funny to hear you talking about surrender and armistices. The Bosche are by no means done. This looks as though it may be the last winter of the war, but we are in for a good deal of fighting next spring in my opinion and we'll do well if we finish them by next autumn. They still fight pretty well with the exception of certain battalions.'* He did not really want the war to end. In this letter, the wish was father to the thought.

Their new fighting colonel joined them on the 27th. And a splendid man he was too. *'Colonel Alex Arbuthnot is our new colonel, CMG, DSO & Legion of Honour. He is very senior and has only just recovered from having both legs shattered 18 months ago. He cannot really get about too well and can hardly get onto a horse. He really has no right to be out here commanding a brigade. He is a most extraordinarily nice man, and will make a first class colonel.'*

But the brigade fired their last barrage of the war at 5.25 am on the 31st October, following which *'a considerable advance was made'*, and during the afternoon the guns were moved forward to positions near Anseghem. They had advanced thirty miles towards Brussels from Ypres in a month.

Just over a week later, the war ended, at eleven o'clock on the eleventh day of November, the eleventh month. It was just another day for Colin.

'Apparently an Armistice was signed at 11 o'clock this morning. Anyway we had orders there was to be no more firing after that hour. It didn't affect us much, as we haven't had a show for these last 8 days, merely been wandering about in the background. Rather sickening, would have liked to have had a last fling at them. Expect there will be some excitement in England tonight.'

| DSO & Bar | MC & Bar | Mons Star with clasp | War and Victory Medals with oak leaf |

Distinguished Service Order	Awarded to Officers for good service Passchendaele 1917, Courtrai 1918.
Military Cross	Awarded to Officers for bravery 2nd Ypres 1915, Spring Offensive 1918.
Mons Star and Clasp	Awarded to all those in action 1914
War and Victory Medals	Given to all servicemen, 1914 to 1918
Oak leaf	Mention in Dispatches for commendation 2nd Ypres 1915, Somme 1916, Passchendaele 1917, Courtrai 1918.

CHAPTER SEVENTEEN

1919 Postscript

'A' Battery, 113ᵗʰ Army Brigade

'The monotony of peace soldiering rather appals one.'

Was Colin happy about it? He was twenty-five years old and had been at war for four years. He faced a very uncertain future. Apart from his mother and his father and the army, he was now almost alone in the world. He had graduated from being a fresh faced youth stunned by the ferocity and confusion of modern war to being commander of a brigade of artillery in a major and successful engagement, a dedicated single minded soldier. From second lieutenant to acting colonel in four years. But he had lost touch with the reality of life at peace. There is no celebration in his last letters. Rather a sadness. He could see no future.

A 'close friend' wrote after the war, *"Colin Hutch was a natural soldier, and the men respected and trusted him absolutely. That he emerged with his whole skin was a surprise to many. That he got two DSOs and two MCs surprised no-one, and many who knew him well were disappointed that he had not received an even higher honour."* One wonders if this was written by Colonel Lambarde. It sounds like him. And there was no hyperbole in this judgement.

But despite his very impressive war record, he was still only just 25. Now was the time to think about staff training and an army career. But he had no division to be loyal too, and no divisional general to look after him. [342] In late 1918, the army unwound very fast. On the 14ᵗʰ

---

342 *'There is talk of all brigades going back to divisions, and the 29ᵗʰ division which is one of the best divisions out here asked Corps if we could go to them if that happened,'* Colin wrote at the end of October, after their heroics at Ypres and Courtrai. He was keen for that to happen. His brigade had been under thirteen different divisions in three different corps in eight months. The divisions looked after their own and he so wanted to be looked after. But it was too late.

November, the brigade batteries were given notice of a cut from six guns to four, and this was actioned on the 17ᵗʰ. They marched towards Brussels, and were posted into the 34ᵗʰ Division, which was itself earmarked for early demobilisation. They hung around in Belgium for a fairly dreary Christmas and went to Germany on the 24ᵗʰ January.

Peace had come, and Colin did not know what to do with it, or how to cope. His men wanted to go home. He was no longer sure what home was.

Army life went on. *'General Plumer is coming to inspect us tomorrow. I shall be thankful when it is over, not that I mind the general. I'm perfectly confidant that we are as good as any brigade in Germany, but it's a strain on the men.'* He does not say *'as good as'* any battery *'in Germany'*. As the army shrank, career soldiers were reverting to their gazetted ranks. He would be back to captain, commanding a wagon line. *'It really would be a good idea to look for a battery commanded by a good major, but I don't know very many that would have me.'* He did not know any.

Meanwhile Uncle Duke succumbed to his wound and died in February, 1919. At almost the same time, Colin received a memento, a silver cigarette case from the mother of Major Gordon, one of his oldest friends, the fellow rugby player he and Tyler had met up with in 1917. He had been killed in almost the last month of the war.

He thought of leaving the army, but had little energy for such a major decision. *'I have very little hankering after the East, but when the time comes, I shall just have to go where I'm sent.'* He was sent out to India in 1920, posted as adjutant to a brigade in Lucknow and remained a captain till he left the army in 1930.

Colin, of course, lives on in his letters. And through them the names of others live on too. Men like Colonel Lambarde, who did leave the army and return to his long suffering wife; like Tyler, now married, who was also sent out to India; like Captain Blackburn, who came up through the ranks, and after the war wanted a small-holding to manage. Men of flesh and blood, but heroes all. Or boys like Subaltern Lancer Royle, fresh out of school, who *'will turn out a splendid fellow, I think, terribly young and inexperienced of course, but game for most things which is what is wanted.'* Major Stapylton might have said the same of Colin in 1914.

But Colonel Lambarde and Captain Blackburn were old enough to return to life without war, and Second Lieutenant Royle was young enough not to be blighted by his teenage adventure. Colin was of the lost generation, changed and matured beyond belief, bereaved, his martial talents honed by combat far beyond peacetime needs, and his scars of war, largely unrecognised, even by himself, born with stoic courage.

He was first in the queue to enlist in 1939 and was killed in North Africa as a brigadier in 1943, aged just 50. I would love to have known my grandfather.

CHAPTER EIGHTEEN

THE ARTILLERY – AN OVERVIEW

'The only thing the whole war I found of use,
is seeing the ground from near your battery, and shooting at what you see.'

This book is based on the letters and journals of just two men, who described what happened on the front line, with awareness of the conventions that guided their deployment. As in every war, military history, politics, personal relationships, and technical developments determined tactical and strategic development. It is necessary in a full history, to be side-tracked into these issues. Bear in mind that this is not a full history.

The Artillery in Defence in France and Flanders

The Western Front was generally static and on the majority of days in most places, there was no expectation on either side that lines would be altered. Colin called this peace warfare and as a general rule it filled the winters of the war, and all those times in the trenches away from where a major battle was taking place. There were however a number of times when the Germans were in the ascendancy and attacking on his front. It is instructive to look first at these battles, because defence generally succeeded. The reason for this success was that the artillery was used effectively.

At Mons and the retreat from Mons, and later at the Aisne in 1914, at Second Ypres in 1915 and at Meteren in 1918 Colin was fighting defensive battles. He was placed close to an advancing enemy and the aim was to prevent any further advance.[343]

---

343 The first battle of the Aisne was a mutual offensive, both sides attacking, but in Colin's sector, he was deployed in a defensive role.

The uniform feature was that his units had autonomy. Circumstances dictated that they picked their own positions, with intelligent use of contours to confer protection and to overlook the infantry in front of them. They identified good observation points and they shot accurately at what they could see. They liaised with the infantry in front of them to provide them with the maximum of support and to disrupt the enemy's intentions.

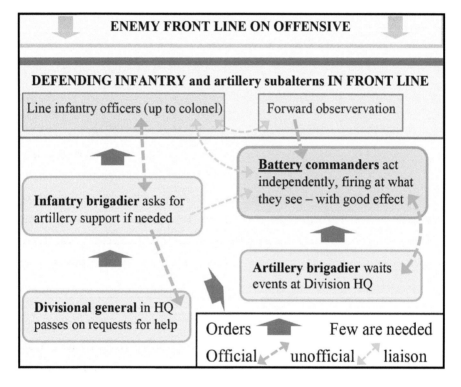

In defence, the artillery observe, liaise and react. There is no reason to wait for orders. Some of the informal pathways shown were formalised later in the war.

The task of the senior generals was simply to get them to an approximate locality, and then leave them to it. Of course, at Mons and Le Cateau, there was divisional control and due to the offensive mentality of the generals they were exposed more than was strictly necessary to enemy counter fire, as they were again in the latter stages of First Ypres in late 1914.[344] But in those early battles, the generals had justified confidence in the competence of their more junior officers to be able to sustain fire, and to withdraw their men calmly under that fire if necessary.

And there is no tactical difference in what Colin did with his two gun detachment on the Aisne in 1914; what Major Lambarde did with his battery at Second Ypres in 1915; or what Colin did with his battery at Meteren in 1918. They identified targets by direct observation from good positions and they fired at them.

This competence in defence was not confined to the British. Local German attacks were repelled relatively easily with considerable loss of life. But so were local British attacks. Great care, on both sides, went in to preparing defensive positions on static fronts throughout the war. The crucial professional skill of an artillery officer was the ability to find good positions for his guns, and good posts for his forward observers.

It is striking how this British competence in defence, and the tactics behind it, never wavered through the war. Even the less experienced brigades did not find it too difficult to defend effectively. The professional competence of artillery colonels and brigadiers was such that they could be relied upon. They prevented the war being lost.

The Artillery in Offence

It is depressing therefore to record how badly the artillery was managed during attacks. There were three main reasons for this.

The first is that in what was a siege war, infantry attacks were planned and then the artillery asked to support. When in 1916, artillery attacks started to be planned with infantry exploiting the results, it was not necessarily done very well. The second is that the quality of the artillery in general, from 1915 onwards, was,

---

344 The very poor quality of the German ordinance for their standard field gun, the 7.7 cm Feldkanone 96, was a significant (and not generally acknowledged) factor in these battles and to a great extent justifies the British tactics of 1914.

unsurprisingly, seldom up to the professional standards of 1914. The third, which follows on from the second, is that, particularly in the new armies of 1915, the quality of the junior artillery staff was desperately poor, and the staff structure such that it isolated and paralysed even the more competent generals.

The relative importance of these three fundamental problems waxed and waned as the war progressed.

1914

In 1914, the British Expeditionary Force was an army sent to Belgium to fight a battle. It was widely expected to fight the Germans, win the battle and finish the war by Christmas. The British army was a very good one, well-schooled in fighting colonial wars in defence of the Empire. But not only was it pitifully small in continental terms, half the size of each of the half dozen armies deployed by both the French and Germans, but it was totally unequipped psychologically and practically for trench (siege) warfare. It had almost no heavy guns.

Offensive tactics were simple. The artillery was deployed as far forward as possible to support the other branches of the army, and was used only to soften the enemy up before the infantry and cavalry did the real work. In some senses, this worked in 1914, but it did so by default. It did so because the quality of the army was so good, and the quality of the German light artillery counter fire so poor. The BEF did not lose a battle and it did not disintegrate. In the circumstances, this was a triumph. But it all happened so fast that nobody had time to digest the lessons.

Yet on the Aisne in 1914, Colin is already advocating a defensive line to be held against oncoming attack for their next campaign at First Ypres. His reasons are clear. He had been posted up in the front line with an infantry battalion at the Marne to combat a nest of machine guns and had seen at first-hand the folly of infantry charging them. He had sat on the heights at the Aisne for a fortnight and picked off both advancing and entrenched German infantry with his howitzers.

And, significantly, the Royal Field Artillery by whom he had been trained were used to digging in. They had a culture of defensive assessment of their positions, unlike either the cavalry or the infantry at that time. They were vulnerable on a battlefield and they knew it.

With the decisiveness of youth, (and would that the British generals had been younger,) Colin decided that the place to be was in defence. They were outnumbered, and the Germans were going to attack in Flanders; so let them, was his attitude. As early as September 1914, he had experienced the stalemate of mutually fortified positions and seen what artillery could do to an infantry attack.

The battle of Ypres in 1914 confirmed both the quality of the British army and the futility of infantry advance against artillery and machine guns. A large proportion of the army was sacrificed as a consequence, with devastating consequences.

In 1914, the staff structure was both a strength, and a weakness, of the small professional army. It was informal, in that all the senior officers knew each other, liaised closely, and were expected to show initiative. Communications were rudimentary, so the generals were as close to their troops as possible. They talked to their young officers (Colin briefed both his senior generals at the Aisne) and expected their staff to do the same. But they got killed.

1915

And by the end of 1914, the loss of experienced officers had become a really serious problem. Well over half had been incapacitated, the remainder were exhausted. The army was expanding exponentially, and this had a devastating effect on staff effectiveness. No experienced front line gunners were given staff jobs. They were needed to fire the guns. New staff officers did not know or socialise with front line officers, thus losing the essential feedback which informed planning. And in the new divisions, they did not even know that this old boy network had existed. They adopted the formal structure, which required separate mess facilities and carried on from there. The only experienced soldiers were the generals and they were isolated.

To compound the problem, battles were planned from an infantry or cavalry viewpoint, with artillery support as an afterthought. So as the artillery moved to offence, they lost liaison with local infantry brigades, and were directed by the divisional artillery brigadier, who learned the infantry plan from the divisional general and then had to plan his supporting fire. He and his staff did so down to battery level. Preparations were hurried; and only rudimentary efforts made to identify enemy positions and threats.

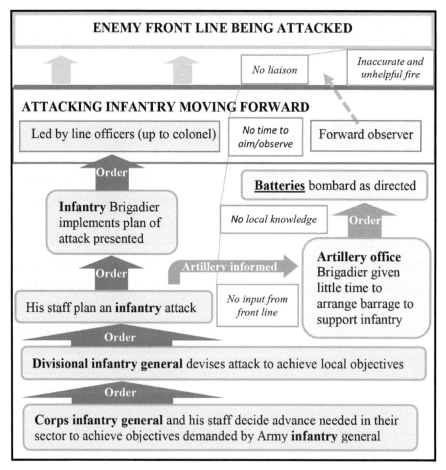

Worst case scenario in attack, a regular occurrence in 1915.

Not only was there insufficient time for planning of targets based on the local knowledge of the batteries, but there was usually insufficient time even for the batteries to run out their wire and register their targets. The artillery brigadier was not senior enough to tell his infantry counterparts to wait until his guns were ready and properly briefed. On the 17th May 1915, Colin observed that the *'poor infantry simply exist to go through the places made for them by the artillery.'* It was at least a year later before this so evident truth was incorporated into the planning of battles.

With the constant repetition of failed infantry attacks, there were plenty of opportunities for generals to come to this same conclusion earlier. It is almost certain that the army of 1914, left alone, would have done so. Experienced middle ranking officers would have spoken to their friends on the staff, and probably to the general himself, ensuring tactical evolvement. But by 1915, the conduit for this informal feedback had dried up.

In the newer divisions, including the 1st Canadian Division, staff officers had been recruited from reservists and territorials who not only did not know that this old boy network had existed, but worse, did not know enough about guns to even ask the right questions of their front line officers.

How could they? They did not come from an artillery background. They had had no training. They did not know how to perform even routine tasks such as arranging transfers or billets. Choosing battery sites or planning fields of fire was way beyond their initial capabilities. They had no experience at all of front line action. The catalogue of errors Colin documents through 1915 would be funny if it was not so tragic. The Canadian Artillery divisional staff managed to lose one of its brigades of artillery; failed to arrange a handover in an active battle; and ordered Colin's brigade to fire on an enemy trench they had no way of seeing, all in the first 48 hours of their move to Festubert. A week or two later, and orders were issued to the batteries to bombard a series of targets in different zones of fire requiring not only a change in observation post with each change of zone, but the necessity of shifting, re-aligning and re-registering the guns as well. Even several months later, the staff, in planned operations, were ordering trench mortars to fire from a swamp without stabilisation, ordering a battery to cut wire outside its arc of fire, and regularly failing to target enemy observation posts to prevent counter fire during infantry attacks.

Of course there were many factors which made life difficult for the staff in 1915. Their maps were inaccurate, and their communications not only poor, but vulnerable. There were shortages of guns, ammunition and other supplies, but this was true of both sides; and had much more impact on training of new units in England than on those at the front.

The failures of 1915 were far more down to misuse of the assets they had, than to lack of resources. There was insufficient reconnaissance from an artillery viewpoint, and the artillery were given insufficient time to set up robust communications, or to target defences in a way that assisted the infantry. The plan for an infantry attack came first. The artillery brigadier was junior to the infantry generals planning the attacks and was side-lined, being presented with an assault plan, for which he was expected to provide support. The inexperience of his staff, allied with their failure to understand the limitations of their own guns, ensured that much of their firing was useless noise.

It was of course far easier for the senior generals to blame their failures on lack of materials than to acknowledge ineptness in their use of them. And so much was made of shortages that every major failure was blamed on them. The army's tactical complacency in late 1915 contrasts with the titanic efforts made in England to provide more ammunition and guns.

The issue of writing reports may seem a small one, but it was not in the culture of the regular army to write an analysis of battles. In a small fast moving colonial army, it was generally unnecessary except to report home. Facts were all that were needed. Everybody knew a failure when they saw one. But in the bigger army of 1915, the generals needed honest reporting. They did not, as they should have done, get it from their staff. And the front line officers simply did not report failure in writing and if they had to, they put the best possible gloss on it.[345] An honest written assessment could be, and was regarded as defeatism.[346] None of the brigade diaries report their own failings in any detail, if at all. Unless a senior officer could read between the lines, or knew the area of operations well, he might well not realise that an attack had been an unmitigated failure.

The front line officers, of course, knew a failure when they saw one, if they survived. They blamed the staff, not unreasonably, given their failure to carry out the 1914 job description. The poor quality of the staff became a standing joke[347] both in England and in France, and relationships at the front became somewhat toxic. The problems should have been vigorously and fundamentally addressed by Kitchener and the senior generals. It would have been relatively easy, even at this stage of the war to demand familiarisation exchanges between the staff and the front line. And, although, disastrously, it had become counter-cultural, it should not have been beyond the wit of any general to set up mechanisms whereby his junior front line officers might have opportunities to report robustly direct to him.

---

345 The operation at Le Touquet (note 140) in late 1915 was a case in point. Duke reports another trench raid in 1916. *'Our bantams raided the Hun line last night and brought back a machine gun, but no prisoners. They claim to have killed many Germans. Colonel Roberts and Captain Butt were killed with about 10 other casualties. I wonder at it being called a great victory. Bit of a failure I would have thought!'* It was written up as a success in the brigade diary and in the Times of the 9th June.

346 This went right to the top. At Ypres, General Smith Dorrien proposed withdrawing from a dangerous and useless salient. He was sacked. General Plumer took over and made the withdrawal anyway.

347 For patriotic reasons, the jokes concentrated more on their perceived love of comfort and safety than on their general competence. This was a pity, because it enabled the hierarchy to reasonably deny the jibes, and to maintain the status quo.

1916

The situation did improve somewhat by early 1916, except in the new divisions coming out from England for the first time. Divisional staff generally became more experienced and front line officers were moving to staff jobs in greater numbers. Problems had also arisen in 1915 in the relationships between New Army, ranker and regular officers. The old school regular army officers did not know how to cope, either socially or professionally with their new colleagues, who often had very different background to themselves.[348] This problem eased slowly with the passage of time and was addressed fairly effectively, with front line familiarisation attachments common, and usually accepted with reasonable grace.

So in the spring of 1916, there was a general realisation that this was an artillery war, and that the artillery had to open the way for the infantry. Crack the city walls and the infantry would break through. There would once more be open war. Leaving aside the second half of this projected scenario, the thinking was good; about a year too late, but at least on the right track.

So the 7th Division in 1916 reconnoitred the front lines in detail, (accurate maps were now becoming available); they prepared an artillery plan tailored to the terrain; and arrangements were made to take out the strong points, the barbed wire and the observation points. The artillery brigades took up good positions and formed strong liaison links with the infantry brigades in front of them. In

---

348 A minority of the new officers were completely unsuitable; and probably more than a minority of the regular officers, at least initially, inexcusably bigoted. It was a collision of two cultures. But Duke Marshall's situation, for instance, is complex. He was 41, officer class and, in peacetime, an experienced project manager. He was a 2nd lieutenant, though clearly he did not act like one. He socialised with captains, majors and colonels, and saw nothing untoward in questioning established army methods on, for instance, water supply or munitions transport. Small wonder that regular army officers found him and his ilk difficult to manage. He should have been in the Army Service Corps.

short, the staff officers got it right, and so did the artillery regimental officers. The surprise in the analysis is not how bad the plan for the first day of the Somme was, but how good. It was not the plan that failed on the day; it was the execution of the plan.

The artillery of the new divisions did not have the skill and experience to succeed at every point in the pre-battle plan. And failure at one point meant failure at the end. So if the artillery staff did not have the expertise to ensure that their guns were well sited with good observation of their targets; or if they failed to provide a complete set of objectives based on good reconnaissance; or if the batteries were incapable of the high degree of technical skill required to take out the barbed wire successfully, then the plan for the first half hour of the battle failed.

The divisions cannot be blamed for failing to be professional soldiers. They weren't. If blame is to be apportioned, it has to fall on the senior generals at army and corps level. They did not check out prior to the attack that the first part of their plan had been adequately executed. Colin, a mere battery commander, knew that other divisions had not achieved their artillery tasks. If one wants to take the blame further back, it was in the tactics of First Ypres, when the professional army was sacrificed in suicidal offensive warfare. There were simply not enough regulars with the necessary skills to train up and provide a backbone to the new divisions.

The first day of the Somme should not have been the disaster that it was. The 7th Division made progress. Their artillery did have the capability to do what was asked of them. They largely destroyed the wire and gave their infantry enough time to get into the enemy positions. Very few of the other divisions made any progress.

Even after the initial barrage of the first morning, the 7th Division maintained close liaison between infantry and artillery, and facilitated the slow advance of the infantry through heavily fortified terrain. Obviously the rolling barrage in the first hour of the infantry assault made sense, but thereafter it was the targeted fire which did the good.

Observation officers were well briefed and got forward to ensure the accuracy and effectiveness of this targeted fire.

But despite the whole battle having been planned around the artillery, even the 7th Division generals reverted quickly to battle mode. They expected a rapid advance to the second main line of German defence, where they knew the artillery would again be needed in close support. But this second line was not reached on the first day, as expected, and the strength of the intermediate trenches between the first and second lines had been badly underestimated. Nobody seemed to realise that a mistake had been made and that the artillery still needed to be equal partners with the infantry to deal with these intermediate defences.

The 7th divisional staff report on their first five days in the line at the Somme, confirms this blindness. It was written in great detail about the infantry. The progress of every battalion is chronicled, in attack and in dealing with counter attack. Those on the ground must have known that they could not progress without artillery support. But there is only one significant mention of the artillery and that on the fourth day when they failed to cut wire before an attack on Bottom Wood. This is the only reference to the diminishing effectiveness of the artillery with increasing range, and it is very understated. Possibly the writer was only looking for a scapegoat for an infantry failure, and had no appreciation of, or interest in, artillery problems.

This reluctance to accept that things were not going to plan has been mentioned before. It applied a disastrous brake to tactical development in 1915, and it did so again in 1916. The facts were that the guns were inaccurate due to excessive wear and long range, and poorly coordinated because of long and vulnerable communications, which hampered both liaison and forward observation. Analysis of the brigade and Divisional war diaries show that these facts are recorded, so certainly the artillery brigadier knew the situation.

But the army plan was that the guns would move forward only when the infantry reached the point from which an assault on the second line could be planned. There is some evidence the 7th Division brigadier tried to change the plan on the second day, but the guns he ordered forward were pulled back within hours. Possibly his wrist was slapped. If the regular 7th Division Artillery was unable to react to changed circumstances on a battlefield, there was no chance of second or third rate divisions being able to do so.

The very slow infantry advance during the first nine days of the Somme was, at least partly, a consequence of deteriorating artillery support. The difficulties at Bottom Wood and the tragedy of the Welsh Division at Mametz Wood were just two examples. Haig did not blame the artillery for the latter as he should have done, or himself for that matter, for not bringing the artillery up. He blamed the Welsh infantry general. As the infantry advanced, they were losing artillery support.

But worse than this, they were pushing the enemy infantry back closer to their own guns, who could, and did, closely support effective counter attacks. And better still for these enemy guns, they were out of range of most of the British artillery. This happened in slow enough motion during the first week of the Somme to highlight the problem. There were two developments, one effective, the other less so.

The obvious and most effective development was to get the guns back up close behind the infantry during their attacks. It was costly, of course, to the artillery, and putting it into practice was not so easy. The front line artillery and their forward observation officers were much more exposed, and they suffered significant casualties. But local attacks with limited objectives immediately became more successful,[349] more so if the general ceded some control to the men on the ground.

But the second development, the long range rolling barrage, became the conventional tactic. The generals did not need to cede

---

349 This was true of both divisional attacks, as at Bazentin, and of smaller battalion attacks, as at Delville Wood.

control to local commanders. The first stage of an infantry attack had always been supported by an initial barrage by the artillery and this was logical and indeed essential, unless the aim was complete surprise. With improved maps and more accurate range estimations, the artillery could make more use of the pre-planned supporting barrage at longer range. This was fine in moderation. Not all the guns could or should been close up.

And at its crudest, a rolling barrage needed no local liaison or even observation of shell fire, with the special and complicating arrangements that needed to be made for both. It could all be arranged on the map from behind. So during major attacks these rolling barrages became longer and longer, with less and less opportunity for the guns to be diverted on to local tactical needs. The longer the rolling barrage went on, the more out of synch it got with events on the ground, and as the range lengthened, the less accurate it became. But it was a technique that even the dimmest cavalry general could understand, and it was an element of the battle that could be micro-managed from above and behind; so unfortunately for the infantry, it was.

It was very unfortunate for the artillery too. The new divisional artillery were not being trained up in the intelligent use of their guns. They got used to the tactic, some content not ever to learn the more demanding alternatives.

The French in contrast were using the creeping barrage, with a well organised signal corps, in close touch with the front line of the infantry, and directing artillery uplifts when objectives were attained. Strict timing was eliminated, and flexibility in forward control achieved. Lacking a signal corps, the British never went down this route.

The British timed rolling barrages were not very effective. They caused friendly casualties if the infantry moved too fast, and left them unsupported if they moved too slowly. The sooner, the artillery finished their initial planned barrage and got down to intelligent observed fire at a reasonable range the more use they were to the infantry.

But unobserved barrages became the norm, even on quiet days. Both Colin and Duke record being bombarded by friendly units in forward observation. Some artillery units in following divisional orders, were ignoring the golden rule of observing fire at all times. Command and control on the battlefield was just not good enough. Nobody forward in the battle zone had the authority to redirect damaging artillery fire. Astonishingly, despite the huge number of friendly fire casualties in 1916 and 1917, this problem was not seriously addressed by the British army for another year.

But, to consider the bigger picture, the object on the Somme was not a grinding advance. It was to win the war. The prevailing wisdom was that the only way to do this was to achieve a breakthrough. So every major assault plan featured a long infantry advance, which inevitably meant that they lost artillery cover. The guns could not advance over the devastated trenches until roads had been built. Without artillery cover for the infantry, enemy counter attacks succeeded.

Every attempt at a breakthrough on the Western Front failed for this basic reason. There were secondary reasons. The advantage in any attack on deep fortified lines is with the defence. Most attacks in 1915 and 1916 were stopped almost before they started. But if they did make progress, the further the attackers advanced, the more of their best troops were used up, the longer and more damaged became their supply lines, and the easier they could be enfiladed. The reverse was true for the defence. The further they were pushed back, the closer they were to artillery and reserves with good undamaged transport networks, and the easier it was to disrupt the tiring enemy progress with effective counter fire and fresh reserves.

Again it is difficult in retrospect to understand why this lesson took so long to learn. Both sides had had defensive success and it should have been relatively easy to analyse the reasons for that success, and by extension come to an understanding of the factors that lead to the failure of attacks. But the senior generals were still fixated on the infantry, and there was a cultural resistance to admitting that no significant advance could be achieved without artillery help every step of the way.

A breakthrough was not the only way to win the war, of course. The key to the war was morale. Both sides recognised this in the concept of attrition. The idea was to wear the enemy down by swapping casualties for a piece of ground that even if it was of dubious strategic value, would hopefully erode the enemy's morale by its capture. One hopes that all the generals grasped this concept, and did not just see attrition as a way of reducing the huge numbers ranged against them, swapping pawns on a chessboard. Enormous counter attacks were launched by both sides to recover lost ground. At the Somme, it was quite usual for a piece of ground to change hands half a dozen times in a few weeks, as at Delville Wood. It was assumed that the loss of territory was demoralising of itself.

It was, but there were other factors at work. In the face of a major massive assault with prolonged build up, just holding the enemy in check is a victory. A titanic defence, all in it together, holding a powerful enemy at bay, is actually inspiring. Morale is likely to hold up, even if ground is being slowly lost.[350] German morale held up on the Somme in 1916 and took into 1917 to dip as they slowly lost ground under continuing pressure. And even then, this was a local problem. The armies involved were so huge, that fresh divisions with reasonable morale were always in reserve and able to counter a major assault. For

---

350 The best example of this was in April 1918, when the last great effort of the German army in Flanders captured strategically important high ground at Kemmel in Flanders. British and French morale, which had been shaky before the expected assault, soared when the Germans were restricted to only a minor advance. A local tactical disaster was treated by the British as a victory and celebrated as such.

the attackers, morale held up while progress was maintained. But in all the major battles, morale was tested when huge attacks with huge losses were made for territory which was of little perceived importance. As a currency, morale was spent during attacks, sometimes dangerously so. The French mutiny in 1917 occurred after a failed offensive.

Colin felt that German morale was not suffering on the Somme in 1916 in their slow hard fought loss of territory, and he observes early in the battle that it seemed bizarre to be attacking where the enemy was strongest. Why not attack somewhere else, where morale boosting gains could be made more easily? Why indeed?

1917

The failures of the Somme resulted in change. About half of all artillery brigades were transferred from division to army control, enabling concentration of artillery where it was most needed, which was sensible. But there were significant disadvantages. As in 1915, when the generals blamed shortages for failure, so now they blamed too few guns at critical spots, yet again drawing a partial veil over tactical ineptness. And worse, it exacerbated the problems of forward artillery control, as the units concerned lost not only their liaison links within a familiar division, but also the protection and stability conferred by a permanent hierarchy of command. Colin's brigade changed divisional general 34 times in twenty-three months.

General Plumer, commanding the British Second Army, was from an infantry background, and was given the task of arranging a limited advance at Messines Ridge, to straighten the British line and occupy the high ground. This would secure the flank for attacks further north. Knowing this, the Germans had resolved to defend the ridge and had prepared very strong defences. No breakthrough was expected, or planned.

General Plumer did not want heavy casualties, and he wanted to hold on to the gains he made. He planned meticulously, and, significantly, he fostered a culture whereby his front line troops were involved in that planning. He resolved to win the artillery battle before the infantry moved forward. This he did by sheer weight of fire from his concentrated guns combined with excellent reconnaissance. He ensured local air supremacy, kept his pre-assault barrage short, and obtained surprise with his mines. Not only were artillery brigades to provide support for the infantry in front of them, but they were to advance at each stage of the attack to closely support the advancing infantry front line. This was the crucial development.

General Plumer retained top down control of the campaign, particularly the artillery, but acknowledged the problems of forward control of the battlefield. He planned pauses in the advance to allow himself time to manage the battle, and to deal with the counter attacks which he knew were inevitable. These delays were also designed to allow time for his artillery to leapfrog forward and provide close support for the infantry. He had logically addressed many of the issues.

Not everything went right. The most obvious problem was the continuing difficulty with forward control. There were fewer casualties than expected in the first attack, causing overcrowding at the first pause, which led to unnecessary losses in the bombardment before the German counter attack. And particularly on the right of the line, the infantry advanced faster or further than planned, and friendly artillery fire caused many casualties. He needed to work out how to address these problems.

But the limited advance was a spectacular success, giving the British a victory to cheer, and further sapping German morale. Earlier in the year, heavy and prolonged pressure on the Somme battlefield had forced a withdrawal by demoralised German troops there. The French had some success with a similar limited objective attack, and the Canadians had taken Vimy Ridge, again in a limited attack.

These 'smacks', as Colin called them, were very demoralising; overwhelming force on one point, almost a hundred per cent casualties for the unfortunate troops in the eye of the local storm, ground the Germans had publicly resolved to hold lost, and then heavy casualties in a failed attempt to recover it. The defenders may have lost no more men than the attackers, perhaps less. But the attackers have clearly 'won'. Morale slumped, out of all proportion to the value of the ground lost.

In the context of these developments on the Western Front in the first half of 1917, it is difficult to find any aspect of the planning or execution of the first month of the Third Battle of Ypres (Passchendaele) which made military sense. The assumptions on which the planning for the battle was based were plain wrong. Wishful thinking overwhelmed military logic. General Haig ignored the evidence of the Somme and other major assaults and decided that a massive attack would cause a terminal collapse in German morale and lead to a breakthrough. He failed to appreciate that a failed break through attempt was a defeat. The Germans could and would claim victory, thus actually improving their morale.

He then selected a battlefield, and commissioned staff reports which determined that the terrain was manifestly unsuitable; that the German position was strong with defence in depth, good communications[351] and reserves in place; and that the British would be cramped into a salient, vulnerable from three sides. These he ignored. Despite perfectly justified misgivings, General Gough accepted and supported the project.

Together they planned a battle of attrition to capture Passchendaele Ridge at whatever the cost, asserting against any reasonable evidence, that success in this endeavour would in some way end the war. General Gough V.C., unquestionably brave, but with a cavalry, not infantry, background, compounded the mistake with archaic and unimaginative tactics. He put his guns close up, out in the open, without protection, (a problem addressed after experience in 1914); enforced a uniform plan of attack across a battlefield which varied

---

351 The German communication links at Messines Ridge had run north-south, and cutting them had severely disadvantaged the defence. The east-west links to Passchendaele Ridge were good.

from firm ground to bog, (a recipe for local disasters); arranged an 8 hour unobserved rolling barrage (a failed tactic from the year before); and made no arrangements to move his guns forward to support the infantry. An artillery dress rehearsal spurned any element of surprise. To make matters worse, he achieved neither artillery dominance, nor air superiority before the infantry battle opened.

He imposed rigid top down control on his front line troops, in marked contrast to General Plumer's culture of involvement in planning at Messines Ridge. Colonel Lambarde's lament that he was not being informed of infantry intentions before firing a barrage sums up the whole problem. The artillery had no freedom to advise on support, and the infantry no freedom to liaise in the planning of attacks. Intelligent and experienced fighting men were treated as mindless pawns, with no say in their destiny.

In the context of the Russian Revolution and the French mutiny, this approach was a huge and completely unappreciated political risk. Even the apolitical Colin mooted the necessity of *'energetic young blood'* to replace the hierarchy imposed on them, a month in to the battle. General Haig acted by sacking General Gough just in time.

In short, the battle, in its first month, was a master class in how not to win a battle in any war. The resilience of the artillery used in the battle, despite their ghastly casualties, indicates that the inexperience and incompetence of past years was now history. Colin of course blamed the staff for the battle, and it is true that staff planning shaped the battle. But they were responding to their generals' direction and authority. Similar staff had planned Messines Ridge. This time it was not the fault of the staff. They were just the messengers.

General Plumer took over.[352] General Haig ordered the battle to

---

352 General Plumer's reaction to command, wanting to abort the offensive, speaks for itself. Whether the battle continued 'to protect the French', or whether it was a matter of British prestige, is still a matter of debate. Probably a bit of both. And Haig gave Gough the command of another army, suggesting that he did not want any blame to be apportioned for either the strategic or the tactical incompetence of the campaign.

continue. Plumer did his best. He changed the focus of his attacks to gain achievable ground on narrower fronts. He did at least try to provide protection for his forward artillery, by allocating machine guns for air protection and by building positions. He deserves credit for rescuing a score draw out of humiliation. But it was still a sorry mess.

Crucially however, learning from Messines Ridge, he oversaw an improved system for forward control of the artillery.

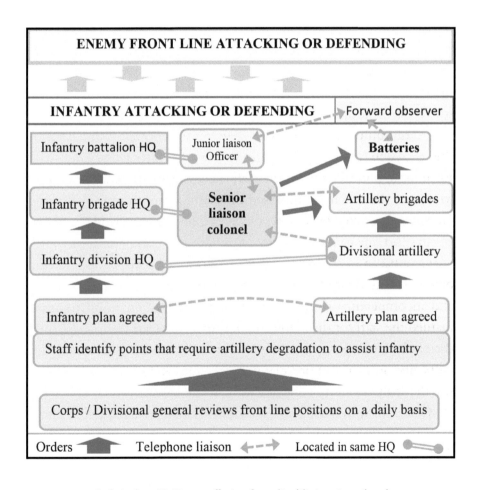

Only in late 1917 was effective formalised liaison introduced, which enabled rapid response to developments on the front line.

Group commanders from the artillery were attached to infantry brigade headquarters. Junior liaison officers from artillery brigades were attached to infantry battalion headquarters, reporting directly, not only to their own guns, but also to him. And he was senior enough to direct units to cooperate, or to discontinue damaging fire in a sector. This was a very long overdue step. Friendly casualties up to then had been huge.

This was the crucial strategic change which enabled the war to be won in 1918. The infantry brigadiers very quickly saw the sense of having close liaison with the artillery. And the artillery brigadiers, with useful artillery input now at all levels of the infantry command, were enabled to be much more proactive. At last, it was a partnership. The artillery were no longer the servants.

But these changes were too late to have an impact on this battle. The weather had broken. The ground behind the British front line was a sea of mud. And the supply routes through this mud so poor and so congested that even a small artillery advance was now impossible. Nevertheless the press in England were still being briefed in October, against all the available military evidence, that a German collapse was pending.

General Haig has to take responsibility for the woeful strategic planning that was the birth of the battle, and the absurd optimism that kept it going. Of course he had to navigate deep political waters and manage expectation, but in so doing, he failed to oversee what should have been up-to-date preparations for a realistic military campaign, or in the context of the early summer of 1917, a series of smaller military campaigns.

But now he was left with a deeply traumatised army that knew it had been fighting a pointless battle for useless territory in an ineffective way. General Plumer did very well to keep his Second Army together. The professionalism with which they reinforced their defences in the last month of 1917 and into 1918 is a testament to that.

1918

Probably the best that can be said is that the Germans, under Ludendorff, did not learn from the mistakes the British had made, though he did improve on their first day tactics. With massive superiority of manpower in early 1918, he also went for a breakthrough, using tactics that had been successful on the Russian Front. He used only a short, very heavy barrage to achieve surprise, and then sent storm troopers forward, who were instructed to penetrate the British lines and not stop to engage strong points. They advanced as far as they could to disrupt gun positions and headquarters behind the infantry lines. Losing coordination and artillery protection, the allied front line infantry were then overwhelmed by a second wave of conventional attackers.

But Ludendorff had to go for a breakthrough. Morale in his own forces was wobbly. The Americans were arriving and he had only limited time before his manpower advantage would be nullified. The initial success of his 'storm troopers' on the first days of his Spring Offensive encouraged him to overreach and the inevitable happened. His best troops sustained the direst casualties. His supply lines became too long. His artillery did not keep up. And the British and French were able to bring up fresh, well positioned reserves.

The only way he could achieve victory was if French or British morale disintegrated. But he was targeting Paris. The French would fight. General Gough had, (unbelievably in view of his reluctance to use front line expertise in 1917), been given command of the Fifth Army which received the full force of the first attack. It is no surprise that it was not ready and not strong enough, though neither were considered entirely his fault. British morale, despite the way it had been squandered at Passchendaele, was however adequate for the task. Just! After a retreat of forty miles, the line held, largely thanks to French reinforcements from further up the line.

At the second attack further north, which progressed ten

miles, the British Artillery yet again proved their competence in defence. All the divisional or army staff needed to do was to tell them approximately where to go and what they had to do. Even the most unintelligent general never suggested holding a defensive line without adequate artillery support. Hopefully there were now no generals left who thought that an offensive could be contemplated without artillery support in all its stages.

Colin's description of the final battles of the war in the Hundred Day Offensive is the vindication of evolving tactics based on the lessons learned on the Somme, at Messines Ridge and in the last six weeks of Passchendaele. German morale was terminally sapped by a succession of reverses, each devastating to their local defence, each unimportant in isolation, but cumulatively damaging to their army as a whole. Damaging also to the senior German generals who not only lost the confidence of their armies and the politicians at home, but lost confidence in themselves as well.

The planning for allied attacks in 1918 differed in almost every respect from the planning for previous battles. The Germans still had big armies and strong defences. They could probably have resisted another prolonged battle of attrition on a ten or fifteen mile front, and have held it till the winter brought fighting to an uneasy end.

But now it was German morale that was being attacked. Surprise and heavy force on a narrow front achieved first day success. Liaison between infantry and artillery was close and effective through all stages of the assaults. Planning was all about getting the guns forward to support realistic infantry advances and to hold onto gains. At Ypres, the artillery brigadier advanced with the infantry until he was out of range of his own guns, and desperate to get them forward as quickly as possible. Labour battalions had advanced yards behind the infantry to start building roads for the guns. And the whole battle was put on hold after just three days to enable consolidation and re-supply.

At Courtrai, the engineers were building a pontoon bridge suitable for artillery within minutes of the first infantry advance, and those infantry waited for their guns to arrive. Colin's brigade there was as close to the infantry as his battery had been at Second Ypres in 1915, intelligently firing, on their own initiative and without any direction from their artillery brigadier in the first stages of the battle, at those targets which were causing most discomfort to the infantry.

This is not in any way to denigrate the infantry. Their losses were heavy and they still had to fight with courage and tenacity. But they fought all the better for knowing that the artillery were close behind them, working with them, and ready to help them out.

Nor of course is it irrelevant that Germany was exhausted after four years at war, its civilian population hungry and discontented, and its army increasingly manned by soldiers too young or too old.

But it was the 'smacks' that did it; a three-day advance, heavy force at one point, using the artillery to make a hole in the enemy lines, following up closely till the supply lines were fully stretched, and then stop. Numerical superiority was used intelligently; the Germans never knew when the next attack would fall. Their morale was shattered in a hundred days.

At last the strategy to win the war had been found. Victory was achieved.

MAIN REFERENCES

War Diaries, sourced from the National Archives at Kew in London.

1914	30th Brigade RFA.	WO-95-1399/5
1915	118th Brigade RFA.	WO-95-3744
	1st Canadian Divisional Artillery – The Canadian Archives	
	113th Brigade RFA	WO 95-2234-2
1916	22nd Brigade RFA.	WO 95-1643-1
	7th Divisional Artillery	WO 95-1639
	35th Brigade RFA.	WO 95-1643-2
	10th Durham Light Infantry	WO 95-1907-2
	159th Brigade RFA.	WO 95-2474-5
	35th Divisional Artillery	WO 95-2471
	1917 113th Brigade RFA	WO 95-295
	16th Divisional Artillery	WO 95-1959-3
1918	33rd Divisional Artillery	WO 95-2410-1
	88th Infantry Brigade	WO 95-2307-4
	29th Divisional Artillery	WO 95-2288-4

The Library of Firepower, the Royal Artillery Museum, was very helpful, providing the list of army brigade placements and much detailed biographical information.

www.1914-1918.net provided an invaluable resource in researching the history and make-up of many units who took part in the war.

'Shoestring Soldiers, the 1st Canadian Division at War, 1914-1915' by Andrew Iarocci gives an excellent account with useful maps of Colin's war in 1915.

'History of the Great War, The British Campaign in France and Flanders', by Sir Arthur Conan Doyle in six volumes, gives a near contemporaneous, very detailed (and rose tinted) account of all the battles. It is available on Project Gutenberg Australia.

'The Horse and the War', by Captain Sidney Galtrey, published in 1918, gives a very informative description of all aspects of the army Vetinary Service and horse management. I used a first edition which was among Colin's papers. It has been re-published.

The library of the National Library of Scotland www.maps.nls.uk has an invaluable reference collection of First World War Trench maps.

Internet references for factual information or pictures are acknowledged in the text. The most valuable were the web-sites of unit museums and I entered too many to acknowledge them all.

This list is short and intentionally so. The book was written as far as possible from the letters and journals of the two protagonists, and their associated official war diaries.

Glossary – The Artillery War

Adjutant 36, 89
Aiming a gun 40, 46
Air observation 30, 208
Air raiding 207, 269
Air warfare 167, 264
Ammunition Column 57, 181
Ammunition faults 110, 118, 125
Ammunition supply 77, 89, 110
Arc of fire 75, 121, 225
Army officer ranks 36
Army Service Corps 17
Army staff 20, 36, 89, 211
Artillery battery R.F.A. xiv, 181
Artillery brigade R.F.A. 2, 36, 181
Artillery groups - R.F.A. 231
Black Maria (slang) 44
Bomb throwing 71
Brigade major 36, 116, 242
British Expeditionary Force 4
Casualty clearing station 176
Casualty counting 208
Censorship xvi, 38
Corps headquarters 224, 238
Counter battery fire 190
Division 2, 36, 184
Dugout (deep) 169, 219
Dugout (conventional) 116, 157
Dugout (observation) 133
First War - origins 1
Enfilade 141
Flamethrower - German 84
Fuse (shell) 8, 44, 133

Gas Chlorine 50
Gas masks 209
Gas Mustard 209, 221
Gas Phosgene 148
Gun emplacement 121
Guns - British
   13 pounder 26
   18 pounder 2, 139
   60 pounder 27, 236
   Howitzer 4.5 inch 2, 58
   Howitzer 6 inch 236
   Howitzer 9.2 inch 59
Guns - French
   90 mm field cannon 47
Guns - German
   Feldkanone 7.7 11, 13, 16
   Feldhaubitze 10.5cm 50, 190
   Feldhaubitze 15cm 16, 27, 190
   Heavy howitzer 21cm 27
   Heavy howitzer 42cm 59
Horses 185 - 187, 247
Horse disease - mange 252
Horse disease - ophthalmia 186
Influenza, 1918 267 - 269
Jack Johnson (slang) 63
Liaison officer 228, 231
Limber 24
Lyddite 44, 110
Machine gun air defence 222
Mapping (trenches) 75, 131, 147, 166
Medals and ribbons 289
Medical board 180

Main Index

Only the first page in any reference sequence is given.
Battles, or units, itemised in chapter headings are not listed here.